Praise for *The Spi*

"Christian understandings of the city h
Sheldrake shows that there is a rich tradi
throughout Christian history. This traditic
and spiritual vision which is essential if citie   ....uc to be human-
ising and hopeful places, spaces of reconciliation rather than alienation.
In dialogue with geographers, philosophers as well as social theorists,
Sheldrake sets out a rich and complex vision of how Christian thinking can
contribute to a worldwide debate."

Tim Gorringe, University of Exeter

"This is an extraordinarily thoughtful book. In carefully tracing the history
of Christian thought on the city, Philip Sheldrake shows how a sense of the
sacred can replenish the urban aesthetic and lives led today largely in environments that push belonging, community and fulfilment to the very edge
of togetherness. A compelling and beautifully written book."

Ash Amin, University of Cambridge

"A quite exceptionally original and timely book, which combines deep
knowledge of the Christian tradition with sensitivity to the issues of
urban life today, and offers fresh insight into what the sacramental
community of Christian faith brings to our current anxieties about social
cohesion, justice and inclusion."

*Rowan Williams, the former Archbishop of Canterbury and
now Master of Magdalene College, University of Cambridge*

Philip Sheldrake is Senior Research Fellow at Westcott House in the
Cambridge Theological Federation, UK and Director, Institute for the Study
of Contemporary Spirituality, Oblate School of Theology, San Antonio Texas,
USA. He has taught and written extensively in the field of Christian spirituality, on the nature of space and place in religion, and on spirituality more
generally. He is involved internationally in inter-religious dialogue. His
dozen books include *Spirituality: A Brief History* (Wiley Blackwell, 2nd edition,
2013), *Explorations in Spirituality: History, Theology and Social Practice* (2010),
Spirituality and History (2nd edition, 1998) and, as editor, *New SCM/Westminster
Dictionary of Christian Spirituality* (2005). He is a Past-President of the international Society for the Study of Christian Spirituality.

The Spiritual City

Theology, Spirituality, and the Urban

Philip Sheldrake

WILEY Blackwell

To Susie

Contents

Contents

Preface

I have been fascinated for many years by the theme of "place" in relation to human identity. My first real opportunity to give this topic some theological and interdisciplinary reflection came when the Divinity Faculty at the University of Cambridge invited me to give the Hulsean Lectures in the academic year 1999–2000. These were published in 2001 jointly by SCM Press and Johns Hopkins University Press as *Spaces for the Sacred: Place, Memory and Identity*. The final lecture and chapter, "Re-placing the city," gathered together a number of my initial thoughts on "place" in reference to our understanding of urban living. I am particularly grateful to Professors David Ford and Denys Turner, who hosted me during the Hulsean Lectures, for encouraging me to develop my thinking on cities into a separate project.

The opportunity to give this idea sustained attention came during 2003–2008 when I held the Leech Professorial Fellowship at Durham University. The Fellowship was supported by the William Leech Foundation set up by the Newcastle philanthropist Sir William Leech. The Fellowship enabled me to concentrate for five years on theological, historical, and urban research in relation to the past, present and potential future of cities. While I have had the opportunity since 2008 to further refine my thinking on cities, and have been invited to speak on the subject in the UK, Ireland, the Netherlands, the USA, and Canada, this book is essentially the product of my time in Durham. I am very grateful to the Leech Trust for appointing me. Additionally, during the Fellowship I was fortunate to work from time to time with Revd Dr Peter Robinson and his urban theology project in Byker, East

Newcastle. I also gave a number of public lectures and other presentations on cities in Durham and Newcastle upon Tyne, two of which were co-presentations with Professor Ash Amin, the founding Director of Durham University's Institute of Advanced Study, and with Professor Fred Robinson, a colleague as Professorial Fellow of St Chad's College in the university. In 2007 I was also privileged to co-organize an international colloquium on "Faith and Spirituality in the Post-Secular City" with Professor Amin and Professors Joe Painter and Stephen Graham of the Department of Geography. This was co-hosted by the Institute of Advanced Study and St Chad's College.

Thanks are also due to Westcott House in the Cambridge Theological Federation, where I am currently Senior Research Fellow. There, I have been able to put the finishing touches to the book and have also been helped by the stimulation of assisting with the Westcott Foundation urban project. I also want to thank my research assistant, August Higgins, at the Oblate School of Theology, San Antonio, for help with compiling the index. As always, I dedicate this book to Susie whose thought-provoking questions as well as loving support have been vital throughout and who contributed significantly to the cover design.

Finally, the image on the cover is a painting *The Ideal City*, attributed to the fifteenth-century Italian artist and Dominican friar Fra Carnevale, now in the Walters Art Museum, Baltimore, MD. The structures and architecture of an imaginary piazza are metaphors for a well-designed and well-governed city. The fountain in the foreground, source of life-giving water, is flanked by four statues on columns portraying the urban virtues of Justice, Moderation, Liberality and Courage.

Philip Sheldrake
Senior Research Fellow
Westcott House, Cambridge Theological Federation

Introduction

The meaning and future of cities is arguably one of the most important and challenging issues of our time. As we shall see, there is a wide-spread sense that we need some kind of compelling urban vision that moves us beyond the limitations of a purely instrumental or utilitarian response to the issue. By a vision I mean a sense that the human city is, or can be, more than an efficient socioeconomic mechanism or convenient but impersonal administrative system conceived by policy-makers and shaped by detached urban planning. In other words, if we accept the need for vision we inevitably point towards frameworks of values based upon some kind of worldview, an understanding of human existence and a horizon of ultimacy.

This book seeks to be a theological and historical "essay" from a Christian perspective on a variety of approaches to cities. In other words, it is not a comprehensive analysis of either urban theory or of other people's theological writings. My purpose is to uncover a few of the rich sources of urban thought and practice in Christianity from a range of different contexts. I hope to suggest ways in which, with due respect to the difference between the various historical and cultural contexts, these may contribute fresh perspectives to the wider human community. As we shall see, I view cities essentially in terms of a "public arena," characterized by the interaction of strangers. Consequently, the

The Spiritual City: Theology, Spirituality, and the Urban, First Edition. Philip Sheldrake.
© 2014 Philip Sheldrake. Published 2014 by John Wiley & Sons, Ltd.

central Judeo-Christian virtue of hospitality to strangers – those who are "other" – is a thread throughout the book.

Engaging the riches of urban thought and expression in Christianity with the contemporary problems of cities is an exercise in what has become known as "postsecularism."[1] The concept counters the ideology known as the "secular project" that held sway in Western countries after the Second World War. This sought to promote a belief in the wholly private nature of religion. Such a viewpoint is rendered implausible both by the simple fact that the majority of the world's population remains religious in some sense and by the recent upsurge in global conflicts with overtly religious dimensions. A critical engagement with religion is now a major global priority. One dominant theme of "postsecularism" is that we must seriously question the argument that any form of shared belief is impossible in plural societies.[2] This clearly has application to the search for shared values in contemporary, diverse urban environments.

Contemporary Cities

The current global growth rate of cities is a critical challenge. By "cities" I mean urban environments characterized not simply by substantial size or large population but also by diversity – social, cultural, ethnic, and religious. The world is rapidly becoming urbanized. In 1950, roughly 29 percent of the world's population lived in urban environments. By 1965 this had risen to 36 percent, by 1990 to 50 percent. This figure is predicted to rise to around 60 percent by 2025, 70 percent by 2050 and at least 75 percent by the end of this century.[3] In the first part of the twenty-first century the "big story" is a worldwide migration of people from rural environments to the city. Humanity for the first time faces a mega-urbanized world. This also means that we are dealing increasingly with mega-cities, many of which are in the new economic giants of India, Brazil, and China. For example, Mumbai has a population of some 18 million, São Paulo is 17+ million, and Shanghai is 14+ million. We increasingly confront sprawling and de-centered cities burdened by crime, congestion, pollution, and social divisions. This means, in effect, that the urbanization of the world is often simultaneously "slumization," to borrow a concept coined by the American philosopher, Eduardo Mendieta. One in six city-dwellers worldwide is currently a slum dweller, and at current rates of increase, by 2050 one in three people – 3 billion – will be.[4]

Cities have a vital role in shaping the human spirit for good or for ill. They represent and create a climate of values that define how we understand human existence and gather together into communities. Conversely, our understanding of what enhances the human spirit shapes the environments we build. As a consequence, their future is not merely a social or economic matter but is also a profound spiritual challenge. Thus, "To read the cities we have built or imagined is, in the end, to read the spiritual biography of our civilization."[5]

This fact was clearly recognized by several late-twentieth-century popes. In the 1971 Apostolic Letter, *Octogesima Adveniens*, Pope Paul VI directed his remarks at social inequality, particularly in reference to contemporary urbanism and its problems. He was concerned with what he called the "irreversible stage" of urbanization associated with social consequences of industrialization in the developing world, and the millions of poor farmers who fled the land for the big cities in hope of a better life. The task of Christians should be "to create new modes of neighborliness" (paragraphs 8–12). He also referred explicitly to the hidden misery to be found in the city which "fosters discrimination and also indifference," homelessness, loneliness, and exploitation of various kinds (paragraph 10).

Pope John Paul II in Chapter IV, section 37 of his 1990 encyclical, *Redemptoris Missio* stated:

> Where before there were stable human and social situations, today everything is in flux. One thinks, for example, of urbanization and the massive growth of cities, especially where demographic pressure is greatest. In not a few countries, over half the population already lives in a few "megalopolises," where human problems are often aggravated by the feeling of anonymity experienced by masses of people.
>
> …. efforts should be concentrated on the big cities, where new customs and styles of living arise together with new forms of culture and communication, which then influence the wider population. It is true that the "option for the neediest" means that we should not overlook the most abandoned and isolated human groups, but it is also true that individual or small groups cannot be evangelized if we neglect the centers where a new humanity, so to speak, is emerging, and where new models of development are taking shape.

In addition, in his 1991 encyclical, *Centissimus Annus*, marking the centenary of Pope Leo XIII's groundbreaking social encyclical, *Rerum Novarum*, Pope John Paul II also underlined the problems of uncontrolled urbanization in the developing world.[6]

As background to our reflections, a positive challenge is offered by Joel Kotkin's provocative study, *The City: A Global History*.[7] He suggests that throughout history successful cities have performed three critical functions in varying ways – the provision of security, the hosting of commerce, and the creation of sacred space. Historically, the latter has been expressed by religious buildings, cathedrals, temples, and mosques, which embody a transcendent horizon in and for the city. However, Kotkin suggests that the city itself is, or should be, a sacred place, that authentically offers an inspiring vision of human existence. He recalls that all major religions have produced models of urban meaning. However, he also notes that the sacred role of cities is regularly ignored in contemporary discussions of the urban condition and the future of cities.

When we confront possible urban futures in the twenty-first century, one key question is "what are cities *for*?" They no longer have strictly practical roles as defense against attack or as the necessary focus for economic systems. If cities are to have *meaning* rather than merely an irreversible existence, there needs to be greater reflection on their civilizing possibilities. Cities have a capacity to focus a range of physical, intellectual, and creative energies simply because they combine differences of age, ethnicity, culture, gender, and religion in unparalleled ways. As Richard Sennett, the eminent sociologist, reminds us in reference to the writings of Aristotle, this is both opportunity and challenge. It is precisely the combination of different people, rather than of similar people, that brings cities into existence.[8] Any attempt to address the conundrum of the city needs more than a mechanical approach. The challenge is how to relate city-making to a vision of the human spirit and what enhances it.

While the "new urbanism" that seeks to respond to current city problems addresses, for example, questions of sustainability, the recovery of a sense of history and the kind of urban design that shapes cohesive neighborhoods, it rarely refers to the need for some kind of moral or spiritual vision with the power to hold cities together.[9] A notable exception is the work of the eminent urban planner, Leonie Sandercock, who writes of "the city of spirit" in her book *Cosmopolis II: Mongrel Cities in the 21st Century*.[10] Yet, as Kotkin notes, what is more important than the creation of new buildings or spaces in isolation is the value city-dwellers actually place on their urban experience. In other words, a successful city is, in the end, a state of mind that offers a vision of a human community that is capable of promoting co-existence between strangers and of learning how to seek a shared code of social behavior. Kotkin critiques all religions, including Christianity, for somehow losing touch with their own historic urban visions. As a result, when religion addresses urban questions it too often tends merely to echo the pragmatic urban language of professional or policy groups. At the same time it largely fails to contribute its own distinctive discourse to the contemporary conversations about the future of cities.

It follows from this that a key challenge to religions such as Christianity in today's radically plural, multicultural, and multireligious Western cities, is to rediscover their own voice – their traditions of urban thinking and practice. This is the building material of ideas, symbols, or experience that is needed to help create a compelling spiritual vision for cities. For, as Kotkin comments starkly at the conclusion of his book, the history of cities teaches us that without some kind of "widely shared belief system it would be exceedingly difficult to envision a viable urban future."[11]

In this context, the phrase "the good city" recently seems to have become common currency. For example, the urban thinker Ash Amin addresses the theme from the perspective of human geography.[12] For Amin the key is to develop the habit of solidarity among strangers built upon a commitment to the common good. Solidarity is shaped by four everyday basics of urban living: repair, relatedness, rights, and re-enchantment. "Repair" refers to the proper maintenance of technological and mechanical infrastructures. The point is that such infrastructures are never purely a matter of mechanics. They are the life-support system of a city that enables effective human orientation and movement. "Relatedness" seeks to counter various forms of human marginalization, exclusion, and disconnection. This may involve a universal provision of the basics of healthy human existence, the creation of social or cultural projects that bring together people of different backgrounds or creatively returning public spaces to effective mixed use. "Rights" again addresses the problem of the effective exclusion and restriction of certain groups in favor of the safety or dominance of others. This needs to be countered by a concept in public culture and civic politics of "the open city" where new voices can emerge and marginalized groups may stake their claim to participate. Finally, "re-enchantment" seeks to make public space more than a context for human socialization created purely by consumerism or tourism. Rather, we should work imaginatively and experimentally with public space to make it the medium for a transformation of imagination and behavior through protest gatherings (nonlegislative "politics"), art, education, and entertainment.

The question "what makes a good city?" also animated the 2006 Church of England Commission on Urban Life and Faith and its report *Faithful Cities*.[13] Among the words and phrases used in response to the question were that a good city is "active," "diverse," "inclusive," "safe," "well-led," "environmentally sensitive," has an "active civil society," "values the inhabitants," offers "opportunities for all," "attracts wealth creators," but also "shares its wealth," is "big enough to be viable" but also is "small enough to be on a human scale." In a sentence, the "good city" enables human aspirations to be enhanced, to be productive, and to be inclusive, rather than for them to be repressed or selfish. Fundamentally, the report *Faithful Cities* suggests that the "good city" is person-centered rather than shaped by abstract approaches to politics, planning, and structural efficiency.

By contrast, the monumental modernist architecture that still characterizes many of today's Western cities does not stand for the value of individual people, for intimate relationships, or for focused community. Rather, it speaks the language of size, money, and power. Commercial complexes such as Canary Wharf in London's Docklands stand in brooding isolation rather than in relationship to anywhere else. Modern cities built in the last 60 years frequently lack proper centers that express the whole life of a multifaceted community. Even the centers of older European cities reconstructed after the devastation of the Second World War can often be described as soulless.

A major part of the problem was the dominance of "zoning" or a cellular view of urban planning (originating in part from the iconic Swiss-born French architect Charles Jeanneret, otherwise known as Le Corbusier) which divided cities into "special areas" or zones for living, working, leisure, and shopping. The immediate consequence of this "zoning" was a fragmentation of human living and of a coherent sense of community diversity. On top of this, the creation of a "city of special areas" has the effect of emptying parts of it at night, especially the centers and commercial districts. This tends to make them dead and sometimes dangerous. Finally, a cellular design demands the separation of areas by distance and clear boundaries. This substantially increases the need for travel and consequently increases pollution.

In more general terms, this differentiation into discrete areas may be said to reflect a growing desacralization of Western culture. There is no longer a centered, let alone spiritually centered, meaning for the city. It is now a commodity, fragmented into multiple activities, multiple ways of organizing time and space, matched by multiple roles for the inhabitants.[14] Overall, zoning or cellular urban design does not invite people out into shared, humane places of encounter. New domestic ghettos are increasingly protected against sterile public spaces that are no longer respected but, at best, treated unimaginatively and, at worst, abandoned to violence and vandalism.

Cities reflect and affect the quality of human relationships. The fact is that in the context of urban environments we cannot separate functional, ethical, and spiritual questions. If places are to be sacred, they must affirm the sacredness of people, community, and a human capacity for transcendence. In an earlier age in European cities the cathedral was an icon of such an urban vision. It offered at the same time an image of God and a symbol of the ideals of the citizens at the heart of the city.

What Counts as Urban?

When we think of what is meant by a city or, more broadly, the urban, we nowadays tend to concentrate on questions of density and size whereas, for example, in England until relatively recently a major criterion for being a city was the presence of a historic cathedral. However, as the seventh-century Christian thinker St Isidore of Seville reminds us, in thinking about what we mean by the urban we need to balance two Latin concepts: *urbs* (cities of stone) and *civitas* (cities of people). Our sense of place refers both to the built environment and the state of mind (or soul) shaped by this, or by geography. The point is that Isidore's use of *urbs* and *civitas* does not refer to alternative concepts of "the city" or two separate planes without interaction. For Isidore, there could be no absolute separation between physical design and urban community. Such a split would have mutilated a reality in which these two dimensions are naturally co-dependent and fused. Yet, according to his philosophy, in the end what makes a place a city is the people, not the architecture in isolation. "A city [*civitas*] is a number of men [*sic*] joined by a social bond. It takes its name from the citizens [*cives*] who dwell in it. As an *urbs* it is only a walled structure, but inhabitants, not building stones, are referred to as a city."[15] Nevertheless, we need to give attention to *urbs* – to the powerful impact on people and human community of design, architecture, and the planning of physical spaces.

In the Western world, from the philosophy of Plato and Aristotle onwards, cities have always been powerful symbols of how we understand and construct human community. In particular, cities are paradigms of our outer, public life. Unfortunately, since the nineteenth century Western culture, particularly in the United Kingdom and the United States, has become deeply polarized. The private sphere (inwardness, family and friends, home) has been idealized as the backstage where individuals are truly themselves, relaxing unobserved before playing different roles on the public stage.[16] However, from a Christian perspective is public living simply a role to be taken up and put down at will? A recent Archbishop of Canterbury, the British theologian Rowan Williams, notes that "we are systematically misled, even corrupted, by a picture of the human agent as divided into an outside and an inside – a 'true self', hidden, buried, to be excavated by one or another kind of therapy."[17] Rather, our identity comes into being from the start through human communication and interaction. An unbalanced *rhetoric* of interiority has had serious moral consequences because it suggests that our social or public life is of secondary importance. However, Christian theology, following St Augustine, affirms that there is no absolutely private identity. To be human embodies a common life and a common task. Without developing a complex point further at this point, it is important to note the intimate link between human identity and the Christian relational theology of God as "Trinity." The core of the Christian life – a paradigm of redeemed human existence overall – is to become united with God, in Jesus Christ, through a Spirit-led communion with one another. God's own relational nature is fundamental to such a life. The doctrine of the Trinity affirms that God *is* persons-in-communion, a mutuality of self-giving love. From this perspective, communion underpins all existence.[18]

Public Living

If to be truly human is to be "in public," in practical terms what does "public" imply? Some social commentators such as José Casanova limit public life to "the arena of moral and political contestation."[19] However, the sociologist Lyn Lofland, who is concerned with a growing American anti-urban, anti-public rhetoric which fosters intolerance and prejudice, uses the word "public" more broadly for places that are dominated by the interaction of strangers or those who are only known casually, for example the newspaper vendor. For her, the city is a powerful paradigm of public existence. Public places are very different from the intimate familiar places of the private or parochial worlds.[20] It is interesting that the Christian tradition suggests that God is often most powerfully experienced in places that are "strange" to us, rather than safely protected. There, people who appear alien challenge our sense of familiarity and security. Scholars sensitive to issues of place-identity in the New Testament, especially in the Synoptic Gospels, have noted that Jesus regularly pushed those closest to him away from familiar places and people towards places that were initially threatening because the people in such places were marginal, Gentiles or in some way "other."[21]

Public life, city life, is the arena where diverse people attempt to establish some form of commonality. This includes the relatively anonymous sociability of local neighborhoods and less anonymous (yet not necessarily intimate) contexts such as the local church. In other words, living publicly goes beyond an incidental sharing of space with others where the individual self is still primary and demands protection. To live publicly implies learning how to be truly hospitable to what is different, unfamiliar, distasteful or even feared. Indeed, to live publicly means letting go of a life focused on the survival of my autonomous self. It involves engaging "the other" in ways that embrace diversity as part of the process of establishing and reinforcing a sense of "who I am." Living publicly implies real encounters with what is different and unfamiliar yet somehow establishing a common life. Social interaction and active citizenship may thus be seen as forms of spiritual practice.

The City as Spiritual Challenge

This central aspect of diversity and difference in cities is picked up by Richard Sennett in his criticism of Christianity's supposed rejection of public life and cities because of its fear of mixture and self-exposure and its concern for purity.[22] In a rich and complex study on the social life of cities, Sennett blames, in part, aspects of Christian theology for the contemporary privatization of space and the soulless nature of modern Western cities. This process began several hundred years ago but reached a particularly powerful climax in the period of urban restoration after the Second World War. Essentially, Sennett argues that modern Western culture suffers from a divide between interiority and exteriority: "It is a divide between subjective experience and worldly experience, self and city."[23] This divide, according to Sennett, is based on an unacknowledged fear of self-exposure. Exposure has the connotation of a threat rather than of the enhancement of life. The result is that, apart from spaces for the celebration of heritage or for consumer needs, city design has concentrated on creating safe divisions between different groups of people. Public space thus becomes bland, as the main purpose is to facilitate movement across it rather than encounters within it.[24] According to Sennett, for the city to recover, we need to reaffirm the inherent value of the outer embodied life.

I agree with much that Sennett says. However, I also believe that he misinterprets Christianity as unequivocally a religion of pilgrimage and dislocation rather than of placement. For Sennett, St Augustine's *City of God* is the classic expression of the triumph of an inner "city" restlessly in search of eternal fulfillment over the everyday human city.[25] Human social places are to be viewed with suspicion. What is most obviously characteristic of these outer places is difference and diversity. Sennett argues, therefore, that by denying the true value of the outside, theology has underpinned the way that Western culture doubts the spiritual value of diversity. If the deep valuation of our inner life found expression externally, it was in church buildings or in cathedrals. For Sennett, these places actually undermined any meaningful definition for the city in itself.[26] He equates "the sacred" with *sanctuary*, which implies not merely special places but an image of protection and refuge from a wider world. According to Sennett, in the premodern city, churches were "sanctuaries" in both senses, and so promoted withdrawal from the outer life. I shall explore a rather different interpretation of the historic role of cathedrals and other urban religious buildings in Chapter 3.

Sennett further suggests that modern urbanism, with its sterile public spaces, stems from what he calls "a Protestant ethic of space." This, he posits, is a further post-Reformation refinement of the Augustinian distinction. According to Sennett, the coming of Protestantism had a long-term impact on what he terms "the compulsive neutralizing of the environment," for example, the way modernist planners designed the "neutral city." This reflected a puritanical suspicion of pleasure and color. "The sacred" should be sober not carnival. As I shall suggest in the next chapter and in Chapter 4, this reading of St Augustine and of subsequent Christian thought, while not wholly inaccurate, is too one-sided. That said, the French Jesuit social scientist and scholar of Christian spirituality, Michel de Certeau, in his writings on spatial practices, also refers to and severely criticizes the impact of a fear of mixing and of the disintegration of social boundaries on modernist urban design (for example in the work of Le Corbusier) that motivated its pursuit of spatial purification. This will be discussed more fully in Chapter 5.[27]

We might also note the degree of ambivalence towards the twentieth-century mega-city present in an urban writer such as Lewis Mumford, where what he calls Megalopolis, the great multimillion city, is simply a staging post on the road to Necropolis, the city of the dead. However such views are not explicitly related to the Christian tradition.[28]

In Western countries over the last sixty years or so, cities have all too often undermined place identity in pursuit of values driven largely by economic considerations. The French anthropologist, Marc Augé, a student of the Jesuit Michel de Certeau, distinguishes between "place," engaged with our identity, full of historical monuments and creative of social life, and what he calls "non-place" – in his words, "curious places which are both everywhere and nowhere." There, no organic social life is possible. By "non-place" he means such contexts as supermarkets, airports, hotels, freeways, working at a computer, or sitting in front of a television. These bring about a fragmentation of awareness and incoherence in relation to "the world."[29] Augé points to urban centers as indicative of the importance of "place." Classic centers contain buildings that resonate with authority and symbolic meaning whether religious (for example a cathedral), civic (the town hall) or historical (for example a war memorial). However, the key feature of such centers is that they are humanly active and hospitable places. People gather and interact there. Significant numbers of cafés, hotels, or businesses concentrate nearby and cross-town routes pass through them. True centers offer "places for living" by being places of encounter,

> ...where individual itineraries can intersect and mingle, where a few words are exchanged and solitudes momentarily forgotten, on the church steps, in front of the town hall, at the café counter or in the baker's doorway.[30]

Cities enable or disable place identity. As we shall see in more detail in Chapter 6, a sense of place is a category of human experience with a strong impact on how we see the world and situate ourselves within it.[31] However "place" is no longer the simple concept that post-Enlightenment thought once proposed. Contemporary urban theorists note that in today's cities, place identity is less fixed and local than hitherto. Community is understood as a never-completed process of becoming, and city life is caught up in a continuous flow.[32] Technology and rapid travel have increased global connections. Cultures previously viewed as homogeneous are revealed as plural and bound up with power issues. In short, "place identity" nowadays embraces a range of associations from the local home or neighborhood to a sense of a single global community. In a world of multifaceted place identity, city-making increasingly needs to attend both to what I call "micro-place" (satisfactory homes and effective neighborhoods) and to "macro-place" (meaningful expressions of wider connections).

Our environments are active partners in the conversation between location and the geographies of the mind and spirit that create "place." Place involves human narrative and memory embedded in place, including deeper narrative currents that absorb the stories of all who have lived there previously. It is, therefore, appropriate to think of places as texts, layered with meaning. A hermeneutics of place continually reveals new interpretations in the interplay between physical environment, memory, and specific people at a particular moment.

Precisely because "place" involves narrative, it is not surprising that it is often contested. We only have to think of Jerusalem, claimed by Israelis and Palestinians and sacred to three faiths. In deconstructing modernity's belief in objective, absolute place, postmodern critiques assert that definition is power. This is also true of cities, their design and their regeneration processes. The French Marxist philosopher Henri Lefebvre's analysis of place also reminds us that systems of spatialization are historically conditioned – not merely physical arrangements of things but also patterns of social action and routine, as well as historical conceptions of the world. The meta-narratives of the people who hold power take over the public places they control. However altruistic or benign the agendas of those with power appear to be, the history of these places sadly often becomes a story of dominance and repression. The notion that place relates to issues of empowerment and disempowerment forces us to think of multilocalities (locations are different "places" simultaneously) and multivocalities (different voices are heard in each place).[33]

If cities are to be places that reinforce a sense that human life is sacred rather than solely a biological phenomenon, they must embrace all dimensions of human existence – functional, ethical, and spiritual. First, we need somewhere to pass effectively through the stages of life and reach our full potential. Second, we need places where we belong to a community. Third, we need cities that continue to facilitate a fruitful relationship with the natural environment. Finally, we need human contexts that offer access to the sacred (however we understand it) – or, better, relate us to life itself as sacred.[34]

The Changing Modern City

Cities have always produced a unique vibrancy. They not only have a particular capacity to create diverse community but, historically, they have been the primary sites of human innovation and creativity. On the whole, as Sir Peter Hall reminds us in his monumental *Cities in*

Civilization, the history of Western civilization is largely the history of cities. Indeed, the very words "civilization" and "civilized" derive from Latin words for "city" (*civitas*) and citizen (*cives*). As Hall argues, in many respects it is precisely the complexity and diversity of cities that forces innovation upon us as the means of solving problems that the very size of cities creates.

Yet, our attempts to reflect on the meaning and future of cities today must take on board a number of radical changes in the nature of cities that go back to the industrial revolution but have accelerated since the end of the Second World War. We not only have to cope with a much higher and growing proportion of the world's population that is urbanized but with a number of important corollaries: the sheer size and rate of expansion of modern cities; the increased mobility and flow of life within them that calls into question any simple notion of place identity; the increasing plurality of communities to which people belong; the global reach of any large city; the radical diversity and pluralism of people and cultures within cities.

This all runs counter to a tendency by some thinkers to link place identity (undoubtedly a vital human need) exclusively to "the local" and to idealize some kind of domestic vision as the primary symbol of a satisfactory life. Even one of the gurus of modern urban theory, Manuel Castells, who previously preached the inevitable triumph of the mega-city over small-scale development, has surprisingly returned to the concept of family and home as the only effective providers of human flourishing "in a world characterized by individuation of work, destruction of civil society and the delegitimization of the state."[35]

The problem with an unbalanced emphasis on the local is that we are left only with lament and nostalgia for something that cannot readily be recaptured and with nothing positive to say about other contemporary urban realities such as flow, the transgression of fixed boundaries, and the presence of distant connections, for example among immigrant communities. However, we need a balanced approach. The geographer Anne Buttimer deplores an overemphasis on mobility in the decades since the Second World War which, for her, is a key element in the contemporary Western disintegration of place-identity. We have de-emphasized place for the sake of economic values such as mobility, centralization, or rationalization. The global relativity of space dissolves the reality of place.

The skyscrapers, airports, freeways and other stereotypical components of modern landscapes – are they not the sacred symbols of a civilization that has deified reach and derided home?[36]

Similar sentiments are expressed by the Scottish Christian ethicist Michael Northcott: "The modern city celebrates and facilitates mobility at the expense of settlement, movement at the expense of place."[37] This is not simply a social issue but a spiritual and theological one. Without a sense of place there is no centering of the human spirit. When human conditions undermine this, the consequent displacement is striking in its effects on individuals and societies. In hardly more than a century, we have moved from a premodern, predominantly rural society through an industrial revolution and urbanized society into what many people call a postmodern, postindustrial world. In an increasingly placeless culture we have become "standardized, removable, replaceable, easily transported and transferred from one location to another."[38] If there is a sense of place, it is predominantly a private one in the face of cynicism about the outer, public world.

Yet, for many people the city is a symbol of social and economic opportunity. It is a symbol of how our origins, caste or class can evaporate. In the city I can become anything I choose to make myself. Equally, what might be called "city experience" dominates the culture and thinking of governments, commerce and the media. This dominant culture insures that groups who do not qualify as urban do not merit the best services – transport, schools, stores, banking, or a post office – because they are not deemed viable.

Cities in the Bible

For better or worse, Western thinking about cities has been deeply influenced over the last thousand years by Christian ideas. As we saw in the case of Richard Sennett, Christianity has sometimes been accused of anti-urban bias. The foundations of Christian response to and thought about cities lie in the Bible. So, briefly, I want to offer a summary overview of the ways that the Hebrew and Christian scriptures have reflected on how cities originated and were constructed.

It is important to begin with the Hebrew scriptures as these are also foundational to Christian thought and sensibilities.

Certainly the Hebrew scriptures (or Old Testament) appear to get off to a tricky start. The Book of Genesis can come across as somewhat gloomy about cities. Arguably, this ambivalence is rooted deeply in the Hebrew memory of being originally (and, according to one viewpoint, ideally) a nomadic people. Cain, symbol of human pride and violence, is portrayed as the founder of Enoch, the first city, an alternative to God's Eden (Genesis 4:16–17). Later the people of Babel in building their tower overreach themselves and seek to replace the authority of God (Genesis 11:1–9). Despite the intercession of Abraham, the cities of Sodom and Gomorrah are destroyed and become classic symbols of corruption. In the Book of Exodus, the wandering Hebrews are portrayed as once again ambivalent about cities: "the city" is the enemy – pagan and also immoral. Cities are abominations that stand against the moral norms of the Covenant between God and Israel (Judges 19:22–30). Such texts are cited by the French sociologist and Protestant thinker, Jacques Ellul, to suggest that the Bible offers no law for the city because the city, far from being sacred, embodies humanity organized against God. For Ellul, "the city" implies a refusal of God's gift of Eden. Thus, in the Hebrew and Christian scriptures "God has cursed, has condemned the city instead of giving us a law for it."[39] While Ellul goes on to express a somewhat more dialectical understanding of the city (he writes of Nineveh saved by Jonah's preaching and God's promise to David in relation to Jerusalem), he does not entirely escape from his anti-urban sentiments.

However, this is a one-sided selection of biblical texts and, indeed, ignores a certain ambiguity even in the texts that Ellul cites. For example, in the story of Babel the city and its tower are also marvels of human creativity and organization. The city is a protection for the people and also ensures some cohesion. The tower is intended as the medium of access to the divine. The very name of the city is actually ambiguous: it is arguably related to "Babylon," in which context it reflects an ancient Akkadian word for "the gate of God," whereas in Hebrew the name is associated with "confusion" or "babbling." The overall implication is that a city may be a preeminent example of human social organization but it is also a potentially unstable association of heterogeneous, rather than homogeneous, people, who may be tempted to go their own way.

There are other positive biblical images of the city in the Hebrew scriptures. Once settled in the Promised Land of Israel, the Jews proclaim Jerusalem as the place of God, a city of peace. Even under the monarchy, Jerusalem is fundamentally ruled by priests and scribes who are the guardians of the divine Covenant. Temple worship shapes cultural life. The Davidic tradition in the Hebrew scriptures was grounded in this settled experience of Jerusalem. At its heart was an assurance that the throne of David would never fail. There was a tendency by royal theologians to link the cultic center of divine power to the throne of the king. That is, political stability became connected with an assurance of God's ritual presence at the heart of the city. The city of Jerusalem becomes the center to which all memory and meaning are bound.

With the rise of Jerusalem as the royal capital of Israel as well as the privileged religious center, the image of cities in Jewish theology improves. The Hebrew bible may be said to create a physical, symbolic and mystical image of the quintessential city – beautiful, rich, and the seat of both political and religious power. In the Book of Psalms, God is enthroned in the sanctuary of Zion (Psalm 9), the city becomes a living reminder of God's power and faithfulness (Psalm 48). Those who live in the city are required to share God's peace with one another (Psalm 122:6–9). Psalm 137 proclaims "If I forget you O Jerusalem, may my right hand wither."[40] Jewish theology of the city as physical place and as human community was based on an ethic rooted in the Covenant. Adherence to the Law, demonstrated by moral behavior in all aspects of material life, determined the Jewish view of cities. When Jewish prophets (for example Amos 8:4–8) proclaimed the renewal of city life, they frequently referred to the quality of care present in the city, especially for orphans, widows, and strangers. Indeed it is a "high" view of the sacredness of the city that leads a prophet like Jeremiah (26:6) to call the inhabitants of Jerusalem to repent. The city is either the true resting place of God or a barren wasteland where God is rejected. In the latter case the city merits destruction.

In the New Testament, although the gospels place Jesus's actions largely in villages, we should recall that in those times a city (for example Jerusalem) and the surrounding villages were united in a single region with strong economic and social ties. Equally, Jerusalem is portrayed as the focal point and climax of Jesus's mission. The Gospel of Luke mentions the city explicitly more than the other gospels. However, as in the prophetic books of the Hebrew scriptures, Jesus's relationship to the city is ambivalent (see, for example, Luke 13:34–35). In the Gospel of Luke, Jesus enters Jerusalem in triumph before his death. There he pronounces prophetic challenges to the religious authorities (Luke 20:45–47). Finally, it is in Jerusalem that his ministry climaxes in the crucifixion. Interestingly, the Gospel of Matthew compares the followers of Jesus to, among other things, "a city on a hill" (Matthew 5:14). Biblical scholars also regularly claim that all three Synoptic Gospels are urban creations – the Gospel of Mark written in Rome, the Gospel of Matthew in Syrian Antioch or in one of the Phoenician cities of South Syria, and the Gospel of Luke also in Syrian Antioch or in one of the cities of Asia Minor. The cities of the Roman Empire subsequently become the centre of Christian mission in the strategy of the Apostle Paul, as outlined in the Book of Acts. Christianity rapidly became an urban religion.[41] Most striking of all, in the last book of the New Testament (Book of Revelation, chapter 21), a new city, perfectly harmonious and peaceful, is made the image of the final establishment of God's reign.

A Map of the Book

With all this in mind, this book seeks to offer a mixture of theoretical and practical perspectives in order to bring urban theory and design into conversation with theology and spirituality which together also embrace elements of history and philosophy. The book has two parts. The first, "The City in Christian Thought," surveys a selection of historical and recent theoretical and practical examples. Chapter 1 reconsiders St Augustine's theology of the human city and critiques Richard Sennett's interpretation of Augustine's *City of God*. Chapter 2 explores the deep connections throughout history between Christian monasticism and utopian urban thinking, from the early Egyptian desert to the city writings of the twentieth-century American monk Thomas Merton. Chapter 3, "The City as Sacred," discusses the understanding of the city as itself a sacred place during the Middle Ages. Chapter 4 explores how positive Christian visions of cities emerge from both the Catholic and Protestant Reformations and then find various forms of expression up to the mid twentieth century. Finally, Chapter 5 focuses on the idea of the city in the provocative urban writings of the French Jesuit social scientist and historian, Michel de Certeau. The second part of the book, "Theological Reflection and the City", brings theology, spirituality and four critical urban themes into conversation. Chapter 6, "Place and The Sacred", addresses the nature of "place", the importance of place identity and shifting ideas on the role and relevance of specifically "sacred place" in urban environments. Chapter 7, "The Art of Community", then explores the nature of community in relation to contemporary urban settings and what Christian thought and experience may contribute to a richer understanding of its critical edges. This leads in Chapter 8, "Reconciliation and Hospitality", to reflection specifically on the challenging theme of reconciliation, including issues of inclusivity and hospitality to the stranger. Chapter 9 explores the notion of "Urban Virtues" and asks what the crucial urban virtues are for the twenty-first century. Finally, the Epilogue begins with a brief exposition of my own vision of what Christian theology and spirituality has to offer to our thinking about cities. From this, the Epilogue concludes by underlining the importance of maintaining a balance between notions of sacramentality and eschatology in any theological approach to the human city.

Notes

English translations are cited wherever available.

1 See for example, John R. Betz. *After Enlightenment: The Post-Secular Vision of J.G. Hamann*. Oxford: Wiley-Blackwell, 2009.
2 For a critique of classic secularization theory, see the work of sociologist José Casanova, *Public Religion in the Modern World*, Chicago: University of Chicago Press, 1994.
3 These figures are cited by Sir Crispin Tickell in his Introduction to Richard Rogers, *Cities for a Small Planet*, London: Faber & Faber 1997, p. vii.
4 The term and the statistics were used by Eduardo Mendieta (SUNY Stony Brook) in his presentation to the colloquium "Faith and Spirituality in the Post-Secular City," hosted at Durham University, England, March 2007.
5 Peter S. Hawkins (ed.), *Civitas: Religious Interpretations of the City*, Atlanta: Scholars' Press, 1986, p. xii.
6 For further comments and details, see Michael Hornsby-Smith, *An Introduction to Catholic Social Thought*, Cambridge: Cambridge University Press, 2006.
7 Joel Kotkin, *The City: A Global History*, New York: Random House, 2006.

8   Richard Sennett, *Together: The Rituals, Pleasures and Politics of Cooperation*, London and New York: Allen Lane, 2012, p. 4.

9   On the "new urbanism," see, for example, Peter Katz, *The New Urbanism: Toward an Architecture of Community*, New York: McGraw-Hill, 1994.

10 Leonie Sandercock, *Cosmopolis II: Mongrel Cities in the 21st Century*, London and New York: Continuum, 2003.

11 Kotkin, *The City*, p. 159.

12 Ash Amin, "The good city," *Urban Studies*, 43(5–6), 1009–1023, 2006.

13 Commission on Urban Life and Faith, *Faithful Cities: A Call for Celebration, Vision and Justice*. London: Church House Publishing, 2006. See especially Chapter 6 "A good city: Urban regeneration with people in mind." This followed upon an earlier and robustly critical Church report *Faith in the City* (1985) during the time of Margaret Thatcher, which focused on the causes of decay and deprivation in "urban priority areas" and an appropriate Christian response.

14 For interesting remarks on the relationship between the fragmentation of intellectual discourse, starting with the medieval separation of theology and spirituality and the contemporary secularization of the city, see James Matthew Ashley, *Interruptions: Mysticism, Politics, and Theology in the work of Johann Baptist Metz*, Notre Dame: University of Notre Dame Press, 1998, pp. 10–12.

15 See Isidore of Seville, *Etymologiarum libri*, 15.2.1, quoted in Chiara Frugoni, *A Distant City: Images of Urban Experience in the Medieval World*, Princeton, NJ: Princeton University Press, 1991, pp. 3–4.

16 José Casanova, *Public Religions in the Modern World*, Chicago: University of Chicago Press, 1994, p. 42.

17 Rowan Williams, *On Christian Theology*, Oxford and Malden, MA: Blackwell, 2000, Chapter 16, "Interiority and epiphany: A reading in New Testament ethics."

18 See, for example, the work of the Orthodox theologian Metropolitan John Zizioulas, *Being as Communion*, New York: St Vladimir's Seminary Press, 1985, and a more detailed discussion of the relationship between God-as-Trinity and human identity in Philip Sheldrake, *Spirituality and Theology: Christian Living and the Doctrine of God*, London: Darton Longman & Todd/ New York: Orbis Books, 1998, especially pp. 75–83.

19 Casanova, *Public Religions*, p. 3.

20 See Lyn Lofland, *The Public Realm: Exploring the City's Quintessential Social Territory*, New York: Aldine de Gruyter, 1998.

21 See Belden Lane, *The Solace of Fierce Landscapes: Exploring Desert and Mountain Spirituality*, New York: Oxford University Press, 1998, pp. 43–46 and his references.

22 Richard Sennett, *The Conscience of the Eye: The Design and Social Life of Cities*, London: Faber & Faber, 1993, Introduction and Chapter 1.

23 Sennett, *The Conscience of the Eye*, p. xii.
24 Sennett, *The Conscience of the Eye*, pp. xii–xiii.
25 Sennett, *The Conscience of the Eye*, pp. 6–10.
26 Sennett, *The Conscience of the Eye*, pp. 10–19.
27 Michel de Certeau, "Practices of space," in *On Signs*, ed. M. Blonsky, Oxford: Blackwell/ Baltimore: Johns Hopkins University Press, 1985, pp. 122–45.
28 Lewis Mumford, *The Culture of Cities*, New York and London: Harcourt Brace, 1970 [originally 1938].
29 Marc Augé, *Non-Places: Introduction to an Anthropology of Supermodernity.* London and New York: Verso, 1997, especially pp. 51–2 and 77.
30 Augé, *Non-Places*, pp. 66–67.
31 For a sustained reflection on the connection between place, memory and identity, see Philip Sheldrake, *Spaces for the Sacred: Place, Memory, and Identity*, Baltimore: Johns Hopkins University Press, 2001. See also Gaston Bachelard, *The Poetics of Space*, Boston: Beacon Press, 1994; Edward S. Casey, "How to get from space to place in a fairly short stretch of time: phenomenological prolegomena," in Steven Feld and Keith H. Basso (eds.), *Senses of Place*, Santa Fe: School of American Research Press, 1997; J.E. Malpas, *Place and Experience: A Philosophical Topography*, Cambridge: Cambridge University Press, 1999.
32 See A. Amin and N. Thrift, *Cities: Reimaging the Urban*, Cambridge: Polity Press, 2002, especially Chapter 2.
33 See Henri Lefebvre, *The Production of Space*, Oxford: Blackwell, 1991.
34 See the comments by architect Robert Mugerauer in *Interpretations on Behalf of Place: Environmental Displacements and Alternative Responses*, Albany: State University of New York Press, 1994, especially Chapter 10.
35 Manuel Castells, *End of Millenium*. Oxford: Blackwell, 1998, p. 349.
36 Anne Buttimer, "Home, reach, and the sense of place," in Anne Buttimer and David Seaman (eds.), *The Human Sense of Space and Place*. London: Croom Helm, 1980, p. 174.
37 See Michael Northcott, "A place of our own?" in Peter Sedgwick (ed.), *God in the City: Essays and Reflections from the Archbishop of Canterbury's Urban Theology Group*, London: Mowbray, 1995, pp. 119–38, especially p. 122.
38 A. Berleant, *The Aesthetics of Environment*, Philadelphia: Temple University Press, 1992, pp. 86–87.
39 Jacques Ellul, *The Meaning of the City*. Grand Rapids: Eerdmans, 1970, p. 16.
40 See Gerald H. Wilson, "Songs for the city: Interpreting biblical psalms in an urban context," Chapter 14 in Stephen Breck Reid (ed.), *Psalms and Practice: Worship, Virtue, and Authority*, Collegeville, MN: The Liturgical Press, 2001.
41 See, for example, Wayne Meeks, "St Paul of the cities," in Peter S. Hawkins (ed.), *Civitas*, 1986, pp. 15–23.

PART ONE

The City in Christian Thought

CHAPTER 1

Augustine's Two Cities

As we saw in the Introduction, Richard Sennett, the American social scientist, critiques Christianity for its supposed rejection of public life and cities based on its fear of mixture and concern for purity.[1] Thus, Sennett interprets Christianity as a religion of pilgrimage towards a purely transcendent eternal horizon rather than a medium of existential placement. For Sennett, Augustine of Hippo's *City of God*, where he develops a theology of Christianity in relation to public life, is the classic expression of the triumph of an inner "city" restlessly in search of eternal fulfillment over the everyday human city.[2] Augustine's book seems to have been provoked in part by the sack of Rome by the Goth Alaric in 410. To be fair, Sennett is not alone in interpreting Augustine's *City of God* in this way as fundamentally a rejection of human cities. However, in my view, this interpretation of Augustine needs significant revision. The idea that Christian faith is unequivocally inward-looking rather than concerned with everyday self-giving and active service of fellow human beings is inaccurate.

Before Augustine

Before turning explicitly to Augustine (354–430 CE), it is interesting to note that he was not the first Christian writer to address the question of the human city. In the period before the conversion of the Roman

The Spiritual City: Theology, Spirituality, and the Urban, First Edition. Philip Sheldrake.
© 2014 Philip Sheldrake. Published 2014 by John Wiley & Sons, Ltd.

Empire to Christianity during the fourth century, the evidence concerning early Christian attitudes is ambiguous. The anonymous "Epistle to Diognetus," which dates from the late second century, describes the Christians who inhabit human cities as "resident aliens." Their presence reminds earthly cities of an ultimate heavenly destiny. The point being made is that Christianity offers a highly paradoxical response to "the urban." The theologian Tertullian (circa 160–circa 225) writes in his *Apology* (chapter 37) that Christians are often accused of being unengaged with the affairs of life because they are too concerned with eternity. However, as Tertullian underlines, in reality Christians participate in the economic and social life of the Empire and offer benefits to it. Because of this, Christianity actively supports the social and moral order. Even a non-Christian Empire is part of God's providence as a means of restraining violence and evil. Tertullian's theological contemporary, Clement of Alexandria (circa 150–circa 215), in his work *Stromata* (4.26) accuses human cities of being cities in name only. Only heaven may properly be described as a city in a perfect sense. However, Clement also believed that the presence of Christians on earth, while an "alien citizenship," is nevertheless a true citizenship. The life of the heavenly city may in some sense be anticipated here on earth. In that sense Christianity's "alien citizenship" is a seed of transformation acting within and on behalf of the world. Similar sentiments are echoed in Origen (circa 185–254) in his *Contra Celsum*. There he asserts that Christians do good to cities, first, by educating their fellow citizens in devotion to God, who is the true guardian of the city, and, second, by enabling those who have lived good lives in even the least of human cities eventually to enter the divine city.

Finally, John Chrysostom, Archbishop of Constantinople (circa 347–407), in his *Homilies* (Homily 16.2) similarly notes that for Christians the only true city is the Heavenly Jerusalem. However, he exhorts his fellow citizens that earthly citizenship should be so informed by a heavenly vision that it is transfigured and the social order is sacralized. In his spiritual ideal for the human city, all the different orders of human society should be mutually dependent. Therefore, the rulers of cities have a duty to protect the weak from the strong (Homily 23). Interestingly, as Augustine did subsequently, John Chrysostom holds up the monastic life as the model for a new approach to human citizenship. Specifically he points to the monasteries of Antioch (Homily 72) as the "city of virtue."[3]

Augustine's Human City

Turning now to Augustine, the German Jewish political philosopher Hannah Arendt commented that "Augustine seems to have been the last to know at least what it once meant to be a citizen."[4] The question is whether he retained hope in the possibilities of human citizenship. It is true that he states at the start of his *City of God*, Book 1 Preface, that the earthly city is marked by a "lust of domination" or a desire for glory.[5] However, this is without question a critique specifically of Imperial Rome which was his historical urban paradigm. In addition, the book was written partly in response to accusations that the growth of Christianity was the cause of Rome's decline because Christian faith was too private and lacked a civic philosophy.

However, Augustine was concerned to counter any suggestion that any political system, even the relatively new Christian Roman Empire, could effectively be canonized as the privileged place of God's presence and purpose. In other words, as the contemporary Augustine scholar Carol Harrison underlines, Augustine clearly breaks with any attempt to create an "imperial theology."[6] In the mind of Augustine, the ongoing flow of history in the period between Christ's ascension and his second coming (or the Parousia) was "secular" in the sense that it manifested no definitive signposts to eternal life or guidelines to the sacred. No human social or political system came closer to God than any other. This aspect of Augustine gives Christianity a great deal of prophetic ammunition to critique attempts to promote specific social and political systems (for example, capitalism, Marxism or religious theocracies) as uniquely effective, let alone notably virtuous. However, Augustine did not deny that God acts equally in every time and place. While for Augustine the true "city" was the community of believers destined to become the City of God, he did not reject the status of "the secular" or of the human city in particular. Indeed he argues that it is incorrect to accuse Christianity of being apolitical. For Augustine, Christianity is neither to dominate public life nor to retreat from it.

The word "secular" (Latin *saeculum*), unlike the word "profane," with which it is often confused, does not have any connotations of being radically opposed to the sacred. In fact, the concept of the "secular" has Christian origins and is simply the shared, common, public space of "the present age" or the here and now. This is, if you like, a zone in which there is an overlap and interchange between religious insiders and outsiders. In the minds of commentators such as Robert Markus and Carol Harrison, the *saeculum* is theologically neutral in that it is not to be taken over either by purely sacred narratives or by those that caricature it as irredeemably separated from the sacred.[7] What is common to all human beings is the public realm. Christians have a stake in its social structures and cultural realities, alongside and with everyone else.

Here, we also need to distinguish carefully between Augustine's theological concept of the "earthly city" (the *civitas terrena*) which is the realm of sin, and the realm of the "secular" – the social and political realities of the everyday human city. The everyday city, a paradigm of the public realm, is a neutral space where the spiritual reality of the city of God and the counter-spiritual reality of the earthly city coexist and contend, like the wheat and tares of the gospel parable, until the end of time. As Augustine comments in his *City of God*, "In truth, those two cities are interwoven and intermixed in this era, and await separation at the last judgment."[8] The theme of mingling the two theological cities in human society is present in other works, for example *De Catechizandis Rudibus*, Augustine's sermons between the years 405 and 408 and his commentary on the Book of Genesis, *De Genesi ad Litteram* (circa 414). In the latter (chapter 11.15.20) Augustine sets out the "city of the just" as social rather than self-centered in nature and with a "regard for the common good for the sake of the community" as opposed to the opposite.[9]

Augustine was far from indifferent to the moral foundations of a human city. He defended a legitimate place for the secular sphere within a Christian interpretation of the world as the theatre of God's action. Indeed, some commentators suggest that in the mind of Augustine the vocation of a human city, both socially and architecturally, was to strive to become an anticipation in the here and now of the eschatological *civitas Dei*. According to this view, while Augustine was neither a city planner nor a political theorist, he effectively redeemed an urban culture in crisis by using the city as his image of heaven. Once again, it is important to bear in mind the context. The *City of God* was written as the city of Rome and Greco-Latin classical culture collapsed in the face of barbarian invaders. In adopting the image of the city as a metaphor for paradise, Augustine effectively uses historic urban civil (and civilized) culture to counter the chaos wrought by what he saw as culturally destructive barbarians. Thus, Augustine was, as it were, imagining a "better Rome." For Augustine, steeped in classical philosophy, no concrete image for paradise embodied the fullness of the human condition better than a city. As we shall see in the next chapter, during centuries following the fall of Rome monastic communities and their buildings effectively took the place of classical urban culture. Monasteries were mini-cities of God, images of the New Jerusalem (Book of Revelation 21) or cities set on a hill (Matthew 5:4). Later, this sacred role was then taken over, as we shall see in Chapter 3, by the medieval city revival.[10]

Human cities are shaped by time and space. Augustine's theology of time and human history was eschatological in the sense that it focused on the ultimate arrival of God's Kingdom at the end of time. Our human cities and our political systems are undoubtedly contingent. Nevertheless, human history is unquestionably God's creation. History is not to be condemned as evil or irrelevant. Augustine's distinction between sacred and secular cities does not render human history or built environments meaningless. What Augustine rejected was a sense that the contingent world or any version of human politics is definitive or of ultimate value. This would be idolatrous. In that sense, the existential human city can never be thought of in idealized, utopian terms. However, this distinction between a "common good" that is achievable in the everyday city and a City of God that is fulfilled only beyond time also counters any attempt to espouse some kind of totalitarian theocracy as the ideal social system.

Because Augustine's *City of God* was more concerned with the city as a community (*civitas*) rather than with it as a physical environment (*urbs*), people have been able to draw from his work a radical distinction between earthly and heavenly cities. As we saw in the Introduction, this image remained etched in the minds of people until the late Middle Ages and, arguably, even into the modern era. In practice, of course, there needs to be a dialectical relationship between the two planes of community and built environment. Only then will there develop a community-centered plan for cities that expresses the various ways in which life is actually lived, or that people hope it may be lived.

For Augustine, human institutions, including city life, are not irrelevant but are both convenient for, and necessary for, our current human purposes. They are also of moral and spiritual value when they are used to frame our human lives more broadly in ways that are focused upon the love of God and are directed at ultimate union with God.[11] Augustine was significantly preoccupied by the question of authority. How were Church authorities (for example, the local bishop) and the civil magistrates to be allowed the necessary freedom to act in relation to their own proper field of authority and according to their own legitimate principles? In his *City of God*, Augustine sought to delineate a sphere in which everyone had a stake. The human secular urban environment was a context in which there was a mixture of both the City of God and the earthly (sinful) city in this contingent life. Augustine sought to define *civitas* – that is, civic community – in a way that enabled Christians to acknowledge its proper claims upon them.

Equally, for Augustine this civic realm was vitally important in order to maintain earthly peace. In one sense civic society was relativized yet it was still of value. Indeed, in Augustine's words, the city of God in its pilgrimage through contingent time and space uses "earthly peace" – social cohesion, we might say – as a useful, even necessary medium for the eventual attainment of the fullness of heavenly peace. There is no question that in the mind of Augustine, *perfect* peace, *perfect* justice and *perfect* community are to be found only in the Church as City of God. However, we need to be clear that this refers to the purified and perfected Christian community of the eschatological age, eternity, not to the contingent, Church institution in the here and now. Like all structures shaped by human action, the institutional Church throughout history is an ambiguous context of high aspirations but also of striking imperfections.[12]

This interpretation of Augustine appears to be somewhat different from the viewpoint put forward by the British theologian John Milbank in the final chapter of his book *Theology and Social Theory: Beyond Secular Reason*. Milbank seems to suggest that any authentic and effective public realm is neither a neutral nor a shared space but must be intimately associated with and shaped by Christianity. In contrast, however, "The realm of the merely practical, cut off from the ecclesial, is quite simply a realm of sin."[13] For Milbank, the material human city is "secular" in this negative sense. This is because it is built solely upon human reason and is therefore inherently involved in a culture of violence – in other words, Augustine's "lust of domination" noted earlier. Given Augustine's relatively sympathetic review of Cicero and his attention to urban virtues in the everyday realm, an important question is whether this negative judgment is *inherently* true of all material cities or is specifically a critique of the decadence of late-imperial Rome. To my mind, part of the problem, as I suggested earlier, is a failure to distinguish effectively between Augustine's unquestionably profane and sinful *civitas terrena* and his understanding of the neutral shared space of the everyday city in the *saeculum*, the here and now. If we accept Milbank's way of seeing things in reference to all human cities, the life of the Christian community would seem to be too sharply set apart from the everyday public world. In the words of the social philosopher Gillian Rose, the danger is that Milbank's approach "effectively destroys the idea of a city."[14] Interestingly, in his brief but astute comments on Augustine's theology of the city, Graham Ward, who is in some ways a theological confrère of Milbank, makes no mention of this interpretation.[15]

I agree with another Augustine scholar, Robert Markus, when he further affirms that any interpretation of Augustine that denies the value of political–social structures in "secular" culture is a misreading. Augustine clearly saw the possibility of moral action and value-driven aspiration within everyday social and political frameworks. It is important to be clear that groups, institutions and societies in the everyday world, such as our human cities, are for Augustine components of his theological–eschatological mixture until the end of time of two cities: the *civitas Dei*, City of God, and the *civitas terrena*, the realm of sin.[16]

To return specifically to his book the *City of God*, Augustine is not essentially a political theorist in a disinterested or theoretical sense. For Augustine, human community, *civitas*, is to be reconceived in terms of the transformation demanded by and facilitated by belonging ideally to the City of God. In the end, the heart of the matter is how we choose to orientate our love. As the theologian Rowan Williams suggests, the *City of God* is a schema for reflecting on the nature of social virtue.[17] Augustine suggests that only if we orientate our love towards God will we discover new ways of relating to the world. He does not really develop detailed ideas about the practical tasks of the urban civic community. The central question for Augustine is how people, whose lives have been transformed by relating to God, approach a life of service within the human city. How is the public realm of a city, human society and politics to be a medium for self-giving? For Augustine, the answer is that if we choose to love rightly the rest will follow. In other words, true citizenship involves observing the dual commandment of Jesus Christ to love God truly and also to love our neighbor (in this case, our fellow citizens) as ourselves. Urban virtue is not purely utilitarian but depends on giving God God's due. Only this way will we give our fellow citizens their full due because their deepest value consists is being images of God.[18] The key is to realize that true human reconciliation and mutual pardon in the city, essential to social justice, can only be produced between people who consistently know themselves to be sinners in need of healing.[19]

Having said this, Augustine does offer a few hints about the tasks and values of a truly common life in the human city. It is clear from reading the *City of God* that Augustine is well aware of Greek and Roman philosophy and enters into conversation with, for example, Aristotle's social ethics and Cicero's *Republic*. For example, in Book 2 he bases himself on Cicero to suggest that Christianity strongly supports the values that are required for effective civil society. Only those who commit themselves to such values will be able to promote a genuinely common life.[20] To create an effective human city there must be some agreement about what constitutes justice and the common good. To speak of the human city as "secular" or "neutral" does not imply that it is a wholly value-free or morally indifferent zone. There must be some reference to the ultimate ends and purpose of human existence. For Augustine this is a theological matter rather than a purely philosophical or political one. Thus, a truly human city needs to be bound together by following the way of Christ, by honoring God and by loving our neighbor in God rather than by focusing on self-interest or power domination. However, the central point is that in this way Christians may contribute to the actual life of real human cities, assist in seeking the civic good and collaboratively work to make the human city an effective, if imperfect, expression of the highest good. This highest good is ultimately reached only beyond time and space in eternal union with God.

One value of civil society is that it promotes consensus or, in Augustine's words, "a certain cohesion of human wills." Clearly, Augustine does not underwrite any form of moral relativism in the human city or the supremacy of freedom of choice or the primacy of individual satisfaction. The further tasks of the civil community are to foster order in the face of chaos and conflict and to create human solidarity. Our common life in the human city is to be more than purely a set of pragmatic institutional arrangements. Equally, a community whose ideal is to be organized around the virtue of mutual love will eschew the temptation to compete for power. For Augustine, true authority is concerned with service rather than with being served and honored. This makes politics a personally demanding and also a spiritual matter. In that Augustine is concerned to foster a particular approach to human life, the human city needs to be orientated towards a sense of ultimate human purpose. The question is, what horizon of human possibility do we promote? For Augustine, Christianity both underlines the limited horizons of Imperial Rome and promotes an alternative narrative of human potential and ultimate destiny. Christianity offers to the human city a unique theology that all people without exception are created in the image of God and are consequently endowed with a fundamental dignity.

The concept of *societas*, "society," in Augustine is the sum total of associations between people ranging from trade to neighborliness, to family and to civic friendship. Interestingly, the family or household is not purely domesticated but is also in some sense a part of "politics" – that is, the life of the *polis* – whose vocation is to build up the whole city. In the *City of God* 19.16, Augustine suggests that the household is the beginning of the city. Domestic harmony contributes to civic harmony. Both individuals and family households contribute to the "common good" and to a more noble civic order. While cities need civic authorities to regulate practical matters and also to mediate between potential conflicts of will, in the end true "society" is made up of a vibrant network of living relationships between people who are seeking to "live rightly" empowered implicitly by their relationship with God. Proper order in the city is built upon, indeed can *only* be built upon, this quest to live rightly.

Augustine also balances the arguably more detached concept of "society" with the more intimate notion of *amicitia*, friendship. In Augustine there is even "civic friendship" – that is, the ideal of a friendship that extends beyond our immediate circle to embrace all those who inhabit the same place in which we live. This ideal of friendship might even be said to extend beyond the city to the whole world "with whom a man is joined by membership of human society" (*City of God*, 19.3). This converges with Augustine's notion in his commentary on the Book of Genesis that it is humanity as a collective whole, rather than isolated individuals, that is created in the image of God and that will be redeemed. As an urban ideal, *amicitia* embraces bonds of real attachment rather than purely pragmatic arrangements or a sense of obligation. It contrasts the self-emptying Christian virtue of *caritas*, self-giving love and service, with the power-driven notion of *libido dominandi* (the lust of domination) as the driving force of an effective city. In this way, Augustine counters a purely utilitarian approach to citizenship.[21] Finally, friendship in a fully Christian sense is bound to transcend social rank and to embrace the virtue of humility. As we shall see, this powerful notion of human equality appears again in the dossier of Augustine's monastic writings.

Although Augustine is bound to say that all human cities fall short of the ideal in relation to the true justice present in the heavenly city, there is a difference between those that fall "somewhat short" and those that fall hopelessly short. In this sense, urban virtues are relativized but not invalidated. It all depends, as Augustine suggests in the *City of God* (19.24), whether an urban society loves "better objects" or not. Augustine also counters any notion that the institutional Church cannot be true to itself in the public realm. The Church is able to proclaim its message of salvation to all while at the same time upholding the general consensus on what makes for a "civilized" life. This counters any rigid polarization of a collaborative against a contestational-prophetic understanding of Christian witness in the human city. The Christian community is a collaborative presence in the city but precisely in order to speak prophetically when required in ways that are true to itself and to its values.

Social Virtues: Augustine's Monastic Vision

Finally, there are also useful pointers to an urban vision in the collection of monastic texts known as "The Rule of St Augustine." The various texts that make up this Rule constitute the most influential monastic guidebook in the Western Church after the Rule of St Benedict. One problem is that Augustine does not mention the Rule in any of his other writings. Consequently, there has been some controversy over authorship, textual variations, and the dating of the various constituent texts. However, nowadays the scholarly consensus is that the male version of the Rule, known as the *Praeceptum*, is authentically by Augustine and dates from around 395–6. Other texts that complete the dossier of the Rule, including a version addressed to women, postdate the *Praeceptum* and may be by Augustine or derive from his immediate monastic circle in Hippo.[22]

In Augustine's *Praeceptum*, which we shall mention again in the next chapter, the monastery is intended to be a mirror for wider society. It therefore models a social way of life where certain virtues are highlighted. Political health, or the security of the human city (*civitas*), is guaranteed by civic virtues which Augustine describes as *fides, concordia*, and *bonum commune*.

Fides, faith or faithfulness, refers back to the important civic Roman goddess of the same name. This urban virtue originally spoke of idealistic citizenship and self-giving patriotism. However, in Christianity "faith" refers specifically to Jesus Christ. It implies living according to faith in Christ. This is not merely a devotional or doctrinal reference but has profound social consequences. The life of a monastery (and by implication, of the human city) was to give off the "good odor" of Christ by exemplary living – witnessing to Christ by living according to his teachings. According to Augustine, true politics in a profound sense demands spirituality. The model he takes is the community of the first Christians in Jerusalem, as portrayed in the Book of Acts Chapter 4, who are described as "one in heart and soul [or mind]." This divinely rooted friendship embraces both love and goodwill or harmony, and brings about authentic "society." This leads naturally a second social virtue, *concordia*.

Concordia, living in concord, also played a central role in the classical Roman public imagination. However, in this ancient imperial context, "living in concord" referred only to the privileged classes. Artisans or slaves were excluded. In the *Praeceptum* Augustine takes this classical notion and radically expands it. For Augustine, living in concord modeled a new ideal of social community. The Rule makes clear that within the monastic community representatives of every social class should live side by side – rich and poor, educated and uneducated, nobility and workers. This deliberately breached the traditional and rigid class boundaries within which people had been conventionally brought up. In one sense, status, distinctions and differences were to be left at the door of the monastery, although the Rule recognized that this was not a simple or pain-free process. Those who came from poorer backgrounds were not to take advantage of their links with people from rich families nor were they to boast to their own families of such grand associations. Conversely, those from rich or noble backgrounds were not to disparage their poorer brethren. Rather they should take pride in living with them. The equality implied by this version of "living in concord" was interestingly balanced with the defense of a certain plurality. Again, referring to the Book of Acts, Augustine noted that the distribution of material goods to each was to be made according to their particular needs. People's needs (or strength or capacities) were not the same across the board and therefore the same things were not necessarily to be provided for everyone in the community.

Augustine's third social virtue as expressed in the Rule, *bonum commune*, or seeking the common good, was once again one of the highest ideals of classical Roman political theory. It is a virtue that seeks to pursue common ideals while honoring individual needs. We find our own good by seeking the good of the other and together we are bound to work for the good of the whole. For, in Augustine's ideal of community or society, the common good is the highest good of all. Nevertheless, Augustine wishes to allow for the uniqueness of each member. In that sense, the common good is not the same as a lowest common denominator. The negotiation between individual personalities and expectations in favor of a common good necessarily involves discernment. That exercise of practical wisdom implies an examination by each person of their desires and aspirations in order to judge whether the needs of other people and of "the whole" might demand some degree of self-forgetfulness. In the light of this, in the *Praeceptum*, Augustine promotes the spiritual principle of self-transcendence – a movement from self-seeking to the higher ideal of seeking the common good.

Epilogue: Augustine's Theology of Self

Underlying Augustine's various approaches to the human city is a theology of human identity which in turn relates to his theological understanding of God.

Importantly, in terms of human identity, Augustine would have found the individualism and privatization that pervades much of contemporary Western urban culture entirely alien. In his contribution to the multiauthor *A History of Private Life*, Peter Brown, the eminent Augustine scholar, reminds us that the earliest approaches to the Christian life, including Augustine's, inherited from late-classical Judaism an intense sense of a vital solidarity between the individual and the social community. The perceived danger was that people would retreat into protected privacy rather than give themselves wholeheartedly to the common good. Hence, Jewish writers turned their attention to the thoughts of "the heart" – the supposed core of human motivation and intention. Human destiny was a state of solidarity with others, expressed by the image of an undivided heart.[23] This biblically-driven perspective was complemented in Augustine by his acceptance of the classical Greek and Roman philosophical understanding (specifically in the writings of Aristotle and Cicero) that humans are essentially social beings rather than solitary by nature.

Augustine adopted this symbol of the heart as a way of expressing "the self." In Book 10 of his *Confessions*, when discussing how well other people may know the truth of a person, Augustine refers to "my heart, where I am whatever it is that I am."[24] The use of the word "heart" suggests that the Christian journey takes us "towards the interior self," the true self, where God dwells. This is away from what St Paul (in his Second Letter to the Corinthians 4:16) refers to as our "outer nature": "Even though our outer nature is wasting away, our inner nature is being renewed day by day." On the face of it, this language appears to be very close to the supposed Christian attitudes to the outer world that are criticized so sharply by Richard Sennett. However, here the notion of "outer" refers to our temptation to live on the surface of life, mistaking what is transitory for what is fundamental. It is not a rejection of the outer world of social relationships.

For Augustine, God created humans with the divine image "in their heart." This *imago Dei* is the measure of the true self and sin disconnects us from it. In his *Tractates* [or *Homilies*] *on the Gospel of John* (18.10) Augustine invites us to reconnect with this real self: "Return to your heart! See there what perhaps you perceive about God because the image of God is there. In the inner man [*sic*] Christ dwells; in the inner man you are renewed according to the image of God."[25] Earlier in the same section, Augustine suggests that in leaving the heart we actually leave ourselves: "Why do you go away from yourselves and perish from yourselves? Why do you go the ways of solitude? You go astray by wandering about... You are wandering without [that is, outside ourselves], an exile from yourself." It is not the journey into the heart that is self-centered and solipsistic; rather what is mistaken is to leave the true self where we engage with God and with all others in God. When Augustine writes about wandering about in our outer landscape, he implies an experience of fragmentation.

Augustine links this wandering to "the body." However, once again it is important to understand that "the body" here means fundamentally "the senses." The senses are plural and therefore have several dimensions that offer distinctive kinds of information. Each dimension, each sense, experiences reality only in part. However, Augustine does not mean that the bodily senses are not important. On the contrary, Augustine describes them as the "assistants" of the heart. Thus the heart stands for "the whole self" or "the true self" in its integrated wholeness. It brings together all these sense impressions and is the principle of unity, harmony, and the means of interpreting reality in the round. To put matters in another way, the outer world, for example the human city, is not the problem. The problem is when we live "exteriorly" – that is, out of our skins. The language of the heart is not evidence of a privatized rather than social spirituality. What is interior to me is, for Augustine, where I am also united in God with the whole human family.

The *imago Dei* in which we are created and which is imprinted on the heart must be read alongside Augustine's doctrine of creation. In Augustine's *Commentary on Genesis*, Adam's original sin was "pleasing himself" and "living for himself" (*secundum se vivere, sibi placere*). Thus, human communion is ruptured by sin – whether our union with God, solidarity with other human beings or harmony with a true self. In other words, sin is essentially a withdrawal into individualistic "privacy," but this should not be confused with inwardness or interiority. Self-seeking pride is the archetypal sin (*Literal Meaning of Genesis*, XI.15.19–20).[26] Original Eden, or the monastic life, or the idealized future City of God are all based on "the love that promotes the common good for the sake of the heavenly society" (*Literal Meaning of Genesis*, XI.15.20). In fact for Augustine the most insidious human sin is self-enclosure. The "private" is seen as the opposite of "common" or "public." In Augustine it is common humanity, rather than entirely autonomous individuals, who are created in God's image. Moral virtue involves defending what is public or held in common. Equally, in Augustine, the Heavenly City was the community in which there would be the fullness of sharing. There will be no room in the eternal kingdom of God for self-enclosed and protected privacy.[27] Within Augustine there is a tension that cannot be resolved. This is between a striking sense of the personal self and an equally striking sense of the fundamentally social nature of human life. "The heart" for Augustine is where a true integration of interiority and exteriority, the spiritual and the fleshly, happens. Equally, Augustine is clear that if anything is claimed to be in the heart or inside us but does not show itself outwardly in love, community, and service, it is illusory. "The return to the heart is but the first step of a conversion process that proves itself in universal and unrestricted – catholic – love."[28]

What exists at the heart of each person is the image of God-as-Trinity. In his treatise *De Trinitate* Augustine focused on the traces of the Trinity (*vestigia Trinitatis*) found in the soul or center of every human person. People are made in the image of God-as-Trinity and are called to be restored to that image which has been obscured by sin (*De Trinitate* 14.19.25[29]). Further, being created in the image of God-as-Trinity involves a call to become a community or society (sharing the inner love of the Trinity). Augustine was concerned with how Christians are transformed interiorly by the indwelling of God-as-Trinity in the human soul. This indwelling of the loving communion of the Trinity brings about our capacity for mutual charity.

The point is that the Christian doctrine of the Trinity is neither an abstract concept nor merely one doctrine among many. To conceive of God as Trinity impacts not only on how we understand and practice the Christian life but also on our understanding of how human society is, or should be, organized.[30] God is to be understood as "persons-in-communion." God's "societal" nature is fundamental. In the Christian doctrine of Trinity, God's unity consists in the interrelationship of persons in free and loving relationships. This understanding of God is rich for our understanding of not only of human identity but also of society and the intimate connection between the two. From this it follows that "communion," *koinonia*, is what makes all things come to be. Nothing and nobody exists without it. It follows that in the thought of Augustine communion, and therefore "society," is structured into the very nature of being human.[31]

Notes

English translations are cited wherever available.

1   Richard Sennett, *The Conscience of the Eye: The Design and Social Life of Cities*, London: Faber & Faber, 1993, Introduction and Chapter 1.
2   Sennett, *The Conscience of the Eye*, pp. 6–10.
3   For a commentary on these early Christian attitudes to cities, see Rowan Greer, "Alien citizens: A marvellous paradox," in Peter S. Hawkins (ed.), *Civitas: Religious Interpretations of the City*, Atlanta: Scholars' Press, 1986, pp. 39–52.

4　Hannah Arendt, *The Human Condition*, Chicago: University of Chicago Press, 1958, p. 14.
5　For an English translation see H. Bettenson (ed.), *St Augustine: City of God*, London: Penguin Classics, New Edition 1984.
6　Carol Harrison, *Augustine: Christian Truth and Fractured Humanity*, Oxford: Oxford University Press 2000, p. 203.
7　For an updated analysis of "the secular realm" in Augustine, see Robert A. Markus, *Christianity and the Secular*, Notre Dame, IN: University of Notre Dame Press, 2006.
8　*City of God*, 1.35.
9　See Gerard O'Daly, *Augustine's City of God: A Reader's Guide*, Oxford: Oxford University Press, 2004, pp. 63–4.
10　David Mayernick, *Timeless Cities: An Architect's Reflections on Renaissance Italy*, Boulder, CO: Westview Press, 2003, pp. 5–13.
11　Augustine, *De Doctrina Christiana*, R.P.H. Green(trans.), Oxford: Oxford University Press, 2.25–38.
12　*City of God*, 19.17.
13　See John Milbank, *Theology and Social Theory: Beyond Secular Reason*, Oxford: Blackwell, 1990, p. 406.
14　Gillian Rose, "Diremption of spirit," p. 48 in Phillipa Berry and Andrew Wernick (eds.), *Shadow of Spirit: Postmodernism and Religion*, London: Routledge, 1993.
15　See Graham Ward, *Cities of God*, London and New York: Routledge, 2000, pp. 227–37.
16　Markus, *Christianity and the Secular*, pp. 41–68.
17　Rowan Williams, "Politics and the soul: A reading of the *City of God*," *Milltown Studies*, 19/20, 1987, p. 57.
18　Williams, "Politics and the soul," p. 59.
19　See Robert Dodaro, "Augustine's secular city," in Robert Dodaro and George Lawless (eds.), *Augustine and His Critics*, London and New York: Routledge 2000, pp. 231–59, especially p. 248.
20　For helpful comments on Augustine's idea of civic virtue, see David Hollenbach, *The Common Good and Christian Ethics*, Cambridge: Cambridge University Press, 2002, pp. 120–129.
21　O'Daly, *Augustine's City of God*, pp. 224ff.
22　See Thomas F. Martin, Chapter 8 "Augustine and the politics of monasticism," in John Doody, Kevin L. Hughes and Kim Paffenroth (eds.), *Augustine and Politics*, Lanham, MD and Oxford: Lexington Books, 2005, pp. 165–86; also Carol Harrison, *Augustine: Christian Truth and Fractured Humanity*, Oxford: Oxford University Press, 2000, pp. 182ff. For a scholarly edition of the Rule, see George Lawless, *Augustine of Hippo and His Monastic Rule*, Oxford: Clarendon Press, 1987.

23 See Peter Brown, "Late antiquity," in Paul Veyne (ed.), *A History of Private Life*, Volume 1, *From Pagan Rome to Byzantium*, Cambridge, MA: Harvard University Press, 1996.

24 *Confessions* Book 10, Chapter 3, section 4 in Albert Outler (ed.), *Augustine: Confessions and Enchiridion*, London: The Library of Christian Classics, SCM Press, 1955.

25 J.W. Rettig (trans.), *The Fathers of the Church*, Volume 92, Washington, DC: Catholic University of America Press, 1995.

26 *De Genesi ad litteram*, Migne Patrologia Latina, 34.245–486. English translation, "The literal meaning of Genesis," in J.H. Taylor (ed.), *Ancient Christian Writers*, pp. 41–2, New York: Newman Press, 1982.

27 On this point see Robert A. Markus, *The End of Ancient Christianity*. Cambridge: Cambridge University Press, 1998, p. 78.

28 Thomas Martin, *Our Restless Heart: The Augustinian Tradition*, London: Darton Longman & Todd, 2003, p. 43.

29 Augustine of Hippo, *The Trinity*, translated and edited Edmund Hill and John Rotelle, New York: Augustine Heritage Institute, New City Press, 2nd edition, 2012.

30 See Catherine LaCugna, *God for Us: The Trinity and Christian Life*, San Francisco: HarperCollins, 1993, p. 1. Also see her comments on Augustine, pp. 10–11 and Chapter 3.

31 For an overview of various theological understandings of the impact of Trinitarian theology on our conceptions of human identity and society, see Philip Sheldrake, *Spirituality and Theology: Christian Living and the Doctrine of God*, London: Darton, Longman & Todd and Maryknoll, NY: Orbis Books, 1998, pp. 48–50 and Chapter 3 "Partners in conversation."

CHAPTER 2

Monasticism and Utopian Visions

It may seem strange to include a chapter on monasticism in a book about Christian visions of "the city." In the minds of many people, monastic life has classically involved people leaving the "human city" in order to seek a purely spiritual "city of God." However, as I intend to show, there are fascinating connections between Christian monasticism and a kind of alternative, utopian urbanism.

A Movement to the Margins

Monasticism is essentially concerned with changing places, literally and metaphorically. At the heart of Christian theology and spirituality is an invitation to enter a new, redeemed world. The Christian community is the carrier of this new world on behalf of wider humanity. Indeed, the community is intended to be an anticipation of it despite the fact that, like all human groups, it is flawed.[1] Historically, monastic life has sought to express this ideal vision of a transformed human community in a particularly intense way. Its specific purpose and power within the Christian community and in wider human society is to be a "place" that, while socially and culturally eccentric, is, paradoxically, where people seek to live out in radical terms, as best they can, the ethos of the future city of God.

The Spiritual City: Theology, Spirituality, and the Urban, First Edition. Philip Sheldrake.
© 2014 Philip Sheldrake. Published 2014 by John Wiley & Sons, Ltd.

The wilderness in its various forms has exercised a peculiar fascination throughout Christian history. This is especially true of the originators of the monastic movement in Syria, Palestine, and Egypt during the fourth century CE.[2] The theme of the desert is common to many early monastic texts. It is a place of trial, where ascetics battle with inner and outer demons.[3] The monastic desert is frontier territory and living there symbolizes a state of spiritual liminality – that is, living between the two dimensions of the everyday world and the spiritual world.

To move to the desert was, metaphorically speaking, both to journey towards the city of God and away from the cities of sin. Indeed, one modern classic study of early desert monasticism is entitled *The Desert A City*.[4] To strive to perfect oneself morally involved a topographical displacement. The early ascetics deliberately sought out the empty spaces of the wilderness. Monastic life from the start was a social and political as well as a spiritual statement. The monastic life represented a disentangling of oneself from conventional social and economic obligations in favor of a reshaping of human relations.[5] In early Egyptian monasticism, we see the gradual development of monastic "villages" or "towns." In their geographical isolation, the monastics recreated the format of social communities and thus became the *oikumene* (human settlement) in the *eremos* (desert).[6]

This expresses not simply a regulation of life in favor of contemplative solitude but also an important vision of a reformed human city. Monasticism received further important input in the thought of Augustine of Hippo during the early part of the fifth century CE. Augustine's theology of grace shifted the ground on which previous understandings of monastic life had rested. In very broad terms, while monasticism continued to involve a degree of renunciation, Augustine moved the earlier concentration on asceticism towards a greater emphasis on promoting the common good, charity, and the virtues of a "common life." In that sense, as we saw in the last chapter, monastic life was to act as a provocative reminder to wider society of the essential human virtues. In terms of directly engaging with wider society, the Rule of St Augustine is quite moderate. For example, in reference to monastic encounters with women, it states "You are not forbidden to see women when you are out of the house. It is wrong, however, to desire women or to wish them to desire you."[7]

In the even more influential Western monastic rule, the Rule of St Benedict (RSB), Chapter 4 "The Tools for Good Works" portrays monastic withdrawal in terms of practicing different behavior:

> Your way of acting should be different from the world's way; the love of Christ must come before all else. You are not to act in anger or nurse a grudge. Rid your heart of all deceit. Never give a hollow greeting of peace or turn away when someone needs your love. Bind yourself to no oath lest it prove false, but speak the truth with heart and tongue. (RSB Chapter 4, verses 20–28.)

Also, in Chapter 4, verse 8, the scriptural injunction to honor one's father and mother is changed to "honor everyone," because a critical element of monasticism was a reformulation of conventional social values. Indeed, Benedict's Rule is not rigid about physical separation from other people, as it lists among the legitimate work of the monks the relief of the poor, clothing the naked, visiting the sick, burying the dead, going to help the troubled and consoling the suffering (RSB 4: 10–19).

Utopias

The liminality of early monasticism is intended to underline a kind of utopian vision for the redemption of the human city. Utopian imagery often portrays a return to a pre-Fall paradise state where people once again live in harmony with wild animals.[8] "Utopia" is a made-up word, based on the Greek, courtesy of Sir Thomas More the sixteenth-century English Christian humanist and politician. It means literally "no place" or "nowhere."[9] In popular understanding, "utopia" often stands for an ideal place but this is a misunderstanding. Utopias are imaginary places that express human desire – positively or negatively. To point the way towards a different kind of place we need to explore the dialectical relationship between the possible and the impossible – which the concept of "utopia" precisely does.[10] Utopias are symbolic places rather than potentially real. In the words of Henri Lefebvre, the eminent French political philosopher mentioned in the Introduction, they allow us to explore the "places of what has no place, or no longer has a place – the absolute, the divine or the possible."[11]

In the early sixteenth century Sir Thomas More wrote his classic work, *Utopia*. The status of his book is a matter of debate. Is it the portrayal of an ideal society, without the benefit of Christian revelation? Is it merely a witty joke? Or is it something in between – a narrative that critiques Christians, who claim the benefit of divine revelation yet manage to do less well than the Utopians, who rely only on their human reason. There is much in More's land of Utopia to admire, but other things fall short of ideal. It seems clear that More intends Christian revelation to provide the yardstick to measure which elements of his vision are to be taken seriously. This supports such details as the absence of poverty, exploitation, luxury, and the idle rich in a land of happy, healthy, and public-spirited people. More's two closest humanist friends, Desiderius Erasmus and Guillaume Budé, a perceptive early commentator on the book, both believed that *Utopia* embodied "divine principles."[12] Budé referred to More's Utopia as *Hagnopolis* or "holy community." The Utopians possessed in the highest degree the important virtues that More had previously described as especially Christian: simplicity, temperance, and frugality. They also had faith in a God whose goodness they trusted. Along with faith went *spes* or hope of eternity and also *charitas* (his spelling of *caritas*) or love. The citizens of Utopia were joined together by "mutual love and charity," *mutuus amor, charitasque* (p. 224, line 8). Utopian institutions were described by More as the most prudent and holy (p. 102, lines 27–28).

More's work is essentially rhetorical, in the humanist style that influenced his intellectual circle. In other words, his *Utopia* is meant not simply to instruct but to *move* the reader to a change of perspective and values. Rhetoric implies a deliberately contrived device to communicate to the reader something of importance beyond the imaginary narrative.[13] Interestingly, More had strong monastic sympathies, and it is not fanciful to see this reflected to some degree in his description of Utopian social life.

All utopias carry the weight of our projections, shaped in particular times and places, of what we long for or loathe. Because of this, as we explore visions of the idealized city what needs to change in the everyday city is an endlessly controversial matter. In particular, religious utopias speak of a world transformed where we may live in perfect harmony, free from suffering, divisions, and injustice. In Christian terms, the ultimate utopia is paradise or the eternal City of God.[14] Theologically speaking, our eschatologies are therefore variations on a utopian theme. Certain kinds of utopianism can be simply a retreat into a blissful realm of pristine separatist imaginings, free from the people we do not like. However, the truth is that this world, this present city, however compromised it is, is the only place we have. Thus, alternative ways forward can only be constructed in the places where we initially find ourselves.

Monasteries are also examples of utopias – places that evoke human aspirations and desires. Although utopias in a formal sense are places of the imagination, the concept merges with places that exist in real time and space. Monastic community is not a substitute for the human city. Rather, monastic life is a rhetorical statement and an act of resistance at the heart of the human city against any diminishment of imagination regarding our potential future. As a form of rhetoric, monasticism invites us to live as if the harmony, the reconciliation, the social transformation implied by the kingdom of God were actually the case. Monastic life lives out the story of God's kingdom in order to give form to a world that is not yet fully realized.[15]

The ideals of Christian monasticism bear an interesting resemblance to the idea of "heterotopias" in the writings of the French postmodern theorist, Michel Foucault. It is important to acknowledge that Foucault himself did not understand monasticism in this way. For him, monasticism was an example, comparable to prisons, of the idealization of repressive "order" and control. This was part of Foucault's characterization of religion as a structure that manipulates and controls people by silencing them.[16] Nevertheless, I believe it is possible to enter into an interesting conversation with Foucault's concept of "heterotopias."[17] In Foucault's words, heterotopias are places that are "outside of all places, even though it may be possible to indicate their location in reality."[18] They exist as real places whose function is to be radically different from the norm. They have the ability to transgress, to undermine and to question the total coherence of our self-contained social systems. Again to quote Foucault, heterotopias are "something like counter-sites, a kind of effectively enacted utopia in which the real sites, all the other real sites that can be found within the culture, are simultaneously represented, contested and inverted."[19]

In other words, heterotopias are places that represent more than simply themselves. Thus, Foucault points to the image of the oriental garden – a tiny place that nevertheless represents the whole world. Symbolic microcosms permeate Christianity as well. As we shall see in the next chapter, medieval cathedrals were deliberately constructed as microcosms of the cosmos. Monastic spaces have also been interpreted in this way, both in terms of their architecture and of the ordered form of life practiced within them.

Spaces of Reconciliation

Monasteries offer alternative visions of human community. They share with many utopian visions a sense that most human divisions are caused by individualism, and the unbalanced priority given to privacy and private property. As we saw in the last chapter, Augustine of Hippo is typical of early Christian thought in believing that it is humanity, rather than autonomous individuals, that is created in the image of God. Virtue consists of defending what is held in common. There is no self-enclosed and protected privacy in the eternal kingdom of God.[20]

The late fourth-century text, the *Ordo Monasterii*, part of the so-called Rule of St Augustine, addressed common life in these terms: "No one is to claim anything as his own, whether clothing or whatever else; we wish to live as the apostles did."[21] In the *Praeceptum*, or Rule proper, the common life is equally stressed. The reference is to the imitation of the early Christian community portrayed in the Book of Acts (2:43–47). However, in the Rule there is also space for individual differences and needs:

> 2. In this way, let no one work for himself alone, but all your work shall be for the common purpose, done with greater zeal and more concentrated effort than if each one worked for his private purpose. The Scriptures tell us: "Love is not self-seeking." We understand this to mean: the common good takes precedence over the individual good, the individual good yields to the common good.[22]

The Rule of St Augustine also offers a quite prolonged treatment of how monastic space is to be one of reconciliation with "the other," particularly by crossing social boundaries:

> 6. Nor should they put their nose in the air because they associate with people they did not dare approach in the world. Instead they should lift up their heart, and not pursue hollow worldly concerns...

7. But on the other hand, those who enjoyed some measure of worldly success ought not to belittle their brothers who come to this holy society from a condition of poverty. They should endeavor to boast about the fellowship of poor brothers, rather than the social standing of rich relations...[23]

A central aspect of monasteries as places of reconciliation concerns the reception of strangers. Receiving the stranger as if they were Christ was an evangelical mandate for all Christians (Matthew 25:35) and thus became integral to monastic identity as a microcosm of the Christian life.[24] All the major figures of early monasticism such as Basil of Caesarea, John Chrysostom, and Jerome founded specialized institutions for hospitality, including pilgrim hospices and hospitals. The collections of sayings and anecdotes from the fourth- and fifth-century Egyptian desert fathers and mothers are also full of examples of hospitality as a rule of life. Charity was an essential rather than additional element of the search for singleness of heart:

> A brother questioned an old man, saying, "Here are two brothers. One of them leads a solitary life for six days a week, giving himself much pain, and the other serves the sick. Whose work does God accept with the greater favor?" The old man said, "Even if the one who withdraws for six days were to hang himself up by the nostrils, he could not equal the one who serves the sick."[25]

In the Rule of St Benedict, Chapter 53 on hospitality, it states: *Omnes supervenientes hospites tamquam Christus suscipiantur* – All are to be received as Christ. However, the Rule goes on to say "for he himself will say, I was the stranger and you took me in." Christ is the stranger. This implies a deeper theology of hospitality, which will be explored further in Chapter 8.

Irish Monasticism

Moving now to northern Europe, early medieval Irish monastic settlements are a particularly potent example of monasticism as an alternative form of urbanism. It is not merely their locations that had spiritual significance. The ways in which such settlements were marked out in the landscape by various kinds of boundaries, as well as the ways in which they were internally ordered, also reveal important aspects of wider Celtic spiritual attitudes.

The hagiographies of the Celtic saints, such as Adomnan's life of St Columba, are helpful in terms of the details of how monastic life was ordered. There were large, wealthy and often mixed religious settlements, but most monastic settlements were relatively small. Two features of the organization of sacred space were similar across all sizes of settlement. First, the inner sanctum, or holy place, was clearly defined. Second, the overall religious space had an enclosing wall. Even the small hermitage of St Cuthbert on the island of Inner Farne exhibited both features. The Venerable Bede's life of St Cuthbert records that the Anglo-Saxon saint built a small "city of God," a *civitas*, designed for his rule and within it houses suited to his city. The essentials were an enclosure wall, a cell to live in, a place to pray and a place to be buried.[26]

The origins of some kind of boundary or enclosure for Christian monastic sites are obscure but seem to go back to the earliest times in the Egyptian desert. With some exceptions, Irish monastic sites favored a circular boundary plan. The circle, because it has no discernible beginning or end point, was a powerful symbol of eternity and of spatial infinity. In other words, a circle represented the cosmos. Circle symbolism was not unique to Celtic culture. We may recall the circular churches and baptisteries of the Mediterranean in late antiquity or the rose windows and labyrinth designs of some medieval cathedrals.[27] The main point here is that the circular design of Irish monastic sites portrayed such places as microcosms of the cosmos. A circular boundary wall spoke eloquently of the desire of the inhabitants to create a place that would exist simultaneously on two planes – the contingent and the cosmic.[28]

The boundaries of monastic enclosures also marked off a *civitas* where spiritual powers, or the power of good, predominated over evil. Within the enclosure raw nature gave way to the sacred powers of ritual and prayer. Beyond the boundary was a "wilderness" that was not only uncultivated and socially untamed but was also believed to be the dwelling place of the forces of evil.[29]

When we interpret Irish monastic sites we need to transcend the classic polarities of secular and sacred, "worldliness" and "withdrawal," that frequently dominated traditional histories of spirituality. Physical boundaries in the Irish monastic context often manifested an interpenetration of spiritual and social relationships rather than the opposite. In no other part of the Western Church did monasticism dominate social systems and cultural life so strongly as in early medieval Ireland.[30] The kinship model of social relationships predominated and was closely associated with place. "Place" in the geographical sense and a person's "place in the world" were intimately connected. It is not surprising, therefore, that this same kinship structure drawn from wider society also governed the ways in which monastic enclosures and sacred spaces were organized.

While the smaller, more ascetic, monastic groups were obviously more socially marginal and distinctive, the larger Irish monastic enclosures contained a fairly representative cross-section of society.[31] Because of the ambiguities in the use of monastic terminology, it seems likely that people of both sexes were considered as "monks" even if they lived within a normal family life. It is inappropriate to consider married monks as evidence of spiritual decline. The fact that senior roles were held by successive members of family groups, many of whom were not clerics, reflects the reality that monastic concepts were in practice expressions of the local Christian and civic community. Everyone in the family was equally a part of the Church and its social world. Such a blurring of divisions was unexceptional when the separation between social, ecclesial, and monastic structures was so indistinct.

The ambiguities were clearly more of a problem after the gradual imposition from the Continent of more structured and "reformed" monasticism (for example, the Cistercians) from the twelfth century onwards. One example is the restructuring under the Rule of St Benedict of the monastic community on the Scottish island of Iona in the early years of the thirteenth century. The evidence from Iona suggests that the traditional family domination of monastic roles such as abbot continued to some degree throughout the Middle Ages. New novices were quite regularly granted dispensations from the impediment of being the son of another monk. This has often been interpreted as an appalling corruption of the monastic ideal, but given the pre-Benedictine history of the monastery such a negative view needs considerable refinement.[32]

Although there were a variety of subdivisions within the basic monastic spaces, monastic enclosures as a whole were also deemed to be sacred spaces. When Maedoc founded the monastic settlement of Druim Letham in the sixth century, the act of consecration stated quite clearly that the chosen site existed in a sacred as well as a physical landscape with an attendant set of spiritual relations that needed to be properly ordered. Such ritual blessings of religious sites were believed to be effective for domestic dwellings as well. A man living close to Ailbe's monastery at Imlech is said to have asked for a similar ritual of foundation to be conducted around his new house. Ailbe granted his request and the blessing promised that the house would be protected from rain, wind, and abandonment. The sanctity of monastic boundaries was perceived as giving the same protection. In other words, all hostile elements were excluded and the positive powers of the place were also locked in within the enclosure.[33]

The boundary walls that enclosed Irish monastic settlements and their Scottish and northern English foundations were partly status symbols delineating the legal area belonging to the group. However, the boundary of the monastic *civitas* also marked out a legal area that was also to be regarded as sacred. This enclosure, or *termon*, was intended to be a place free from all aggression. Violence was excluded. Because of this ban, monastic settlements also functioned as a kind of bank in which people's valuables could be stored for safe-keeping. Some of them also served as the equivalent of an open prison. Large settlements had groups of penitents attached to them, some of whom had committed serious crimes against society, including murder.[34]

Consequently, the boundaries around religious sites did not function as enclosures to shut out the world or to separate monastics from the rest of the population. Because of this relative lack of separation from wider society, the evidence suggests that within the wider boundary, solitaries or groups of celibate ascetics occupied a distinct enclosure. Sometimes small groups moved apart from such settlements to live in more remote locations. Overall, however, a monastic enclosure was simply a privileged space within which a particular vision of society could be lived out. Thus, monks in the tradition of Columbanus saw monastic settlements as anticipations of paradise in which the forces of division, violence, and evil were excluded. Wild beasts were tamed and nature was regulated. The privileges of Adam and Eve in Eden, received from God but lost by the Fall, were reclaimed.

To live out this vision of an alternative world involved all of the people who were brought within the enclosed space. It was not something that concerned merely the professional ascetics. The tradition of Columbanus, for example, believed that all people without exception were called from birth to the experience of contemplation. So, monastic enclosures were places of spiritual experience and also places of education, wisdom, and art. Ideally speaking, within the enclosures an integration of all elements of human life took place as well as of all classes of human society.[35]

In Ireland, there was no regular layout of buildings around a rectangular cloister as there was in later medieval monastic traditions, nor a general segregation of monastics or clergy from the general populace in the great monastic "cities." Even so, Irish religious settlements did employ some internal zoning of the enclosed space to provide areas of lesser and greater privacy.[36] Usually, there were one or more small churches, a graveyard, a standing cross or two, probably a separate abbot's dwelling, a *scriptorium* (where manuscripts were copied) and a collection of small huts where the monks lived either alone or in small groups. The general choice of sites and overall layout did not make neatness or standardization possible. As we have already noted, there were different kinds of people including families who were described as "monks." However, while they may have inhabited distinct areas they frequently lived within the same overall enclosure. The monastic centre of Kells in Ireland appears to have been an integral part of local society. Ancient charters relate the buying and selling of private property within the enclosure. There was a market there, and craftsmen were attached to the monastery. Kells was also a great education centre and its monastic school had a high reputation. The street pattern of the present-day town reflects the old monastery layout. There were public areas and a specially sacred area (where, for example, there was a "desert" for the ascetics) whose perimeter was marked by crosses.[37]

Irish church laws around the seventh century appear to recognize the different spaces within the overall sacred precinct of the monastic enclosure. The most sacred space contained the relics of the saints. There was another area for clergy and a third for laymen and all the women, whether monastic ascetics or not. As at Kells, the strict ascetics might live separately from the rest of the settlement. The Annals of Ulster for 1162 indicate that the beginnings of the twelfth-century reforms of monastic life in Ireland involved a move away from the old hereditary system and towards a greater professionalization of clergy and monastics. This in turn meant that, as for example in the city of Derry, a clear distinction came to be introduced between secular and religious buildings and areas. There was now to be a total separation of ordinary houses from the area of the churches and a wall was built around the sacred center. This delineated a special area of sanctuary.[38]

As we have noted, not all the people within a sacred enclosure led celibate or explicitly ascetical lives. Space for monastic settlements had often been provided by whole kin groups. Some of its members then led an ascetical life and formed the inner circle of Church officers, including the abbot or abbess and the bishops. Some settlements were more traditionally monastic in that they included only celibate ascetics, but most of the larger ones also included *manaig* who married and farmed the land. This implied that some monastic personnel (perhaps the majority in some settlements) were born into the system. The *manaig* were not tenants but were within the monastic family. It is true that it is somewhat misleading to think of such settlements as monasteries in our conventional understanding of the word. However, there is evidence that some married, nonclerical *manaig* actually became abbots or the overall leader of a religious settlement. The *manaig* had a spiritual regime even though the legal tracts concerning them that are appended, for example, to the Rule of Tallaght speak of men, women, boys, and girls. This clearly implies normal family life.

So far we have only described what may be thought of as permanent insiders within the monastic enclosures. However, there were also various categories of short-term or long-term visitors. What formal education that existed in Ireland was provided by these monastic settlements. Some of the students were the children of the *manaig*, but the Venerable Bede, for example, implies that famous scholars attracted pupils from far away. It seems that some settlements, such as the island of Nendrum in Northern Ireland, had schools in distinct buildings. In others the individual monks taught students in their cells and pupils even boarded with them – thus living in the heart of the monastic space. This carried on the great tradition of the "colleges" and culture of the ancient druids and bards. It may even be that one of the motives behind the development of such large monastic settlements was to accommodate pupils in sufficient numbers for schools to flourish.[39]

There were also other passing guests to be accommodated. It seems that these were accorded a kind of semi-spiritual status and housed within the sacred enclosure. Often the guest house was given the choicest site within the settlement and yet was somehow set apart, sometimes within its own enclosure. The guest quarters, or *hospitium*, was therefore within the sacred space yet separated from the monastic living quarters. The guest quarters became in this way a kind of liminal or boundary place between inner and outer worlds.[40]

Thomas Merton and Cities

If we move forward to the twentieth century, the American Cistercian monk Thomas Merton perhaps surprisingly offers us some significant reflections on the meaning of the city. In his writings, there is a clear development from the very traditional pre-Vatican II spirituality of his early autobiographical volume *The Seven Storey Mountain* (1948) to the sympathetic observations on the public world in *Conjectures of a Guilty Bystander* (1966). In the first, Merton's presuppositions were in terms of a sharp dichotomy between monastery and world. As he later commented, on entering the monastery effectively he "spurned New York, spat on Chicago, tromped on Louisville" ... "heading for the woods" with the mystical writings of John of the Cross in his pocket, and "holding the Bible open at the Apocalypse"!

When Merton entered the Cistercian Abbey of Gethsemani in Kentucky during the Second World War, the city for him meant a prison, defined by human egotism. Some of Merton's early poems, both before and after he entered Gethsemani, are revealing. For example, his "Hymn of Not Much Praise for New York City" portrays city life as meaningless and self-destructive. "Sentence us for life to the penitentiaries of thy bars and nightclubs, / And leave us stupefied forever by the blue, objective lights / That fill the pale infirmaries of thy restaurants... ." In 1947 in "Figures for an Apocalypse" he writes a poem of advice to his friends to escape New York "the city full of sulphur" and flee while they can "From the wide walks where antichrist / Slips us his cruel snare."[41]

By 1958 his journal shows that Merton had changed his attitude massively. He records a visit to downtown Louisville:

> Yesterday in Louisville, at the corner of 4th and Walnut, suddenly realized that I loved all the people and that none of them were, or could be, totally alien to me. As if waking from a dream – the dream of my separateness, of my "special" vocation to be different.

In his 1966 *Conjectures of a Guilty Bystander* Merton again described this second conversion experience when he was overwhelmed by a realization of his unity with all the people on the sidewalks.[42]

Some of Merton's most engaging comments on the city appear in an essay "The Street is for Celebration," written originally for a community action book in 1967 and made widely available in his posthumously published essays, *Love and Living*, edited by Naomi Burton Stone and Patrick Hart.[43] The sentiments still speak powerfully to our contemporary urban condition and highlight themes of hospitality, inclusivity and solidarity. Interestingly, the question of racial distinctions is never mentioned. Overall, the essay suggests that how we arrange and navigate our cities reveals a great deal about who we are and what we value as a society. "A city is something you do with space ... It is a crowd of occupied spaces. Occupied or inhabited? Filled or lived in? ... The quality of a city depends on whether these spaces are 'inhabited' or just 'occupied'." Merton remarks on the distinction between inhabiting a place and merely existing there or "being dumped." He comments "When a street is like a tunnel, a passage, a tube from someplace to someplace else, the people who 'live' on it do not really live on it. The street is not where they live but where they have been dumped." "Somebody says the street belongs to the city. It is everybody's public street. All right. Is it? You can move around it under certain conditions. But the conditions are such that you do not feel it is *your* street, because you are not safe, you are not wanted, you are not noticed ..." "Can a street be an inhabited space? A space where people enjoy being? A space where people are present to themselves, with full identities, as real people, as happy people?" "To acquire inhabitants, the street will have to be changed. Something must *happen* to the street. Something must be *done to it*. The people who are merely provisionally present ... must now become really present on the street as *themselves*. They must be recognizable as people. Hence they must recognize each other as people." "Instead of submitting to the street, they must change it."

For further inspiration, Merton turned to the ancient Mayan cities in Mexico of around 500–300 BCE, which were contemporary with the city states of ancient Greece. His purpose is to highlight a vision of the city as built by the people, for themselves, as a place of celebration. Mayan cities were partly ritual centers. Merton notes that the architecture and planning of these cities made the streets into pathways leading to "open spaces that were free for everybody, not to closed buildings reserved for the few." What these early Mayan cities did with space "made human life joyous." Merton draws parallels between this and the Bible (presumably the Book of Revelation, Chapter 21) where, he suggests, the text tells us that in the end it will be like that once again, in a city of pure celebration.[44] For Merton, there is a close connection between the quality of public space – a space for celebration rather than violence and fear – and a full human identity. He further develops these thoughts on ancient Mexican cities in a separate 1968 essay "The Sacred City."[45]

Finally, during the last ten years of his life, Thomas Merton became fascinated by the Shakers, a Christian religious movement that originated in ecstatic millenarian Quaker circles in early industrial England during the eighteenth century. The founder, Ann Lee, moved with a few disciples to America just before the American Revolution. Shakers lived in ways that both reflected similarities with monasticism (on the margins, separated from what they saw as the corruption of wider society) and also with a utopian urbanism. One historic Shaker township, Pleasant Hill, lies close to the Abbey of Gethsemani. The Shaker community itself died out by 1910 and the township is now a heritage site. Thomas Merton first visited it in 1959 and then records at least six further visits until the last one in April 1968. He also mentions the Shakers and Pleasant Hill frequently in his journals. The small collection of his essays, talks and letters on the Shakers have been published.[46] Merton noted that Shaker buildings always fitted closely into their locations. As he put it, a building "manifests the logos of the place where it is built, grasps and expresses the hidden logos of the valley, or hillside ... which forms its site."[47] I will return to the subject of the Shakers in Chapter 4.

Overall, from well before he entered the Abbey of Gethsemani, Thomas Merton was deeply preoccupied with the question of where the "real" city was to be found.[48] Initially, for example in a journal entry for April 7, 1941, he says of his monastery "This is the only real city in America." However, later on he was deeply affected by reading the Jewish philosopher Hannah Arendt's book *The Human Condition*, in which she critiques Christianity for having a near-fatal effect on the whole idea of civic life. On the one hand classic civilization had understood the "polis" as the space in which humans develop cooperative action. On the other hand, a Christian suspicion of "the world" leads to an undervaluing of "political" action. In the end, Merton agrees with Arendt that in Western countries we have made ourselves into a culture in which what is genuinely public has virtually disappeared. In the ancient classical Greek and Roman cities, the pursuit of politics was grounded in public debate about values and in nurturing admirable public lives that were deserving of imitation. However, in Merton's view, Western modernity offers no real debate about values, no concept of public greatness; it simply focuses on systems and management. Merton concluded that the task of the modern monastic contemplative is to expiate this history and to recover a sense of public greatness. This implied, in the spirit of Aristotle and Aquinas, promoting a vision of "greatness of soul." What Thomas Merton suggests is that a monastic community is, or should seek to be, an authentic *polis*, an exemplary *civitas* pointing towards values relevant to the human city and wider society.[49]

Notes

English translations are cited wherever available.

1 Robin Gill, "Churches as moral communities," in *Moral Communities: The Prideaux Lectures for 1992*, Exeter: Exeter University Press, 1992, pp. 63–80.
2 Richard Morris, *Churches in the Landscape*, London: Dent, 1989, p. 104.
3 Andrew Louth in *The Wilderness of God*, London: Darton Longman & Todd, 1991, represents a recent attempt to describe the special qualities of the religion of the desert. The essay "The wilderness in the medieval West" by Jacques Le Goff in his *The Medieval Imagination*, Chicago and London: University of Chicago Press, 1988, has some illuminating remarks on the understanding of "desert" in Western monasticism, including the Celtic tradition.
4 Derwas Chitty, *The Desert a City: An Introduction to the Study of Egyptian and Palestinian Monasticism Under the Christian Empire*, Crestwood, NY: St Vladimir's Seminary Press, 1995 [1966].
5 See Peter Brown, "From the heavens to the desert: Anthony and Pachomius," Chapter 4 in *The Making of Late Antiquity*, Cambridge, MA: Harvard University Press, 1993.
6 On the geographics of monastic "style," see Peter Brown, *Society and the Holy in Late Antiquity*, Berkeley: University of California Press, 1989, pp. 110–114.
7 George Lawless, "Regulations for a monastery," Chapter 4 in *Augustine of Hippo and his Monastic Rule*, Oxford: Clarendon Press, 1987, p. 89 (cited as "Rule").
8 See, for example, the experience of monastic space as paradise restored in "The life of St Onophrius," in Tim Vivian (ed.), *Journeying into God: Seven Early Monastic Lives*, Minneapolis: Fortress Press, 1996.

9   For a critical edition of the text of More's *Utopia*, see Edward Surtz and J.H. Hexter (eds.), *Utopia*, The Complete Works of St Thomas More, Volume 4, New Haven, CT: Yale University Press, 1965.

10 See Henri Lefebvre's comments on utopias in his philosophical study of "daily life," urbanism, and architecture, *The Production of Space*, Oxford: Blackwell, 1991, p. 60.

11 Lefebvre, *Production of Space*, pp. 163–64.

12 See Surtz and Hexter, *Utopia*, Introduction, pp. xlviii and lxxv–lxxvii.

13 For some illuminating remarks on Renaissance rhetoric, particularly in reference to the connections between rhetoric and place, see Marjorie O'Rourke Boyle, *Loyola's Acts: The Rhetoric of the Self*, Berkeley: University of California Press, 1997, especially pp. 7–10.

14 For an illuminating essay on the nature of utopias, see Professor Carey's Introduction in *The Faber Book of Utopias*, pp. xi–xxvi.

15 See Belden Lane, *The Solace of Fierce Landscapes: Exploring Desert and Mountain Spirituality*, New York: Oxford University Press, 1998, pp. 141–47.

16 See for example, Michel Foucault, *Discipline and Punish: The Birth of the Prison*, London: Penguin Books, 1991 (originally published in 1975).

17 The validity of theological interpretations of such a post-Christian (and probably atheist) thinker, albeit one fascinated by the history of Christianity and by theology, is discussed intelligently by his main English-speaking interpreter, Jeremy R. Carrette, in his *Foucault and Religion: Spiritual Corporeality and Political Spirituality*, London and New York: Routledge, 2000, pp. ix–xii and 1–6. There is a critical appraisal of Foucault's writing on monasticism on pp. 112–113 and 118–122.

18 Quoted in Katherine Gibson and Sophie Watson, "An introduction," in Katherine Gibson and Sophie Watson (eds.), *Postmodern Cities and Spaces*, Oxford: Blackwell, 1995, p. 2.

19 Michel Foucault, "Of other spaces," 1967, quoted in Edward W. Soja "Heterotopologies: A remembrance of other spaces in the Citadel-LA," in Gibson and Watson, 1995, *Postmodern Cites and Spaces*, p. 14.

20 This is the emphasis of Augustine's commentary on Genesis, and is cited in Robert A. Markus, *The End of Ancient Christianity*, Cambridge: Cambridge University Press, 1990, p. 78.

21 Reference to Acts 4:32. See "Rule," 4, p. 75 in Lawless, 1987.

22 Lawless, "Rule," Chapter 5, 2, p. 95.

23 Lawless, "Rule," Chapter 1, 6 and 7, p. 83.

24 For a historical and theological reflection on the Christian tradition of hospitality, see Christine D. Pohl, *Making Room: Recovering Hospitality as a Christian Tradition*, Grand Rapids, MI: Eerdmans 1999.

25 Benedicta Ward, *The Wisdom of the Desert Fathers*, Fairacres Publications, 48, Oxford: SLG Press 1986 edition, no. 224.

26 Cited in Morris, *Churches in the Landscape*, p. 104.

27 See, for example, Painton Cowan, *Rose Windows*, London: Thames and Hudson, 1979.

28 See Lisa Bitel, *Isle of the Saints: Monastic Settlement and Christian Community in Early Ireland*, Ithaca, NY: Cornell University Press, 1990, pp. 58–60.

29 See Bitel, *Isle of the Saints*, p. 82.

30 Philip Sheldrake, *Living Between Worlds: Place and Journey in Celtic Spirituality*, London: Darton, Longman & Todd/ Cambridge, MA: Cowley, 1995, Chapter 1.

31 See Michael Maher (ed.), *Irish Spirituality*, Dublin, 1981, p. 11; Bitel, 1990, pp. 1 and 80–94; also Kathleen Hughes and Ann Hamlin, *Celtic Monasticism: The Modern Traveller to the Irish Church*, New York: Seabury, 1981, pp. 6 and 16.

32 For details of monastic life at Iona Abbey during the Middle Ages, see Alan Macquarrie, *Iona Through the Ages*, Society of West Highland and Island Historical Research, Isle of Coll, 2nd Edition, 1992, pp. 13–23.

33 See Bitel, *Isle of the Saints*, pp. 61–63.

34 See Hughes and Hamlin, *Celtic Monasticism*, pp. 13–15 and 54; also Kathleen Hughes (edited by D.N. Dumville), *Church and Society in Ireland, AD 400–1200*, Aldershot: Variorum, 1987, section 8 "The Church and the world in early Christian Ireland," p. 111.

35 See Hughes, *Church and Society in Ireland*, p. 111; also Pierre Riché, "Spirituality in Germanic and Celtic society," in Bernard McGinn, John Meyendorff, and Jean Leclercq (eds.), *Christian Spirituality 1: Origins to the Twelfth Century*, New York: Crossroad Publishing, 1985, pp. 169–70.

36 See Morris, *Churches in the Landscape*, p. 118; Hughes and Hamlin, *Celtic Monasticism*, 1981, p. 73; and Hughes, *Church and Society in Ireland*, section 8, p. 109.

37 Màire Herbert, *Iona, Kells and Derry: The History and Hagiography of the Monastic Familia of Columba*, Oxford: Oxford University Press, 1988, pp. 105–106.

38 Kathleen Hughes, *Early Christian Ireland: Introduction to the Sources*, London: Hodder & Stoughton, 1972, pp. 267–68. On the twelfth-century changes, see the *Annals of Ulster*, ed. B MacCarthy, Dublin, 1893, Volume II, p. 141.

39 On education, see Bede's *Ecclesiastical History of the English People*, London and New York: Penguin, revised edition 1990, book III, section 27; Hughes and Hamlin, *Celtic Monasticism*, pp. 9–11 and 75.

40 Bitel, *Isle of the Saints*, pp. 201–202; Hughes and Hamlin, *Celtic Monasticism*, pp. 14 and 75.

41 See *The Collected Poems of Thomas Merton*, New York: New Directions Publishing Corp, 1980.

42 Thomas Merton *Conjectures of a Guilty Bystander*, New York: Doubleday, 1966, pp. 140–41.

43 "The street is for celebration," in Naomi Burton Stone and Patrick Hart (eds.), *Thomas Merton: Love and Living*, New York: Harcourt Brace Jovanovich, 1979, pp. 46–53.

44 "The street is for celebration," p. 51.

45 Thomas Merton, "The sacred city," in *Ishi Means Man*, Greensboro NC: Unicorn Press, 1976, pp. 53–71.

46 See Paul M. Pearson (ed.), *Thomas Merton, Seeking Paradise: The Spirit of the Shakers*, Maryknoll, NY: Orbis Books, 2003.

47 Pearson, ed., *Seeking Paradise*, pp. 40–41.

48 See Rowan Williams, "The Only Real City: Monasticism and the social vision," Chapter 4 in *A Silent Action: Engagement with Thomas Merton*, Louisville: Fons Vitae, 2011.

49 See V. Kramer (ed.), *Turning Towards the World: The Pivotal Years (1960–1963)*, The Journals of Thomas Merton, Volume 4, San Francisco: Harper, 1996, pp. 5–6.

CHAPTER 3

The City as Sacred

In the hundred years from approximately 1150 to 1250 Europe underwent the first major urban revival since the collapse of the Western Roman Empire during the fifth century CE. During this period, the population of cities increased roughly eight-fold, even though by 1250 they still embraced only about 5 percent of the total population, which remained predominantly rural and feudal. However, the new urbanism created increasingly literate social classes of merchants and skilled artisans and this had a major impact on wider religious perspectives. As we shall see, it is precisely the needs of these groups that partly explain the proliferation of new forms of spiritual theory and practice outside the traditional monastic cloister. This new spiritual climate involved a search for what was known as the *vita evangelica* (the evangelical life) in imitation of the way of life of Jesus and his early disciples. This spiritual trend, while not a defined movement, led to the foundation of new preaching and pastoral religious orders such as the Franciscans and Dominicans as well as to the emergence of new urban lay-groups such as the Beguines.

The new cities also produced a growing differentiation of spheres of activity, with related institutions and discourse (the "vernacular") organized around these multiple axes. People's lives were divided increasingly into several roles. No longer were they merely religious

The Spiritual City: Theology, Spirituality, and the Urban, First Edition. Philip Sheldrake.
© 2014 Philip Sheldrake. Published 2014 by John Wiley & Sons, Ltd.

believers and family members: they were now citizens, consumers, workers, merchants, intellectuals, governors, and lawyers. Each role had its own way of organizing time and space as well as its sources of authority that were less in harmony with inherited religious patterns. The Church, rather than being automatically the dominant framework for human society, now had to reshape its own distinct space within increasingly multifaceted cities. There was also a growth of optimism about material, this-worldly, existence. The concept of "heaven" lost some of its philosophical abstraction and its imagery shifted increasingly from the re-creation of a Garden of Eden as portrayed in the Book of Genesis to the new heavenly city of Jerusalem described in the Book of Revelation. The imagery of "heaven" moved increasingly from the world of nature to culture, from the rural to the urban.[1]

Even so, the new cities continued to need favorable rural environments because city dwellers were great consumers. Medieval cities were still inextricably part of their surrounding landscapes, and the boundary between urban and rural life was permeable. It is, therefore, not surprising that the decoration of medieval cathedrals, for example at Chartres, was dominated by rural imagery in reference to the seasons, harvesting, and vine-growing. This strongly contrasts with today's cities which are often disconnected not only from the surrounding countryside but also from their global sources of food production.

Interestingly, the landscape imagery for heaven in a number of texts mixed a paradise garden with a heavenly city. For example, the visionary material of the twelfth-century English Cistercian monk Gunthelm offers two versions of paradise – a walled city which, within its walls, turns out to be a garden with plants, trees, birds, and fragrant flowers. Thus paradise is a city from the outside but a garden within.[2] Other late medieval portrayals of heaven also mingle the city with natural landscapes. Gerardesca of Pisa (1210–69) envisaged heaven as an Italian hilltop city state where God dwelt with the angels and major saints (the Virgin Mary and Apostles), surrounded by castles on nearby hilltops for the saints of second degree and minor forts for the remainder of the blessed. However, the central walled city was accessible to everyone. The whole of this paradise landscape was surrounded by a celestial park and open fields.[3]

Cathedrals

One of the most obvious physical reflections of the new urbanism was the development of the great Gothic cathedrals. Medieval cathedrals are "texts" in the broad sense implied by semiotics. We need a key in order to "read" their sign systems and thus to interpret them. Such buildings were constructed with various levels of meaning built into the stonework. Because such medieval religious buildings may be understood as acts of worship in themselves, as well as spaces for liturgy, their art and architecture were directly at the service of theology. For example, Gothic architecture is a bearer of quite specific religious ideas – not least about the nature of God and God's relationship to the material world and to human beings. It is also important to note that the citizens of medieval cities had an integrated worldview rather than a differentiated one. They believed in the ultimate unity of the cosmos. Thus the ground plan and decorative details in the great cathedrals reflect a grand architectonic design of the structure as a whole. The architecture echoes an overall approach to life which conceives the whole as somehow reflected in each single part.

In the cathedral, paradise was in a conscious way symbolically evoked and also brought down to earth in the heart of the city.[4] To enter the cathedral was to be transported psychologically and spiritually into a transcendent realm by the vast spaces, the flooding of light through the growing dematerialization of walls with stained glass and by increasingly elaborate rituals. The thirteenth-century writer Guillielmus Durandus in his *Rationale Divinorum Officiorum* suggested, in reference to solemn processions through the cathedral, "When entering the church while we sing we arrive with great joy in our [heavenly] fatherland... The chanters or clerics in their white robes are the rejoicing angels."[5] For Abbot Suger of St Denis in Paris, the great theorist often associated with the formal birth of French Gothic, churches were the gateway to heaven and had to be more impressive than all other city buildings. Equally, for him the clergy officiating at the sacred liturgy, like the blessed in heaven, should dress in rich silks and gold.

It is now widely recognized that there was a diversity of aesthetics, and therefore of theological symbolism, during the Middle Ages, not least during the development of Gothic architecture. This has been emphasized in important studies such as those by Umberto Eco.[6] Gothic "space" has been characterized as, among other things, dematerialized and spiritualized. It thereby expressed the limitless quality of an infinite God through the soaring verticality of arches and vaults. These were a deliberate antithesis to human scale. The medieval fascination with the symbolism of numbers cannot be ignored either. The basic three-storey elevation of Gothic church architectural form (main arcade, triforium, and clerestory) cannot be explained purely by a progress in engineering techniques. Both Rupert of Deutz and Abbot Suger in the twelfth century drew explicit attention to the Trinitarian symbolism of three-storey elevation. Later Gothic buildings, for example King's College Chapel in Cambridge, are notable for another characteristic: the stone walls were progressively reduced to a minimum and replaced by vast expanses of stained glass. The biblical stories portrayed in the windows taught the worshippers much about the doctrine of God and the history of salvation. However there was also a sense in which colored glass, and its patterned effect on the stonework of the interior of the building, reinforced a "metaphysics of light." In this way, God was proclaimed as the one who dwelt in inaccessible light yet whose saving light illuminated the city.[7]

The aesthetics of the early Christian thinkers Augustine and the Syrian mystical theologian known as pseudo-Dionysius played an important part in the theology of medieval cathedrals.[8] As a result the notion of *harmonia*, or the "fitting order" of reality established by God, was a central theme. This fitting order referred both to the layout of a cathedral building and to the worshipping community of citizens that it contained. Abbot Suger referred to "perspicacious order" as the key to his vision for Saint Denis – and *ordo* is the characteristic word in the writings of Augustine for the harmonious beauty of the cosmos.[9] In the mind of someone like Suger, a church building in the heart of the city should evoke wonder and point beyond itself to the eternal "house of God." The building was an access point to eternity and its harmony is represented not simply by its geometry or architectural coherence but by the degree to which it fulfilled its function as a gateway to heaven.

In Suger's theory, the inner meaning of material signs always pointed beyond the building to something higher. The aesthetic of a church building was not based merely on its physical beauty: rather, such buildings facilitated a transition from the material to the spiritual dimension of reality. Suger actually quoted Augustine in the inscription he placed on the great west door of Saint Denis through which the citizens of Paris entered:

> Whoever you are, if you seek to extol the glory of these doors
> Do not marvel at the gold and the expense but at the craftsmanship of the work.
> Bright is the noble work; but, being nobly bright, the work
> Should brighten the minds so that they may travel through the true lights...
> To the true light where Christ is the true door.
> The gold door defines the manner in which it is inherent.
> The dull mind rises to truth through what is material
> And, in seeing this light, is resurrected from its former submersion.

The implication was that the citizens should see the physical doors of the building as the "door of Paradise." There is also a passage in Chapter 5 of Suger's *Libellus Alter De Consecratione Ecclesiae Sancti Dionysii* that explicitly links the lofty architecture of the building to the way that it leads believers to access higher meaning. Suger was clear that material realities were necessary rather than incidental to an apprehension of the divine.

> The whole building – whether spiritual or material – grows into one holy temple in the Lord. In whom we, too, are taught to be builded together for an habitation of God through the Holy Spirit by ourselves in a spiritual way, the more loftily and fitly we strive to build in a material way.[10]

It has been said of the medieval city-dwellers who entered the great cathedrals that "they were the enraptured witnesses of a new way of seeing."[11] In a sense, cathedrals were thought to contain all the information in the world and about the world for people who knew the codes. The "new way of seeing" involved visual aids that drew the viewer from an awareness of the mundane to an awareness of God. The twelfth-century Paris theologian, Richard of St Victor, described four different modes of vision in his commentary on the Book of Revelation.[12] In the first mode, we open our eyes to what is physically there – the colors and the shapes of the building. In the second mode, we see through the outward appearances to their potential mystical significance. The movement is from immediate perception to a deeper knowledge. In the third mode, we discover the truth of hidden things.

Finally, in the fourth mode, we reach the deepest level of spiritual seeing – the mystical. Here the viewer has been drawn to a pure and naked vision of divine reality.

The architecture of the cathedrals acted as a kind of symbolic landscape, a microcosm in stone and artwork of the whole cosmos evoking a peaceable oneness between Creator and creation. This was a utopian space where a heavenly harmony was anticipated in the here and now.[13] However, the harmony was undoubtedly idealized. As Georges Duby, the eminent French medieval historian, reminds us, "Yet it would be a mistake to assume that the thirteenth century wore the beaming face of the crowned Virgin or the smiling angels. The times were hard, tense, and very wild, and it is important that we recognize all that was tumultuous and rending about them."[14]

The social symbolism of medieval cathedrals was also ambiguous. We cannot ignore the fact that while the architecture of cathedrals portrayed divine–human unity it also manifested the divisions of the social order. Within the building, the space was carefully divided up, sanctioning the new urban wealth from which such a building derived.

> Cathedrals also demarcated interior spaces; some parts were reserved for clergy alone, and in the laity's space, subdivisions reflected ranks and distinctions, and substantiated a hierarchical order with seats given over to the powerful who did not wish to stand and could afford particular proximity to the holy. Special chapels served select groups, and pictorial representations, by privileging certain groups and implicitly rejecting others, contributed to the cathedral's role in organizing, enacting, and publicizing a hierarchy of social differentiation.[15]

Equally, representations of heaven in the art of cathedrals tended to reproduce rather than subvert social separations – for example, of the peasantry from the wealthy or the nobility. Thus, on the West front of Chartres above the great door,

> ...elongated figures of "saints" thinned out of the world to reach a God above, and stout, stocky figures of this-worldly artisans and peasants supporting with the sweat of their brows that other "leisure class" who have all the time and energy for liturgies and mystical contemplation, point to a conception of spirituality indelibly sculptured in the cathedrals of our collective unconscious.[16]

Yet, at its best, cathedral design promoted something more than a two-dimensional, static, urban "map." It portrayed a third and a fourth dimension – movement through space on both vertical and horizontal planes and a process of human transformation through time. Cathedrals were repositories for the cumulative memory and constantly renewed aspirations of the urban community where people engage with decades or even centuries of human pain, achievements, hopes, and ideals. These "memory palaces" are a constant reminder that the act of remembering is itself vital to a healthy sense of identity.

In his outline of an urban aesthetic, the American philosopher Arnold Berleant suggests that in the pre-modern city, cathedrals (and other great churches) acted as guides to an urban ecology that contrasts with the monotony of the modern city "thus helping transform it from a place where one's humanity is constantly threatened into a place where it is continually achieved and enlarged."[17] Such an urban icon speaks of the "condition of the world" and offers communion with something more profound than merely a well-ordered city.

While all this is true, it is not the whole story. The theological symbolism and the use of such buildings for sacred rituals also have to be placed in a wider context. It is worth remembering that medieval churches were used for a variety of purposes other than worship or pilgrimage. As the major public buildings of a city, they housed business meetings of the city guilds, hosted neighborhood feasts, held markets in the nave and even allowed boisterous and subversive festivities such as the Feast of Fools, where people's conventional social status was turned upside down.[18]

The City as Sacred

Medieval urban growth also led to the development of the notion that "the city" itself could be understood as a holy place. Thus, it was not simply the religious buildings that conveyed a sacred meaning. On the contrary, the medieval city as a whole was the expression of a definite plan which was intended to express a clear idea of the meaning and purpose of human existence.[19] Notions of "the sacred" in the city were also not restricted to churches. There was a sense that the whole of a city embraced a wider sacred landscape of the streets. Even today, streets in culturally Catholic southern European countries frequently retain medieval examples of religious street shrines. For example, the rich collection of street-corner shrines in the *città vecchia* of the southern Italian city of Bari, ranging in age from the twelfth century to the present day, has been the subject of scholarly writing.[20]

The sense that the city was a sacred landscape was also reinforced by processions and blessings. In medieval cities the central Christian ritual of the Eucharist was a public drama, not only in the many churches but also the associated feast-day pageants, mystery plays, and street processions, for example on the feast of Corpus Christi. Street processions, held before Lent and on Rogation Days (days of prayer in early summer to protect crops), or the traditional ceremonies to mark out the boundaries of each parish (known in England as "beating the bounds") together symbolized a continual purification of the city landscape from the spirit of evil.[21] Medieval society was quite at home with a dialectical vision of reality that encompassed the sacred and sinful, light and dark, at the same time and in the same space.

Medieval cities sometimes even made the heavenly Jerusalem of the Book of Revelation, Chapter 21 a model for urban planning and design. Thus the Statutes of Florence of 1339 emphasized the existence of the sacred number of twelve gates even though by then the city had actually expanded to fifteen gates. The 1334 Statutes of Imola also described that city entirely in terms of the sacred number twelve, which was derived from the Book of Revelation. Thus there were twelve chapels, three in each of the four city quarters.[22] In the same way as Italian cities, other European cities also defended the ideal that city life, with its citizenry living in concord, was just as much a way to God as monastic life.[23] The city was seen as an ideal form of social life that provided an image in this world of the heavenly Jerusalem. In terms of architecture, such cities as Utrecht, Bamberg, and Paderborn placed a number of churches in design arrangements that reproduced the figure of a cross. This served as a visible sign of the holiness of the city.[24]

Later in the Middle Ages, the development of the great Italian city piazzas owed much to the new religious orders, such as the Franciscans, Dominicans, and Servites and their preaching churches. These buildings opened onto large open spaces that enabled crowds to listen to sermons (for example, in Florence the famous piazzas outside the churches of

Santa Croce, San Marco, Santa Maria Novella, and Santissima Annunziata). Just as the colonnades of ancient Rome gave birth to the design of the monastic cloister, so in the new laicized city spirituality of the later Middle Ages, the monastic cloister in turn moved out into the city to give birth to the colonnaded piazza. This space offered a vision of the city, metaphorically (because it engendered a concept of public space for intermingling) and also practically (because it opened up new urban vistas).

A genre of medieval poetry, the *laudes civitatis* or the *laudes urbium* (hymns of the city), articulated a utopian ideal of civic life. The value of these *laudes* as significant historical sources has been positively reevaluated in recent years.[25] The hymns depict the human city as a place where, like the Heavenly City, diverse people live together in peace. This "urban peace" is explicitly related to the *pax monastica* of the preceding centuries. In these hymns cities were praised for the quality of their communal life in which each citizen, like the monks of old, had a particular place that contributed to building up the whole. The faith of the citizenry underpinned a city's claim to holiness. A Milanese hymn of circa 740 praised the inhabitants because they fulfilled all the requirements of the Gospel of Matthew, Chapter 25 – the hungry are fed, strangers welcomed, the sick cared for. However, having said this, we also need to acknowledge that in practice medieval European cities were not notably hospitable to members of other faiths, creating physical ghettoes for Jews, limiting the civic rights of other faiths and even at times "purifying" cities by expelling religious minorities. Cities were also regularly praised as places of hard work. In terms of a spirituality of place, the *laudes civitatis* also portrayed particular cities as the center of the world, the *axis mundi*. This notion was related to the perceived geographical and topographical perfection specific to each city. Thus in a poem by Heinric van Veldeke, the location of the city of Maastricht is described as perfectly balanced in a range of different ways. It is located between a large and a small river, is in a valley in which both grass and wheat grow, and is on the crossroads between Cologne and England and between Saxony and France.[26]

The idea of the city as a holy place depended on three elements. First, cities were often portrayed as moral centers with a particularly good share of the world's delights or, as in Thomas à Becket's biographer William FitzStephen's immodest praise of London, it was founded by Brutus, descendant of the Trojans, thus predating the foundation of

Rome! Second, cities often based their sacred quality on some special religious foundation. Thus, Paris claimed to be the burial place of St Dionysius the Areopagite, converted by St Paul in Athens, supposedly apostle of the Gauls and a martyr on the hill Montmartre under the emperor Domitian. Thus St Denis, patron saint of Paris, became identified, in a sublime disregard for chronology, with a convert of St Paul (first century CE), with Dionysius, first Bishop of Paris (circa 250 CE) and also with pseudo-Dionysius the Greek mystical theologian (circa 500 CE). Whatever the case, this spiritual conflation established Paris firmly as a holy center and the source of Christianity in France. By a strange coincidence this also enhanced the reputation of the Abbey of St Denis and its Gothic rebuilding program, where the amalgamated figure was reputedly buried, and also the emerging national French monarchy, whose kings, now to be buried at St Denis, became invested with almost apostolic authority. Third, it was the faith of the people that marked the holiness of the place. Especially in Italy, a country that had never totally lost its civic life, it was not simply clergy or monastics but the life of the whole citizenry that underpinned a city's claim to holiness.

Interestingly, the heavenly city was often imaged in terms of actual human cities. For example descriptions of heaven were inspired by the recent flourishing cities of walls, towers, cathedrals, busy market places, public squares, workshops, and wealthy merchants' houses. For example, the thirteenth-century Franciscan friar and poet, Giacomo de Verona, in the elegant Italian of his text "On Heavenly Jerusalem," describes heaven in terms of the avenues and piazzas of a beautiful city. His writing clearly reflects his significant knowledge of urban architecture, especially in his native city of Verona.[27]

Universities as Sacred Space

It is interesting that the *laudes civitatis* mentioned earlier also sometimes count "teachers" among the categories of people who lend a sacred quality to city life. Guido of Bazoches, writing to one of his former pupils, urges him to return to Paris because there the seven sisters, the liberal arts, have made their home but also because the city is the source of the three rivers that "irrigate the mind" – that is the historical, allegorical, and moral senses of Holy Scripture.

During the twelfth century, the centers of intellectual and theological enquiry increasingly moved from rural monasteries to urban cathedral "schools." These eventually gave birth to the great European universities. This involved a geographical shift of learning from the countryside to the new cities that paralleled the movement of economic power from agricultural manorial estates to the growing commerce of cities. However, the move involved more than geography. The new city universities existed primarily to foster teaching and learning. Thus theology was no longer focused on monastic centers explicitly dedicated to the pursuit of a spiritual way of life. Despite the work of such outstanding theologians as Thomas Aquinas and Bonaventure, the "new theology" appeared to encourage a sense that the discipline of the mind could be separated from an ordered spiritual lifestyle.

As already noted, the new religious orders, such as the Franciscans and the Dominicans, were essentially an urban phenomenon, and their foundation parallels the birth of the universities. It was not long before they became deeply involved in teaching, often taking a leading role in university development. For example, the Dominicans entered the new universities initially to train their own members to be more effective preachers. Gradually, however, they developed an intellectual ministry in its own right – exploring how to cope theologically and spiritually with the rediscovery of Greek philosophy, especially the work of Aristotle. Throughout the greater part of the Middle Ages, it was the city universities that acted as vital carriers of religious thought for the wider Christian world.

The Vita Evangelica

The growth of cities was accompanied by a number of significant spiritual trends. The so-called *vita evangelica*, that coincided more or less with the growth of cities, was not really an organized movement but is a way of describing a diverse and widespread spiritual fervor. This was provoked, at least in part, by the papal-directed "Gregorian" reforms. These concentrated on the organization of the Church and its relationship with political systems, but failed adequately to address more popular spiritual concerns. The spiritual fervor of the *vita evangelica* centered on a return to gospel values expressed in simplicity, the literal imitation of the poor and homeless Jesus (mendicancy and wandering) and in preaching. It is noticeable that women played an active role at the start, although eventually this was curtailed in significant ways. This can be seen with the eventual monastic enclosure imposed on some evangelical women's groups (for example the Poor Clares) and a general suspicion of other female spiritual movements (for example, the Beguines).

In the case of the various elements that went to make up the *vita evangelica*, some were absorbed into the spiritual mainstream. Thus, the mendicant groups found an accepted place through formal recognition of new religious orders such as the Franciscans in the thirteenth century. However, they continued close connections with lay urban Christians by founding associated groups, known as Tertiaries (or "Third Orders"), for men and women who were unable to take on the full lifestyle of the parent order. Some Tertiaries lived in community, but the majority continued to live at home in normal married and working environments while undertaking a life of prayer and charitable work compatible with everyday commitments.

The new urban spiritual movements, gathered around an ideal of the evangelical life, expressed the sensibilities and the complexities of the merchant classes. It has been said that Francis of Assisi's choice of radical poverty as the predominant gospel value was not solely the result (as suggested in Bonaventure's biography) of a sudden inspiration while listening to the reading of scripture in church.[28] Rather, it was at least partly a spiritual reaction to the growing wealth and power of urban society and to the characteristic sins of Francis' own social groups. Eventually this evangelical way of life solidified into a number of new religious orders whose male members were popularly known as "friars" (from the Latin *fratres*, brothers).

Close ties grew up between the new mendicant orders and the new city political classes in ways that gave birth to a kind of civic religion in which local city saints (not least members of the new orders themselves) were venerated and their love of the local commune was emphasized. The mendicant movement responded to two contemporary urban needs. First, it attempted to free spirituality from an older monastic dominance. Second, there was a realization that the Church in the new cities needed preachers who were not tied down by owning large country estates like the older monastic communities. The new friars were free to move around the streets and to be absorbed into the flow, a transgression of fixed boundaries which, even at such an early stage, was characteristic of city life.

As exponents of a mixed, contemplative–active life, the new orders made contemplative values accessible to their urban contemporaries. They not only engaged with the general population in ways that traditional monasticism had not done, by preaching, teaching, and spiritual guidance. In addition, their religious complexes were architecturally more accessible to the outside world, and their churches were built with the spiritual needs of the city populations in mind. They were characterized by large, open preaching naves and relatively small and unpretentious areas for the community's prayer.[29]

Francis of Assisi's desire to live a gospel existence embraced the theme of the imitation of Christ who was the brother of all, but especially of the poor. His spirituality focused on serving Christ in poor and marginalized people. The famous story of Francis embracing the leper whom he met on the road was, in medieval terms, a challenging encounter with the excluded "other" or social outcast. Lepers were not simply people with a feared disease. They symbolized the dark side of human existence onto which medieval people projected a variety of fears, suspicions, and guilty sinfulness that must be excluded from a community of the spiritually pure. Lepers were outcasts banished from the city. In his *Earlier Rule*, Francis enjoins the brothers that he gathered around him that they "must rejoice when they live among people of little worth and who are looked down upon, among the poor and the powerless, the sick and the lepers, and the beggars by the wayside."[30]

The Beguines

A further striking expression of the new urban spirituality and the classic values of the *vita evangelica* were informal lay groups of women known as the Beguines. Originally there were related groups of men, known as Beghards, but these do not seem to have survived long or made a major impact. The Beguines emerged towards the end of the twelfth century and flourished in northern Germany, the Netherlands, Belgium, and northern France. Some scholars now extend the term to groups of lay-women in Italy and in Norwich, England. It was not a cohesive movement in that there was no single founder and no single written rule of life.

The important point is that the Beguines were essentially an urban phenomenon. Their emergence reflects the appeal of the new spiritual reform movement to lay-people, especially to educated and relatively affluent ones, and coincides with a more lively participation in matters of faith by urban citizens who were often dissatisfied by the ministrations of poorly educated priests, and who had had relatively little access to the spirituality of traditional monastic life. As a result, numbers of literate laypeople became involved in spiritual teaching and even informal preaching. They also created associations for prayer and charitable works, and began to read the Bible in the vernacular. In the specific case of women, there was a move towards associations for mutual spiritual support as an alternative to traditional convent life.

The life of Beguines offered women the possibility of shaping their own spiritual experience and a degree of freedom from clerical control. While some continued to live with their families, others banded together in city houses which they bought by pooling their resources. Eventually during the thirteenth century two dominant forms emerged. In Germany there were very few large units but small houses or tenements of between three to twenty individuals. In Flanders the Beguines tended to create fairly sizeable building complexes popularly known as *beguinages*, which often became independent parishes. These might resemble a walled city within a city, with a large church at its hub, as in Bruges, or be simply a tree-covered square hardly distinguishable from other public squares in the city, as in Ghent. In either case the architecture was domestic and urban rather than classically monastic. Indeed, a recent study of the Beguines refers to them as single-sex cities.[31] Despite the close trading connections between Flanders and Norwich, the only English city thought to have housed Beguines during the fifteenth century, the style of the three known groups reflected the German rather than the Flemish model. All of them were small, two were in tenements and one was in a parish churchyard. This may reflect a purely local development, in that there was a custom in that part of England for recluses sometimes to live together.[32]

Beguines expressed two particular religious motivations – a cult of chastity and a desire for voluntary poverty. The latter led not simply to a simple style of life but also to the virtue of self-sufficiency achieved by the labor of their own hands. Eventually the Beguines became famous for the quality of their weaving and lace-making. To this may be added a lively interest in serving the poor and devotion to the Eucharist that expressed both a desire for greater affectivity in spirituality and an emphasis on the humanity of Christ.

Thomas Aquinas and Civic Life

Finally, on a more theoretical level, the writings of the great thirteenth-century theologian Thomas Aquinas reflected the renewed preoccupation with the meaning and value of cities and urban life. Arguably, they are among the most articulate religious expressions of the idea of a city as the pinnacle of human community. According to Thomas Aquinas, the study of cities is "politics" whose aim is to be a practical philosophy for procuring goodness in human affairs through the use of reason.[33] For Aquinas, cities and politics were important because he understood community as vital to human flourishing. Aquinas even borrowed from his hero, Aristotle, plans for constructing cities aimed at making the good life realizable. Aquinas offered a Christian reading of Aristotle's sense that to create the *polis* was a fundamental human vocation. Based on Aristotle's notion of cities as creative of the virtues, Aquinas noted that cities originate initially for pragmatic reasons but continue for the sake of "the good life" – that is, in his words, the uniquely human goals of courage, temperance, liberality, greatness of soul, and companionable modesty. These goals are only achieved in cities because virtue is most effectively learned by interaction with other people in a mixed community. Based on this vision, Aquinas also believed that it was unnatural for humans to live outside community.[34] Not surprisingly, the work of Thomas Aquinas had a significant impact on the development of Christian social teaching from the nineteenth century onwards. As we shall see in Chapter 8, the writings of Aristotle and Thomas Aquinas have particular relevance to the development of a contemporary notion of "urban virtue."

Conclusion

Overall, the notion of "community" was expanded in the religious dimension of the medieval city. Almshouses, hospitals, and the houses of religious communities all opened their doors to strangers – the homeless, the sick, the mentally ill, and the abandoned. While the ethos of religious community did not, in practice, embrace the whole of a city, in its various forms from the local parish to the almshouse it did act as a moral reference point. A religious vision of community evoked moral and spiritual standards that measured human behavior in the city more broadly. This vision stood in stark contrast to the aggressive commercial behavior prevalent among the urban mercantile classes. The values of the new religious and spiritual movements that developed in the medieval cities spoke of community as sanctuary in the sense of "a place where compassion bonded strangers."[35]

Notes

English translations are cited wherever available.

1 See Colleen McDannell and Berhard Lang, *Heaven: A History*, New Haven, CT: Yale University Press, 1988, pp. 70–80.
2 Cited in Jeffrey Burton Russell, *A History of Heaven: The Singing Silence*, Princeton, NJ: Princeton University Press, 1997, p. 106.
3 See McDannell and Long, *Heaven: A History*, pp. 74–76.
4 See Philip Sheldrake, "Reading cathedrals as spiritual texts," *Studies in Spirituality*, 11, 2001, pp. 187–204.
5 Quoted in translation in McDannell and Long, p. 79.
6 Umberto Eco, *Art and Beauty in the Middle Ages*, New Haven, CT: Yale University Press, 1986.
7 For some reflections on what might be called the theology of Gothic, see Christopher Wilson, *The Gothic Cathedral*, London and New York: Thames & Hudson, 1990, especially the Introduction, pp. 64–66, 219–220, 262–63.
8 On this mixture of theological aesthetics see the essay by Bernard McGinn "From admirable tabernacle to the house of God: Some theological reflections on medieval architectural integration," in Virginia Chieffo Raguin, Kathryn Brush, and Peter Draper (eds.), *Artistic Integration in Gothic Buildings*, Toronto: University of Toronto Press, 1995.
9 *Libellus Alter De Consecratione Ecclesiae Sancti Dionysii*, IV, translated in Erwin Panofsky, *Abbot Suger on the Abbey Church of St Denis and its Art treasures*, Princeton, NJ: Princeton University Press, 1979, pp. 100–101.
10 Translation by Bernard McGinn in his essay above, p. 49. from the Latin text in Panofsky, *Abbot Suger*, p. 104.
11 Michael Camille, *Gothic Art: Visions and Revelations of the Medieval World*, London: Weidenfeld & Nicolson 1996, p. 12.

12 See Camille, *Gothic Art*, pp. 16–17.

13 For a study of the medieval cathedral as a spiritual "text" see Sheldrake, "Reading cathedrals as spiritual texts."

14 Georges Duby, *The Age of the Cathedrals: Art and Society 980–1420*, Chicago: University of Chicago Press, 1981, p. 95.

15 Brigette Bedos-Rozak, "Form as social process," in Raguin *et al.* (eds.), *Artistic Integration in Gothic Buildings*, pp. 243–44.

16 Aloysius Pieris, *An Asian Theology of Liberation*, Edinburgh: T. and T. Clark / Maryknoll, NY: Orbis Books, 1988, p. 7.

17 See A. Berleant, *The Aesthetics of Environment*, Philadelphia: Temple University Press, 1992, p. 62.

18 See J.G. Davies, *The Secular Use of Church Buildings*, London: SCM Press, 1968.

19 See Peter Raedts, "The medieval city as a holy place," in Charles Caspers and Marc Schneiders (eds.), *Omnes Circumadstantes: Contributions towards a History of the Role of the People in the Liturgy*. Kampen: Uitgeversmaatschappij J.H. Kok, 1990, p. 144.

20 See N. Cortone and N. Lavermicocca, *Santi di Strada: Le Edicole Religiose della Città Vecchia di Bari*, 5 volumes, Bari: Edizione BA Graphis, 2001–2003.

21 See P. Ackroyd, *The Life of Thomas More*, London: Random House, 1999, p. 111.

22 C. Frugoni, *A Distant City: Images of Urban Experience in the Medieval World*, Princeton, NJ: Princeton University Press, 1991, p. 27.

23 On the development of medieval cities see Jacques Le Goff, *Medieval Civilisation*, Oxford: Blackwell 1988, pp. 70–78.

24 Raedts, "The medieval city as a holy place," p. 145.

25 See Raedts, "The medieval city as a holy place," pp. 144–54.

26 Raedts, "The medieval city as a holy place," pp. 147–8.

27 See McDannell and Lang, *Heaven*, pp. 69–80.

28 For Bonaventure's biography of Francis, see E. Cousins (ed.), *Bonaventure: The Soul's Journey into God; The Tree of Life; The Life of St Francis*, New York: Paulist Press, 1978.

29 On the mendicant orders and their spiritualities, see Chapter 2 "The mendicants," in Jill Raitt (ed.), *Christian Spirituality II: High Middle Ages and Reformation*, New York: Crossroad Publishing, 1987; and C.H. Lawrence, *The Friars: The Impact of the Early Mendicant Movement on Western Society*, London: Longman, 1994.

30 See R. Armstrong and I. Brady (eds.), *Francis and Clare: The Complete Works*, New York: Paulist Press, 1982.

31 See Walter Simons, *Cities of Ladies: Beguine Communities in the Medieval Low Countries, 1200–1565*, Philadelphia: University of Pennsylvania Press, 2003.

32 See F. I Dunn, "Hermits, anchorites and recluses: A study with reference to medieval Norwich" in Frank Dale Sayer (ed.), *Julian and her*

Norwich: Commemorative Essays and Handbook to the Exhibition "Revelations of Divine Love," Norwich: Julian of Norwich 1973 Celebration Committee, pp. 18–27.

33   *Sententia Libri Politicorum. Opera Omnia*, VIII, Paris 1891, Prologue A, 69–70.

34   See *Sententia Libri Politicorum. Opera Omnia*, VIII, Prologue A 69–70 and also *De Regimine Principum*, Chapter II in R.W. Dyson (ed.), *Aquinas: Political Writings*, Cambridge: Cambridge University Press, 2002, pp. 8–10.

35   Richard Sennett, *Flesh and Stone: The Body and the City in Western Civilization*, London: Faber, 1994, p. 159.

CHAPTER 4

The City and the Reformations

The European Reformations of the sixteenth century, both Protestant and Catholic, were largely urban phenomena. This was a natural consequence of the major revival of European cities during the twelfth and thirteenth centuries which we explored in the last chapter. The rebirth of cities created new literate and wealthy urban social classes, which led to a shift in religious perspectives, gave birth to new religious movements that were accessible to laypeople, and brought about a move of theological and intellectual centers from the largely rural monasteries to the new urban universities. Turning back to the origin of the Protestant and Catholic Reformations, it was largely in this urban lay context that a number of earlier movements of Church reform, such as the *Devotio Moderna* (literally, "modern devotion") or the Christian humanism associated with Desiderius Erasmus and his circle, arose during the fifteenth and early sixteenth centuries. In large measure, the later Protestant and Catholic Reformations grew out of these reforming trends. Interestingly, as we shall see, by the middle of the sixteenth century the Society of Jesus (or Jesuits), a major religious order of reformed clergy associated with the Catholic Reformation, had almost no interest in the rural world compared to their significant engagement with cities.[1]

The Spiritual City: Theology, Spirituality, and the Urban, First Edition. Philip Sheldrake.
© 2014 Philip Sheldrake. Published 2014 by John Wiley & Sons, Ltd.

A Protestant Ethic of Space?

Turning first to the Protestant Reformation, even though this was focused largely on urban environments, the "high" view of city life that permeated the European Middle Ages was somewhat diluted under its impact in large parts of Europe. To some extent Richard Sennett's notion of a "Protestant ethic of space" which we noted in the Introduction, even if somewhat overstated, reflected a degree of suspicion of the material world. Classical Protestant theology affirmed an unbridgeable gulf between the holiness of God and the world of sinful creatures. It also relocated "the sacred" to the community of believers and downgraded physical mediations of God's presence. Rudolph Bultmann, the twentieth-century German theologian, describes this Protestant ambivalence towards the physical world in the following terms:

> Luther has taught us that there are no holy places in the world, that the world as a whole is indeed a profane place. This is true in spite of Luther's "the earth everywhere is the Lord's" (*terra ubique Domini*) for this, too, can be believed only in spite of all the evidence.

> In the same way the whole of nature and history is profane. It is only in the light of the proclaimed word that what has happened or what is happening here and there assumes the character of God's action for the believer... Nevertheless the world is God's world and the sphere of God as acting. Therefore our relation to the world as believers is paradoxical.[2]

Whether this is a fully balanced interpretation of Martin Luther or not, some elements of Protestantism tended to question the value of physical symbols and material mediations of the sacred. This shift in sensibilities during the sixteenth century was the beginning of the end of the religious street shrines and processions that had revealed the medieval city as a sacred landscape. Over time "the sacred" retreated from public places and public life (which became increasingly secularized) into the purified spaces of religious buildings and into the private or domestic realm. This opposition between the sacred and everyday spheres of human life was further developed and consolidated during the eighteenth-century intellectual movement known as the Enlightenment.

It is worth noting that many conventional modern interpretations of "the sacred," at least implicitly, reflect the approach of the great twentieth-century historian of religion, Mircea Eliade.[3] In Eliade's words, "the sacred" is something that is "wholly other" than the mundane or everyday life – to quote, "something of a wholly different order, a reality that does not belong to our world."[4] For Eliade, manifestations of the sacred (what he called "hierophanies") are associated with special places and special activities. It is worth bearing in mind that Eliade's ideas were strongly influenced by Rudolph Otto's classic work *Das Heilige* (in English *The Idea of the Holy*[5]). Otto, for all his work in comparative religion, was fundamentally a Protestant theologian influenced by a conservative understanding of Martin Luther's distinction between two kingdoms, God's kingdom and the kingdom of this world, and by a theology of God who was imaged as awesome mystery and sovereign power (*mysterium tremendum et fascinans*).

Interestingly, one expression of the association of "the sacred" with places set apart from the outer, public world, was the idealization of "the home." The home was a private space protected from the evils of the streets. Although the widespread Western mystique of "home" has a variety of origins, it became particularly prominent in the early Victorian era in Britain and North America. For many people, domesticity became the shaping symbol of a satisfactory life. In part this reflects a sense of loss in the face of the Industrial Revolution and the growing squalor, crowding, and noise of ever-expanding cityscapes. It also reflects a growing shift towards a sense that private spaces, reflecting a new form of interiority, are where human beings are most truly themselves. In England there were particular links to the nineteenth-century Protestant Evangelical revival and the sense that the way people organized their most intimate spaces reflected their moral character and spiritual temperament. Interior design expressed who people thought they were or what they valued, and at the same time was itself creative of vision and value. Clergy were even involved as design consultants. As one commentator recently noted, it was a time when the priests chose the drapes [or curtains]![6]

Sweden – A Lutheran Test Case

On a more constructive note, some recent scholarship has challenged Richard Sennett's somewhat critical interpretation of Protestant approaches to city space. The core of his viewpoint is that Protestantism tended to generate a kind of urban disengagement as well as a spiritual individualism. Sennett in fact focuses predominantly on Calvinism and Puritanism rather than Lutheranism. In an important scholarly essay, Hilary Stanworth offers Sweden as a critical case study in relation to Sennett's perspective. She suggests that Scandinavian Lutheranism, while sharing with other elements of Protestantism certain moral and spiritual anxieties about human nature, was also able to generate a positive approach to civic community and its responsibilities. For 300 years, from the Swedish Reformation in the mid sixteenth century to the middle of the nineteenth century, the parish was the key unit of Swedish local government as well as of religious administration. As a country, Sweden is famous for its tendency to document environmental and social realities in considerable detail. Rather than interpret this in terms of Richard Sennett's emphasis on social control in Protestantism, Stanworth marshals a great deal of evidence to promote an alternative perspective. In her view, such close documenting both of nature and of society reflects a positive Lutheran belief that, in continuity with the pre-Reformation worldview, we can learn about God by reading the natural world as the second book of divine revelation alongside the scriptures. Even the smallest and most trivial natural elements are revelations of the transcendent reality that lies behind them. In this spirit, Stanworth notes that the contemporary Gothenburg official city booklet refers to the cultural landscape as always having something to tell us.

Equally, in terms of cities, the Swedish concern to rationally order the built environment should not be interpreted solely in terms of control but also in terms of protecting what remains good about human nature in our fallen world. We also have a duty to continue the *missio Dei*, the mission of God, and therefore to try to complete God's work in our everyday existence. In concrete terms, after the 1950s there was a major movement to end the chronic housing shortage in Sweden and to modernize city centers in order to better suit contemporary needs. By the 1970s the Swedes had ended up as among the best housed people in Western Europe. In terms of individual homes there was an emphasis on spaciousness and on individual garden plots. In terms of the socially mixed neighborhoods there was an emphasis on developing common facilities and on providing shared external public space. The official Swedish housing policy has been based on an ambition to integrate communities, to be just and to be equal. Sweden seeks to prevent people being separated into different groups based on social or economic factors. Open access is the prevailing virtue, and gated communities are deemed to be very un-Swedish. There are even exhortations to citizens by local government not to repaint the outside of a house before walking down the road with a paint-chart to see one's house as "part of the landscape"! In the case of Sweden, Stanworth suggests that the emphasis on "common responsibility" for the built environment in an egalitarian rather than hierarchical way is actually fundamentally Lutheran in its origins rather than simply the product of the post-war social democratic political system.[7]

John Calvin's Geneva

In terms of the Reformed tradition, John Calvin seems to have been even more comfortable than Martin Luther with the notion that the world of both natural and human places is a *theatrum gloriae Dei* – a theater full of wonders, in which God's glory becomes apparent. The *loci communes*, the ordinary places of the world, become the stage on which divine revelation is acted out.

> Meanwhile, being placed in this most beautiful theater, let us not decline to take a pious delight in the clear and manifest works of God. For, as we have elsewhere observed, though not the chief, it is, in point of order, the first evidence of faith, to remember to which side soever we turn, that all which meets the eye is the work of God, and at the same time to meditate with pious care on the end which God had in view in creating it.[8]

John Calvin's spirituality engaged strongly with society. The Reformed Church had a major impact on the city of Geneva under Calvin. He explicitly intended this symbiosis. In Geneva, spirituality became a public matter. In particular, the city was intended to be a Christian state in which citizenship and spirituality infused each other. The role of magistrates and elders was to administer faithfully the covenant between God and Christian citizens. A moral and spiritual life touched all elements of existence – public and personal. Behind this lay a sense that the Spirit of God was at work in the world and in all human activities.

In some respects, the relationship between religion and the city was ambiguous. On the one hand, Calvin took the ideal of the city seriously. On the other hand he was suspicious of the role of "play" or entertainment in city life. In his view, too much leisure leads to vice, as we shall see later in the attitudes of Reformed pastors in America during the Industrial Revolution. If we are not dominated by necessary duties, the danger is that we give way to natural passions. Thus, Calvin's Geneva was organized in such a way that there was little opportunity to sin. Calvin's idea of the small city was as a perfect theocracy. It was an economically viable environment and also offered protection to its citizens against war and violence. However, it was also small enough to permit constant surveillance of its citizens by Church and civil government, and was thus a secure tool for the repression of natural human baseness.[9]

The Church had the pulpit, which, in the context of the times, was the major vehicle of mass communication, especially because there was a legal obligation to attend Sunday sermons. Pastors and other Church functionaries taught the youth of the city. Indeed the Church sponsored and the city paid for the academy which educated the citizens. The Church "consistory" oversaw the moral behavior of the city. Church deacons looked after the poor and the sick in the city. Overall, citizenship was effectively equated with membership of the Church. John Calvin's *Institutes of the Christian Religion* made no essential distinction between public and private morality. The Church and the city government were to cooperate in maintaining God's underlying governance of the world.

Having said this, civil government was seen as autonomous. The civil authorities had no role in maintaining the spiritual life of the citizens – that was the task of the Church. However, city government did have a specific role in maintaining civil justice and outward morality. The city magistrates were seen as having a specific mandate from God, as invested with divine authority and as being God's vice-regents in the city. The main point is that John Calvin had an overwhelmingly positive view of civil society and city government. The Church and city authorities were not competing rivals but were ideally speaking two cooperative spheres.[10]

Alternative Community: The Shakers

Finally, a number of communitarian Anabaptist groups arising from the so-called Radical Reformation and other groups from the later Quaker tradition found their way to North America during the eighteenth and nineteenth centuries. There they founded distinctive communes or townships based on their religious principles. The best-known Anabaptist communes belonged to groups known as the Amish and the Hutterites. As we have seen, the Cistercian monk, Thomas Merton, became fascinated by another group known as the Shakers, that is the Shaking Quakers or, to give them their official title, "The United Society of Believers in Christ's Second Appearing." The origins of the Shakers lie in a religious movement that began in ecstatic millenarian Quaker circles in England during the eighteenth century. An illiterate factory worker in newly industrialized Manchester, Ann Lee (1736–84) joined this group and eventually emerged as their leader. She was a visionary who, among other things, promoted a simple communal celibate lifestyle as the pathway to the renewed Kingdom of God. Mother Ann, as she became known, moved with a few disciples to America just before the Revolution. They settled near Albany in what is now New York State and during the War of Independence suffered for their strictly pacifist beliefs. A number of communes or townships were founded in New York and New England and later, during the nineteenth century, Shaker communities also spread to Kentucky and to the Midwest. Nowadays, there is only one surviving yet still influential Shaker community, at Sabbathday Lake in Maine.

The Shakers lived, and still live, in ways that reflected similarities with monasticism, that is to say, on the margins, separated from what they saw as the corruption of wider society but also with the spirit of utopian urbanism. While in one sense set apart from the American cultural mainstream, Shakers made commerce and neighborly hospitality an expression of solidarity with American cities. They created a form of counter-urbanism, establishing a new society based on a community of goods, the sacredness of work (indeed, work was seen as an act of worship), and on excelling as craftspeople. Shakers believed strongly in human solidarity. They were pacifists and also had equal rights within their townships, with no distinction between male and female, black or white. Their villages or townships manifested a strong sense of relationship to the place where they lived and the natural world they shared with that place. A sense of place also embraced the design of their buildings which were characterized by beautiful simplicity and by a conscious harmony of architecture, building materials, and the use of light. Shaker buildings always fitted comfortably into their environments.

Ignatian Urbanism

Turning now to the Catholic Reformation, one of the major strands of pastoral life and spiritual renewal was the tradition associated with the Society of Jesus, or Jesuits, a religious order of reformed priests founded by Ignatius Loyola and formally endorsed by the Pope in 1540. The Jesuits were strikingly urban in their priorities and attitudes. There are various versions of a famous dictum of unknown origin: *"Bernadus valles, montes Benedictus amabat, oppida Franciscus, magnas Ignatius urbes"*: "Bernard loved the valleys, Benedict the hills, Francis the towns, and Ignatius the great cities."

Ignatius was the first founder of a major religious order to locate its headquarters in the center of Rome, and also the first to seek to insert the order's work and life into the center of the urban fabric. This was not a casual step but quite deliberate. Ignatius placed the Society of Jesus at the psychological heart of Catholic Christianity, creating, as it were, a sacred circle at the heart of the human city.[11]

What might be called a preferential option for urban ministry is sketched out at certain points in the *Formula of the Institute* and the *Constitutions of the Society of Jesus*, or Rule (fairly explicitly in paragraph 625).[12] Overall, Ignatius's main spiritual principle for discerning which work should have priority was always "the greater service of God and the more universal good." The phrase "more universal good" seems to be a variation and expansion of Thomas Aquinas' famous urban principle, based on Aristotle, of seeking "the common good" as the central civic virtue. This will be explained further in Chapter 9. As a further extension, the Jesuit *Constitutions* (Part VII, Chapter 2, paragraph 622) are clear that preference should be given to those persons and places which, through their own improvement, may potentially become the source of an even wider "good" for many other people.

This theme is built upon in a number of Ignatius Loyola's extant letters, for example in his ten-year long and 76-letter correspondence with the city rulers concerning the potential foundation of a Jesuit college in the Italian city of Florence. He is clear why he wishes to locate a college in the heart of this great city. First, according to Ignatius, a college would be a great public advantage to the city. For it is important that the children of the citizens should be taught doctrine and sound morals alongside "letters" (that is, the humanities). Second, there were a greater number of poor people in the city who could not afford to go elsewhere to be educated. Finally, in general, a Jesuit college would lead to better pastoral care being available to the citizens. In summary, Ignatius's vision is that all social classes would be served, that the work would not be merely educational but also more broadly pastoral, that it would lead to a greater service to greater numbers and that, in cooperation with the civic authorities, there would be the "edification" of a whole city.[13]

In Rome itself, the Jesuit work embraced the entire spectrum of urban society – from Popes to prostitutes, from eminent scholars to small children, from the nobility to the poor, from the respectable citizens to marginalized Jews. The Jesuits worked mainly in pastoral, social, and pedagogical fields. They preached not only in the great urban churches but in the open-air piazzas. They worked in city hospitals and in the prisons. During the severe famine of the winter of 1538–9, the Jesuit residence of Frangipani was opened up to provide food and housing for hundreds of needy people. The Opera di Santa Marta provided a home for former prostitutes. The Jesuits also helped to set up two centers for street children and, at the other end of the spectrum, they not only founded the Roman College and what eventually became the Gregorian University, but also founded numerous other colleges in European cities for which they created a manual of educational theory and practice known as the *Ratio Studiorum*.

Ignatius's letters speak in fairly stereotypical terms of cities promoting the "common good," and frequently describe cities as being contexts of social and spiritual "edification." Overall, Ignatius Loyola does not promote any kind of utopian urban vision. For him, "edification," for all its pious resonances, actually implied a thoroughly pragmatic renewal of existing urban situations from the inside.[14]

As well as contributing significantly to the further development of late-sixteenth-century and seventeenth-century Baroque cities in Europe, the Jesuits were also responsible for founding new "cities" in the Spanish colonies of Latin America. The strategy of the Spanish imperial authorities had been to gather indigenous groups into centers known as *Reducciones* (Reductions) in order to govern them more efficiently. The Jesuits interpreted this strategy in a rather different way. They also built "Reductions" in present-day Paraguay, and later in what are now Argentina, Bolivia, and Brazil. The Jesuit approach involved conversion to Christianity but not necessarily to European culture. The leadership of such townships was partly Jesuit and partly indigenous.

The most famous examples are the Reductions in Paraguay, built for the semi-nomadic Guaraní peoples. These began to emerge around 1609, were firmly established by the 1640s and survived until the expulsion of the Jesuits in 1767. The Jesuits built a network of 30 complete mission towns along the Uruguay and Paraná rivers. These townships became semi-autonomous in relation to the colonial authorities, and were economically successful. The Jesuits even created an indigenous militia to enable the local peoples to defend themselves against the incursions of colonial slave-traders. These settlements were considered by some philosophers to be ideal communities of "noble savages," for example in the anti-slavery *La défense de l'esprit des lois* (1750) by the late seventeenth and early eighteenth-century French political thinker Michel de Montesquieu.

At their peak, the Jesuit Reductions numbered a total of around 40 townships, and housed upwards of 150,000 indigenous people. These Reductions were planned and laid out according to a standard pattern, marked by large churches and prolific workshops or factories concentrated around a central square or plaza. Although they always had a Jesuit residence, and were ultimately controlled by the Jesuits, the Reductions were generally governed by indigenous chiefs. Their architectural style was broadly European Baroque. However, there was also a certain artistic mingling with the presence of vegetable ornamentation in the mestizo style and also the presence of an unusual number of designs with angels playing musical instruments, reflecting the centrality of music to the Guaraní and to the life of the towns.

To take one example, the town of Trinidad in Paraguay spread over some eight hectares. It was centered on a large plaza or town square, formal in style and suited to the traditional Guaraní love of dance and music, with a main church, a Jesuit residence, workshops, ten apartment blocks, a smaller secondary church, and a massive stone bell-tower.

Even full-scale operas were composed to be performed in the Reductions. All the residential quarters in the town were designed to suit traditional Guaraní family and kinship groups. Each family had its own cubicle, and these were surrounded by verandahs which enabled people to spend most of their time outside. A number of trades and skills were taught and practiced, including printing to produce religious texts in the indigenous languages, often illustrated by indigenous artists. The earnings from goods that were sold were put into a common fund for the workers and their dependents. Given the particular traditions of the Jesuits, it is not surprising that a great deal of emphasis was placed on education, as this was seen as the key to future success for the inhabitants.

The nature of these Jesuit Reductions may appear to the contemporary observer as controlling and paternalistic – little more than attempts by a colonial Church to Europeanize the Guaraní. However, in the context of the times the actual motivation and purpose for the Reductions was more complex. In practical terms the Reductions protected the Guaraní from Spanish colonial exploitation and from slave labor. The Jesuits were in practice also proclaiming clearly that indigenous people such as the Guaraní had equal human status with Europeans, deserved planned settlements like the Spaniards and should be treated with proper dignity.[15]

Industrial Revolution and Urban Change

A second major Western urban expansion took place during the eighteenth and nineteenth century as a result of the Industrial Revolution. This evoked religious visions of the city in a new way. There was a renewal of paradise imagery in some Protestant circles, particularly in North America. However, the idea of heaven in religious literature no longer focused on visual imagery. Rather, it was now characterized as an active place, modeled on the productivity of the industrial cities. The morally righteous should not expect heaven to be a place of eternal rest for that would be lazy and frivolous. Rather, they should expect to lead industrious and busy lives of decent work and public service. This is especially striking in the book *Physical Theory of Another Life* by Scott Isaac Taylor in the 1830s. William Clark Wyatt a nineteenth-century New York pastor also suggested that "Heaven will be a busy hive, a center of industry."[16]

After the cataclysmic trauma of the American Civil War (1861–65), American religion took on a much stronger social consciousness in the face of the abolition of slavery, the expansion of cities and massive American industrial developments. The weakness of a purely private religion and individualistic piety had been exposed and a new kind of social awakening took place. Previously unquestioned assumptions about inevitable progress and the perfection of the American way of life were confronted by a spirituality that insisted on examining the underside of America. The Baptist pastor Walter Rauschenbusch (1861–1918) was one of best-known figures of the social gospel movement who worked among the urban poor of New York. He sought to hold together classic evangelical revivalism, with its emphasis on personal testimony and conversion, and social concern. He anticipated an important theme in twentieth-century spiritualities of liberation by asserting that true social change would only be substantial if nourished by a deep religious life. Rauschenbusch's most popular work was *Prayers for the Social Awakening* (1910). His own deep commitment to personal prayer and spirituality led him to found the "Little Society of Jesus" in 1887 with two friends Leighton Williams and Nathaniel Schmidt. They were influenced by what they saw as the zeal and enthusiasm of the Jesuit Order and sought to emulate its cohesion without compromising individual initiative. The aim was a voluntary association, based on a Jesus-centered spirituality that combined Protestant doctrine with Catholic devotion. The "Little Society" eventually became the Brotherhood of the Kingdom, with both social and spiritual values.[17]

In England Christian urban visions took an unexpected turn. Where modern buildings and public spaces attempted to offer people something special, there was the possibility of their expressing what lay beyond the everyday, even if not in a formal or religious sense. While at first it may sound odd, the expansion of the London Underground railway system during the 1930s had distinctly religious overtones. For example, the Tube stations that Charles Holden (1875–1960) designed for the Piccadilly Line extensions for the London Passenger Transport Board are not so very far from being the parish churches of their day. Not only were (and are) they focal points in the suburbs they quietly adorn, but they were clearly designed to raise the spirits of local people. It is hardly a surprise to discover that their architect, Charles Holden, was a Quaker and a deeply religious person, or that the director of London Transport who commissioned the stations, Frank Pick (1878–1941), was a Congregationalist lay minister who preached the gospel not only of Jesus Christ but also of the ethical business corporation. For Pick, the design of a train or Tube station was both a highly practical matter and, at the same time, an act of spiritual devotion. The world for Pick and Holden was full of the presence of God.[18]

There were also a number of examples of model towns created during the nineteenth century and based on explicitly Christian principles. Two examples are Port Sunlight, on the Wirral peninsula near Liverpool, and Bournville, just outside Birmingham, England's second-largest city. Both were built by business families to house the workers in their factories in conditions that were healthy and humane.

Port Sunlight was created in 1888 by William Lever, a devout Congregationalist who applied his Christian ideals to his business life, to accommodate workers in his new soap factory (now part of Unilever). The name is derived from Lever Brothers' most popular brand of cleaning agent, called "Sunlight." Today, Port Sunlight contains nine hundred Grade II listed buildings, was declared an official conservation area in 1978 and has been informally suggested for World Heritage Site status to protect it from excessive development. The township had a prime location between the river and a railway line. William Lever personally supervised planning the model township and employed nearly thirty different architects. Between 1899 and 1914, eight hundred houses were built to house a population of 3,500. The garden township had allotments and public buildings including an art gallery, a small hospital, schools, a concert hall, open air swimming pool, church, and a non-alcoholic hotel. Lever introduced welfare schemes and provided for the education and entertainment of his workforce, with a special emphasis on encouraging organizations which promoted art, literature, science or music.

William Lever's stated aims were "to socialize and Christianize business relations and get back to that close family brotherhood that existed in the good old days of hand labour." He proposed that Port Sunlight should be an exercise in profit sharing in the sense that he invested his profits in the township. He said, "It would not do you much good if you send it down your throats in the form of bottles of whisky, bags of sweets, or fat geese at Christmas. On the other hand, if you leave the money with me, I shall use it to provide for you everything that makes life pleasant – nice houses, comfortable homes, and healthy recreation." The historical significance of Port Sunlight lies in its combination of model industrial housing, providing materially decent conditions for working people, with the architectural and landscape values of the Arts and Crafts movement. Each block of houses was designed by a different architect with every house being unique. In terms of architectural features, there is half-timbering, carved woodwork and masonry, pargetting (ornamental plaster work), molded and twisted chimneys, and leaded glazed patterns. Some houses were built in Flemish style, with bricks imported from Belgium. Until the 1980s, all residents were employees of Unilever plus their families, but during this decade the houses began to be sold privately.[19]

In 1824, a Quaker called John Cadbury began producing tea, coffee and drinking chocolate in Birmingham. He later moved into the production of a variety of cocoa and drinking chocolates, sold mainly to the wealthy because of the high cost of production. John Cadbury became a partner with his brother Benjamin in the company Cadbury Brothers of Birmingham. By 1854 they had received the Royal Warrant as manufacturers of chocolate and cocoa to Queen Victoria. In the 1850s, with the reduction in the high import taxes on cocoa, chocolate became more affordable for the wider public. John Cadbury's sons, Richard and George, decided in 1878 that they needed new premises and better transport access both for the milk and for the cocoa they used. As a result, in 1879 they acquired the Bournbrook estate, comprising 14.5 acres south of the outskirts of Birmingham. In 1893, George Cadbury bought 120 acres of land close to the works and planned, at his own expense, a model town which would "alleviate the evils of modern more cramped living conditions." They renamed the area Bournville, with "ville" (the French for town) making clear that this was intended to be a freestanding, self-contained township, rather than just a suburban housing estate. By 1900 the township included over 300 cottages and houses set in 330 acres of land. The houses were in an Arts and Crafts style, with large gardens and modern interiors. These became a blueprint for other model villages around Britain. Because the Cadbury family were Quakers there were no pubs in the estate. In fact it was their Quaker beliefs that first led them to sell tea, coffee, and cocoa as alternatives to alcohol.

Cadbury also pioneered social schemes such as a pension system, work committees, and a fully staffed medical service well in advance of the advent of universal healthcare. The Cadbury family was particularly concerned with health and fitness, and so Bournville incorporated parkland and recreation areas to encourage swimming, walking and outdoor sports. In 1900 the Bournville Village Trust was formally set up to control future development. This was independent both of

George Cadbury and of the Cadbury company. The Trust focused on the provision of schools, medical facilities, a library, swimming baths, and a museum, and also rigorously monitored all plans for extensions to buildings. The Bournville Trust continues to exercise an international influence on approaches to housing development and to the ideals of town planning.[20]

Finally, however, Christian urban visions did not always work positively. Modern cities built or rebuilt after the Second World War frequently lack effective centers. Where does this tendency come from? As we shall see in the next chapter, the influence of the Swiss architect Le Corbusier was very powerful. However, paradoxically, the tendency began somewhat earlier with a Christian-inspired quest for more beautiful and healthier cities to counter nineteenth-century industrialized cities dominated by crowded slums and smoke-belching factories.[21] The prophet was a certain Dana Webster Bartlett, a Congregationalist pastor, who had ministered in the tenements of St Louis Missouri and was one of the founders of the City Beautiful movement. He went to work in Los Angeles at the beginning of the twentieth century and promoted the movement of manufacturing away from city centers to the periphery, and the move of working class people from tenements to single-family homes with gardens. Thus were born suburbia and urban sprawl. By the 1930s Los Angeles demonstrated a new urban vision – dispersed and multicentered. There was a downside. In the long term, the City Beautiful movement, by idealizing suburbs as a new kind of urban gospel, encouraged car ownership and increased pollution. The further consequence was the absence of any of the great public areas of earlier cities and the loss of compact community.[22]

In the next chapter, our attention will turn to the French Jesuit social scientist, Michel de Certeau, and in particular to two of his urban essays. In these he severely critiques the antisocial elements of European urban regeneration projects after the Second World War, and particularly in the 1960s. As we shall see, it seems likely that de Certeau in part targets Le Corbusier, who not only had a powerful influence on European urban regeneration during the mid twentieth century but also promoted a further sterilization of public space and a philosophy of urbanism which, while significantly different from that espoused by the City Beautiful movement, had similar consequences.

Notes

English translations are cited wherever available.

1   See D. Bertrand, *La Politique de S. Ignace de Loyola: L'Analyse Sociale*, Paris: Les Editions du Cerf, 1985.

2   Rudolph Bultmann, *Jesus Christ and Mythology*, New York: Scribner, 1958, pp. 84–85.

3   See especially, M. Eliade, *The Sacred and the Profane: The Nature of Religion*, New York: Harcourt Brace Jovanovich, 1987, Introduction.

4   Eliade, *The Sacred and the Profane*, p. 11.

5   R. Otto, *The Idea of the Holy*, Oxford: Oxford University Press, 1958.

6   See the fascinating book by Deborah Cohen, *Household Gods: The British and their Possessions*, New Haven, CT: Yale University Press 2006.

7   Hilary Stanworth, "Protestantism, anxiety and orientations in the environment: Sweden as a test case for the ideas of Richard Sennett," *Worldviews: Environment, Culture, Religion*, 10, 3, 2006, pp. 295–325.

8   John Calvin, *Institutes of The Christian Religion*, Grand Rapids, MI: Eerdmans 1995, I, XIV, 20.

9   See Richard Sennett, *The Fall of Public Man*, London: Penguin Books, 2002, pp. 116–117.

10   See Roger Haight, *Christian Community in History*, Volume 2, New York: Continuum, 2005, pp. 121–31.

11   For a broad, but somewhat fragmented study of Jesuit urbanism, see Thomas M. Lucas, *Landmarking: City, Church and Jesuit Urban Strategy*, Chicago: Loyola University Press, 1997.

12   For the classic modern English translation, see George E. Ganss (ed.), *The Constitutions of the Society of Jesus*, St Louis, MO: The Institute of Jesuit Sources, 1970.

13   See especially Sancti Ignatii de Loyola, *Epistolae et Instructiones, Monumenta Historica Societatis Jesu*, Madrid 1903–11, Volume 3, Letter 2047, pp. 637–8.

14   See Michael Sievernich, "The evangelization of the great city: Ignatius Loyola's urban vision," *CIS Review of Ignatian Spirituality*, XXVI, 3, n 80 (1995), pp. 26–45.

15   See Gaurin Alexander Bailey, "Jesuit architecture in colonial Latin America," in Thomas Worcester (ed.), *The Cambridge Companion to the Jesuits*, Cambridge: Cambridge University Press, 2008, pp. 217–42.

16   See Colleen McDannell and Bernhard Lang, *Heaven, A History*, New Haven, CT: Yale University Press, 1988, pp. 280 ff.

17   See W.S. Hudson, ed., *Walter Rauschenbusch*: Selected Writings, New York: Paulist Press, 1984.

18　See David Lawrence, *Bright Underground Spaces: The Railway Stations of Charles Holden*, Capital Transport, 2008. Also Christian Barman, *The Man Who Built London Transport: A Biography of Frank Pick*, Newton Abbot: David & Charles, 1979.

19　See A. Macqueen, *The King of Sunlight: How William Lever Cleaned up the World*. London: Bantam, 2004.

20　Michael Harrison, *Bournville, Model Village to Garden Suburb*, Chichester: Phillimore, 1999.

21　Joel Kotkin, *The City: A Global History*. New York: Random House, 2006, Chapters 14 and 15.

22　Dana Webster Bartlett, *The Better City: A Sociological Study of a Modern City*, Los Angeles: Neuner Company Press, 1907.

CHAPTER 5

Michel de Certeau:
Everyday Practices
and the City

As we saw briefly in the last chapter, the city as a place for the virtuous life
appears in a nonsystematic way in the writings and spirituality of Ignatius
Loyola. Both he and the early Jesuits more broadly may also be said to
have had a significant urban strategy at the heart of their work. In this
chapter I want to turn my attention to another Jesuit, the eminent
twentieth-century French scholar Michel de Certeau, who died aged
only 61 in 1986. De Certeau was a highly original writer on the history
of Christian spirituality and on mysticism, and was an expert on early Ignatian
sources. He also became one of the most creative interdisciplinary
intellectuals of the late twentieth century – philosopher, historian, cultural
theorist, and prominent social scientist, with a particular and creative
interest in cities, their design and their vibrant communities.

Michel Jean Emmanuel de la Barge de Certeau was born in Chambéry
(Savoie), the oldest of four children in a close-knit family of minor
nobility. He studied at different universities, Grenoble, Lyon, and Paris,
obtaining degrees in classics and philosophy, and subsequently began
theology at the Catholic faculty in Lyon, where he met the great Jesuit
theologian Henri de Lubac (who became his mentor). De Certeau entered
the Society of Jesus in 1950 and was ordained in 1956. De Certeau's
original hope had been to undertake missionary work in China but he
became involved in editing both the monthly journal *Etudes* and the
Ignatian spirituality journal *Christus*. He undertook research on Ignatian

The Spiritual City: Theology, Spirituality, and the Urban, First Edition. Philip Sheldrake.
© 2014 Philip Sheldrake. Published 2014 by John Wiley & Sons, Ltd.

historical studies and gained his doctorate from the Sorbonne with a thesis on the *Memoriale* or spiritual diary of one of Ignatius Loyola's early companions, Pierre Favre. De Certeau then moved on to edit the mystical writings and letters of the seventeenth-century Jesuit Jean-Joseph Surin, who was famous as the exorcist of Loudun. Surin haunted de Certeau for the rest of his life and plays a key role in de Certeau's unfinished analysis of Christian mysticism, *The Mystic Fable* which was his final and incomplete work. Studying Surin, who suffered a severe psychological breakdown after his experiences at the convent at Loudun, led de Certeau to become interested in Freudian analysis and to become, with another Jesuit expert on the Spiritual Exercises, François Roustang, a founding member of the informal circle associated with the French psychoanalyst, Jacques Lacan. A further critical turning point in de Certeau's life and thought was brought about by the political upheavals of May 1968.This led him to become a public and politicized figure, to engage with new intellectual networks, and to become involved in studying the social sciences. From 1970 he wrote, published, and taught on a wide range of areas, including anthropology and history. He also moved somewhat to the margins of Jesuit life, as he began to live on his own. He went to teach at the University of California in 1978 but in 1984 became director of studies at the École des hautes études en sciences sociales in Paris – a remarkable feat for a priest given the institution's overtly secular ethos. Sadly, it was less than a year before de Certeau was diagnosed with cancer and, despite surgery, he died in January 1986.

For many social scientists and cultural theorists, particularly in the English-speaking world, it is de Certeau's later social scientific work, and the fact that he became director of the École des hautes études, that receives exclusive attention. This leaves people with the impression that the later de Certeau ceased to be interested in spirituality or theology and is to be thought of solely as an important cultural theorist and social scientist. As a result what drops from view are de Certeau's enduring membership until his death (albeit in a somewhat detached way) of a religious order, the Jesuits, and his unwavering preoccupation with Christian belief and its place in secular culture (as attested to by Professor Luce Giard his close collaborator and literary executor).[1] According to this interpretation, Michel de Certeau's life and writings can be divided neatly into two parts. The first period was dominated by religious faith and theological and spirituality scholarship, while in the second period, after the early 1970s, religion and spirituality were fundamentally abandoned both personally and intellectually. However, I strongly question this interpretation. In my judgment, apart from the testimony of Luce Giard, it can be demonstrated that key values from Ignatian spirituality also underpinned de Certeau's later work as social scientist and urban thinker.

However, at the same time I also have some questions about one recent attempt to retrieve de Certeau as a religious thinker by the theological grouping known as "Radical Orthodoxy." I will simply mention three things. First, this retrieval concentrates largely on de Certeau's religious or quasi-religious writings and does not really address the religious underpinning implicit in his later social scientific work. Second, there is too strong an emphasis on an ecclesial and eschatological reading of de Certeau's "spiritual spaces."[2] Such an emphasis underplays de Certeau's later focus on everyday practices (which I believe has Ignatian origins) and also de Certeau's primary symbol in later life for discipleship as the empty tomb.[3] The Christian call is to wander with no security apart from a story of Christ that is to be "practiced" and lived rather than authoritatively stated.[4] Finally, while there has been some reference to de Certeau's debt to Ignatian spirituality this is not pursued in any detail.[5]

As a consequence, in this chapter I want, first, to outline briefly some key Ignatian values that leave a "trace" in de Certeau and will note how this Ignatian thread relates to his emphasis on "the practices of everyday life." Then, second, I will turn specifically to de Certeau's writing on cities, both his critique of Modernist planning's totalizing tendencies and his suspicion of urban utopianism.

Ignatian Resources

Luce Giard, de Certeau's collaborator, notes in several places his early fascination with solitary journeys and with the desire to be an itinerant.[6] As we shall see, this sensibility in relation to movement rather than fixity plays a role in the way de Certeau approached the nature of cities. The theme of journeying and movement is, of course, at the heart of Ignatian spirituality from its origins – not least the characteristic lifestyle of the Jesuit order to which de Certeau belonged. Solemnly professed members of the order take a fourth vow to journey anywhere in the world to undertake mission. Its specific content is freedom to travel.

> This is a vow to go anywhere His Holiness will order, whether among the faithful or the infidels, without pleading an excuse and without requesting any expenses for the journey.[7]

"One should attend to the first characteristic of our Institute... this is to travel." (*Constitutions*, paragraph 626). Ignatius Loyola's assistant, Jeronimo Nadal, wrote a commentary on the deeper meaning of the Fourth Vow. For Nadal the "best house" of the Jesuits was their journeying.

> The principal and most characteristic dwelling for Jesuits is not the professed houses, but in journeyings. They consider that they are in their most peaceful and pleasant house when they are constantly on the move, when they travel throughout the earth, when they have no place to call their own.[8]

Again, according to Nadal, "The world is our house."

In broad terms, this value is also evident in de Certeau's later religious writings. In "The weakness of believing: from the body to writing, a Christian transit" Christian spirituality must avoid the temptation to settle down into a fixed and definitive "place."

> The temptation of the "spiritual" is to constitute the act of difference as a site, to transform the conversion into an establishment, to replace the "poem" [of Christ] which states the hyperbole with the strength to make history or to be the truth which takes history's place, or, lastly, as in evangelical transfiguration (a metaphoric movement), to take the "vision" as a "tent" and the word as a new land. In its countless writings along many different trajectories, Christian spirituality offers a huge inventory of difference, and ceaselessly criticises this trap; it has insisted particularly on the impossibility for the believer of stopping on the "moment" of the break – a practice, a departure, a work, an ecstasy – and of identifying faith with a site.[9]

In another later religious essay, "How is Christianity thinkable today?" de Certeau draws implicitly upon the Ignatian mysticism of practice. For de Certeau this was mediated particularly through the *Memoriale* of Ignatius Loyola's early companion, Pierre Favre which de Certeau edited in a critical edition for his doctoral research, and also through the writings of the seventeenth-century Jesuit, Jean-Joseph Surin which, as I have already noted, fascinated de Certeau until the end of his life.[10] This "mysticism of practice" offered de Certeau among other things the Ignatian language of the *magis*, God as the *semper maior*, the always greater, the always more, the always beyond. "Practice" is the quest for this perpetually elusive "more." Hence, for de Certeau, the prominent values are of movement, the transgression of boundaries and the process of always exceeding limits.

> Within the Christian experience, the boundary or limit is a place for the action which ensures the step from a particular situation to a progress (opening a future and creating a new past), from a being "there" to a being "elsewhere," from one stage to another... A particular place – our present place – is required if there is to be a departure. Both elements, the place and the departure, are interrelated because it is the withdrawal from a place that allows one to recognise the enclosure implicit in the initial position, and as a result it is this limited field which makes possible a further investigation. Boundaries are the place of the Christian work, and their displacements are the result of this work... It is this action which transcends, whereas speeches and institutions circumscribe each place successively occupied.

And again:

> In order to pass from one place to another, something must be *done* (not only *said*) that affects the boundary: namely *praxis*. It is this action which transcends, whereas speeches and institutions circumscribe each place successively occupied.[11]

These sentiments could apply as much to the temptation of policy-makers and planners to totalize cities as to religious institutions. De Certeau became suspicious of both. Thus, paradoxically, the radical role of Christian practice and of mysticism is to be a disruptive act of resistance at the heart of all systems and attempts at definitive statements about reality. As we shall see, this emphasis relates to the concept of "indeterminacy" in de Certeau's later writing on everyday practices in cities, and its corollary – that such everyday practices are powerfully subversive.

One particular phrase from the Ignatian tradition which also echoes the value of movement appears directly or indirectly at a number of places in de Certeau – that is, "procedures" or "ways of proceeding." The Jesuit Constitutions employ this language at several points to embody the Jesuit way of life. The Preamble, paragraph 134, describes the purpose of the Constitutions as "to aid us to proceed better... along the path of divine service." In the Declaration, the core of the Constitutions is described as "our procedure" and in the Constitutions proper, Part 1, chapter 2, paragraph 152, the overall Jesuit way of life is described as "our manner [or way] of proceeding."[12]

In de Certeau, this phraseology is echoed in some of his later religious writings. In "Weakness of believing" (p. 215) Christianity itself is "a way of proceeding" and more generally a fluid "practice" as opposed to a fixed site, an establishment, a locus of authority. In "Mystic speech" (originally *L'énonciation mystique*, 1976) he refers to mysticism as "practices" or "a domain in which specific procedures are followed" as opposed to a body of doctrines, and suggests that "mystic procedures" produce "endless narrativity."[13] I shall return to de Certeau's fascination with the importance and power of narrative shortly.

Equally, in his Preface and General Introduction to the first volume of *The Practice of Everyday Life*, de Certeau uses similar language in his evaluation of everyday practices and the importance of "tactics" in shaping city life in contrast to the totalizing strategies of the socially and politically powerful. Thus the Preface talks of working out a "science of singularity" – the "relationship that links everyday pursuits to particular circumstances." This is not merely descriptive but value-laden: only here can "one grasp how... these pursuits unfailingly establish relational tactics (a struggle for life), artistic creations (an aesthetic) and autonomous initiatives (an ethic)."[14] The purpose, for de Certeau, is to inspire readers "to uncover for themselves, in their own situation, their own tactics, their own creations and their own initiatives." In this context, it is notable that the Jesuit Constitutions limit their own normativity by noting that everything must be adapted to "times, places and persons."[15] In the General Introduction, p xiv, de Certeau's subtitle is "The procedures of everyday creativity" and the theme of popular everyday "procedures" (or sometimes, "ways of operating") is present throughout. In de Certeau's Conclusion to his collection of essays on political themes, *Culture in the Plural*, the "everyday" has an almost transcendent, even mystical quality. As he puts it, "daily life is scattered with marvels" and these wonders are to be found everywhere, not least on the streets. Luce Giard explicitly notes that de Certeau was predisposed to see wonder in the everyday ordinary by the Ignatian Spiritual Exercises.[16] She also suggests elsewhere that *The Practice of Everyday Life* discloses ordinary life as mystical and was a kind of reflection on "other ways" of believing beyond the explicit boundaries of the Church.[17]

It is thus not difficult to detect in de Certeau clear echoes of the Ignatian understanding of spirituality as "practice" – particularly in the context of the everyday. We need to recall that de Certeau, like many of his generation of French Jesuits, was strongly influenced by Maurice Giuliani, one of the most important French Jesuit exponents during the 1960s and 1970s of new approaches to the Ignatian Spiritual Exercises. One of Giuliani's most striking themes was that, in the Ignatian spiritual "economy," everyday life was itself intended to become a spiritual exercise.[18]

The climax of the text of the *Spiritual Exercises* themselves (specifically the prayer exercise known as the "Contemplation to attain love" or "Contemplatio," Exercises, paragraphs 230–237) invites the retreatant to "find God in all things" without exception and to carry this sensibility back into everyday life. In an article on the French Jesuit website as part of the 25th anniversary of de Certeau's death, his fellow Jesuit Philippe Lécrivan underlined that in so many ways de Certeau's particular "take" on Ignatian spirituality and its mystical dimension of finding God in all things and of action–praxis lays the foundations for his later social thought.[19] He draws attention particularly to de Certeau's seminal 1966 article in the Ignatian spirituality journal *Christus*, "L'universalisme ignatien, mystique et mission,"[20] in which the "Contemplatio" meditation is the key. There are three main elements. First, the impulse is always to find God in the present moment. Second, Ignatian discernment is a movement from contemplation to a "spiritual reading" of the everyday world as the source of a mysticism of practice. Finally, in Ignatian mysticism one learns through encounters with "otherness" – including people who are strange to us – to seek ceaselessly a God who is always "more." Lécrivan then draws parallels between the vision embodied in the two volumes of *The Practice of Everyday Life* and de Certeau's late work on the history of mysticism, *The Mystic Fable*, which he refers to as two diptychs of the same *rétable* (that is, an altar-piece).

Interestingly the only explicit reference to Ignatian spirituality in *The Practice of Everyday Life* is in the multi-author Volume 2 and is not written by de Certeau himself but by his colleague Pierre Mayol. However, I do not believe this is coincidental. Mayol is discussing the concept of "neighborhood" and focuses on one street in the Croix-Rousse district of Lyon.

> I realize that by focusing my information on just one family group on one street, the rue Rivet, I have respected the first preamble (or prelude)

from the First Exercise of the Spiritual Exercises of St Ignatius Loyola about "a contemplation of the place" which fixes the imagination on "the physical location of the object contemplated" or, more humbly, understood or analyzed.[21]

Everyday Subversive Practices

One of the most influential ideas in de Certeau's first volume of *The Practice of Everyday Life* is his distinction between the concepts of "strategy" and "tactics," particularly in the context of everyday life on the streets. Strategy is linked to institutions and to structures of power; tactics are utilized by ordinary individuals to create space for themselves in environments defined by other people's strategies. This notion of the tactics of the marginalized and "weak" is powerfully illustrated in his urban writing but is also clearly present in *The Mystic Fable*. The "privileged places" for the development of mystical practice belonged with people of little or no power in the public realm. Indeed, de Certeau sees these people whose lives affirm the elusiveness and "otherness" of God as outsiders to the modern project yet with the capacity to challenge traditional centers of power.[22]

In *The Practice of Everyday Life* the emphasis on "tactics" is not simply a detached sociologist's observation of how people behave; it articulates an ethical and political *imperative* which I believe is also implicitly religious. In other words, it invites us to understand not merely *what* we know but also that *how* we come to know things is not value-free. It is important to recall something about de Certeau that is regularly overlooked. His engagement with the "political" actually pre-dates the events of May 1968 and his overt espousal of left-wing views. It is important to remember that from an early age, well before he entered the Society of Jesus, de Certeau was inspired by the social humanism and political vision of Emmanuel Mounier (who was strongly influenced by Catholic Social Teaching[23]) and continued to write for Mounier's journal *Esprit* (with which his collaborator Pierre Mayol was closely associated) in later life. *The Practice of Everyday Life* does not merely note "other voices" but seeks to make proper space for them to be heard and thus to become empowered.

De Certeau, Le Corbusier and the Modern City

Michel de Certeau's writings continue to be prescient and provocative in relation to contemporary urban realities.[24] In important ways, de Certeau's approach echoes the thinking of the seventh-century Christian bishop, Isidore of Seville. Like Isidore, for de Certeau *urbs* implies the mapped, planned, and architecturally conceived concept-city. In contrast, *civitas* implies a space shaped by the urban narratives of a community of people. This is the city as a dynamic organism. Such a view reflects de Certeau's overall aim as stated in his General Introduction to the first volume of *The Practice of Everyday Life* – "a continuing investigation of the ways in which users – commonly assumed to be passive and guided by established rules – operate."[25]

I now want to focus directly on two of de Certeau's urban essays. First, in his famous essay for architects, "Ghosts in the city," it seems probable that one target was the Swiss architect Le Corbusier, who had a powerful influence on European urban regeneration during the mid twentieth century.[26] Le Corbusier stood for two aspects of modernist planning that de Certeau abhorred: a tendency to erase the past, and a tendency to subordinate the realities of people's lives to abstract concepts of space. Le Corbusier was influenced by Christian symbolism, and even the writings of the Jesuit, Pierre Teilhard de Chardin, but fundamentally he believed in a kind of mystical neo-Platonist utopianism and (as a supposed descendent of medieval Cathars) a version of Gnostic matter–spirit dualism.[27] Le Corbusier sought to create an ideal world through the perfection of design and planning. In his vision, the architect became a version of Plato's all-powerful philosopher-king.

For Le Corbusier, true knowledge and value were to be found in the inner, individual life. The outer, public, world of self-exposure, mixture, and engagement with strangers was of dubious worth. His city theory sought to eliminate anything that reinforced public life as a determining factor in human identity. In this sense, Le Corbusier is an important source of the fear of mixture and the decay of public life that Sennett critiques and which we noted in the Introduction. Consequently, his city schemes made it difficult for people to congregate casually, and tended to create sterile public space because he believed that uncontrolled socializing was a distraction. Not surprisingly, Le Corbusier disliked participatory politics. Authoritarian systems offered efficient bureaucracy without the need for political debate.[28] Le Corbusier's almost mystical emphasis on the "radiant city" with glass towers reaching to the sky appealed to a transcendent horizon where the *city itself* becomes the Temple. Le Corbusier's city plans had no churches because he believed that all human desires could be met and realized in his utopian urban environment. In this spirit, Le Corbusier called the skyscrapers of Manhattan "new white cathedrals." They engineered a kind of euphoria and not only embodied transcendence in their sublime height but offered a "total vision" of reality, symbolized by their panoramic vistas.

In contrast, de Certeau was concerned that the modernist "restoration" of Paris (that is, regeneration driven by planners and politicians) simply created upmarket apartments and shopping malls while displacing existing communities and forcing them to disperse to outer areas. There the low cost, high-density housing projects, *banlieues*, of the 1960s created new instruments of isolation which continue to remain socially problematic today. For de Certeau, such city-centre gentrification was simply a form of social colonialism by another name. De Certeau was also sharply critical of "fresh start" architecture which he saw as vain and grandiose. He was also concerned by the ruthless erasure of the past and the belief that regeneration should begin with the bulldozers creating a *tabula rasa* – a "blank canvas" – without consideration for the existing inhabitants. Similar criticisms have been made of regeneration projects in England, for example in Newcastle upon Tyne. For de Certeau, "the new" could only be welcomed when it fostered a healthy present-day context by respecting the past. Without such respect, the "ghosts" of the past (hence the title of the essay) will haunt the new spaces and make them dysfunctional and ultimately unliveable. What de Certeau objected to was the quest for what he called "rational geometries" that eliminate the "opaque ambivalence" of the human oddities that make cities liveable.

"Restoration" or regeneration in this sense implied for de Certeau a separation of design from human lives. "Through its own movement, the restoration economy tends to separate places from their practitioners... In this particular case, it is not surprising that technical administrations are so interested in buildings and so little in the inhabitants" (p. 139). De Certeau was a prophet of the "ineffable something" that a poetics of everyday life brings to a city in opposition to what he called "utilitarian and technocratic transparency." In short, de Certeau may be said to have a person-centered rather than a design-centered and policy-driven approach to planning. For him, a healthy city is a richly textured fabric woven by its "users" – their ways of proceeding, their walking, their chance encounters, the stories they tell, the dreams they nurture. As he said, "Gestures are the true archives of the city, if one understands by 'archives' the past that is selected and reused according to present custom. They remake the urban landscape every day" (p. 141).

De Certeau's attacks on Modernist planning for destroying history were not merely nostalgic. On the contrary, he strongly emphasized the vital importance and power of narrative, including the inherited memories and narratives of neighborhoods, to shape environments and to transform them. Indeed, in terms of everyday life, it is story and memory as much as architecture and planning that enables people to *use* the city as a means of creative living.For example, in his essay "Spatial Stories" de Certeau comments:

> In modern Athens, the vehicles of mass transportation are called *metapho-rai*. To go to work or come home, one takes a "metaphor" – a bus or a train. Stories could also take this noble name: every day, they traverse and organize places; they select and link them together; they make sentences and itineraries out of them. They are spatial trajectories.[29]

Stories are more than descriptions. They take ownership of spaces, define boundaries, and create bridges between individuals. The narrative structure of local communities enables people to shape the world that surrounds them, rather than be passively controlled by it.[30] As another eminent French thinker, the Christian philosopher Paul Ricoeur, notes, narrative is power and without it we risk two things. First, we undermine a key element of human solidarity (because we bond together by sharing stories) and, second, we reduce or remove a key incentive for changing the status quo as well as an important means of bringing this about. In the words of Ricoeur: "We tell stories because in the last analysis human lives need and merit being narrated. The whole history of suffering cries out for vengeance and calls for narrative."[31] For de Certeau, making space for narrative is a vital factor in creating the city as a community rather than simply a collection of buildings and spaces.[32] As he quotes elsewhere from Pierre Janet, "Narration created humanity."[33] The essay "Ghosts in the City" is rhetorical in the ancient sense that it seeks to evoke our sympathies and to focus attention on our human stories and practices rather than on what he calls "the law of the market" as the driving force of urban regeneration.

This viewpoint was not purely political. There was an essentially spiritual underpinning for de Certeau's pleading with architects and planners.[34] His defense of provisionality and objection to totalizing utopian visions accords with his implicitly Augustinian view, inherited from his theological mentor Henri de Lubac, that a harmonious arrangement of human environments implies more than mechanical order. Part of the aesthetics of a healthy city, in contrast to an efficient "urban mechanics," is the way it facilitates the transcendence of static order. De Certeau believed that the kinds of fixed space theories that urban planners can impose on city environments in order to "make sense" of them are frequently totalitarian because they are top-down rather than authentically consultative.

Modern cities were constructed primarily with a sense of ordered efficiency. Yet a harmonious arrangement of human environments implies more than order. A healthy city will actually facilitate movement and change as opposed to static order. In a second of his urban essays, "Walking in the City," de Certeau expressed another of his favorite themes, present throughout his writings, that of "resistance" to systems that leave no room for otherness and transgression.[35] The "weak," in this case those who actually live in the city rather than stand to one side and plan it, find ways to make space for themselves and to express their self-determination. What de Certeau calls "the urbanistic system" attempts to define a literal meaning of geometrical space that is similar to the "proper" meanings in language constructed by grammarians rather than by usage! Influenced by Roland Barthes' essay on Paris as seen from the Eiffel Tower, de Certeau describes standing on the 107th floor of the World Trade Center in New York. He contrasts the geographical space of panoptic visions and theoretical constructions of the city with the "practices of space" and "ways of operating" (or proceeding) that shape the "lived" city.

De Certeau writes of the almost erotic pleasure and temptation of "seeing the whole," of looking down upon the city and thereby totalizing it. There we are (or once were, given 9/11) lifted out of Manhattan's grasp – becoming *voyeurs* not walkers. We "read" the city as a simple text but this is an illusion. As de Certeau puts it, "The fiction of this kind of knowledge is related to a lust to be a viewpoint and nothing more."[36] "Lust" clearly relates to desire in a certain sense. The notion of "desire," true or false, is a key one in de Certeau. There are strong Ignatian echoes here too. In the *Spiritual Exercises*, desire refers to the inner "movements" or motivations that drive us and govern our ways of acting and seeing. The point is to distinguish between superficial "wants" and life-directing desire, related to our life purpose. For de Certeau the "lust to be a viewpoint and nothing more" is partly the desire to be above the world – to escape the limits of the body. In this sense it is the desire to feel God-like as opposed to a true experience of the divine revealed in the everyday practices of people on the sidewalks.

Meanwhile, according to de Certeau, the ordinary practitioners of the city are the walkers "down below." For de Certeau, what he called "the Concept-city" of Modernist abstraction was decaying. What outlives this decay are "the microbe-like, singular and plural practices which an urbanistic system was supposed to control or suppress."[37] These everyday practices by ordinary people are what make the city lived space as opposed to mere concept-space. Such urban practices are plural and defy differentiation, classification, and the imposition of social hierarchies.

Those who "practice" the city are the people who walk its streets. "The act of walking is to the urban system what the speech act is to language" (p. 97). In other words language is only actualized in the act of speech and walking actualizes the city. The walker "makes the urban exist as well as emerge" (p. 98). This dimension of the city is what de Certeau called the "noise" – the "difference" that is a city's life blood and without which it becomes an empty shell. That is why he believed in the role of indeterminacy or casual time. For "to eliminate the unforeseen or expel it from calculations as an illegitimate accident and an obstacle to rationality is to interdict the possibility of a living and 'mythical' practice of the city."[38]

De Certeau rejected the urban utopias of people like Le Corbusier partly because they reduced transcendence to abstractions about "space" and "light" but most of all because they overestimated the possibility of ultimate fulfillment engineered purely by design. Equally, humanly-constructed utopias are contrary to the "ineffable something" that de Certeau espoused which underpins urban-social indeterminacy and resists all forms of totalization in human existence. For de Certeau, the "ineffable something," apart from God, referred to people and their communications. Interestingly, for de Certeau the events of May 1968 on the Paris streets were not an excuse to construct a new political utopia; they saw the release into the wind of this "ineffable something."[39] That is, in de Certeau's words, people were "starting to speak" – speak for themselves. This speech act had greater power than theoretical utopias. In this context, de Certeau's emphasis on resistance and "tactics" becomes something like a mystical sign indicating the power of a God working through the everyday. In my view, de Certeau's anti-utopianism is really a believer's counterblast to false gods.

De Certeau's refusal to entertain an earthly, final and definitive urban utopia (such as he interpreted Le Corbusier's vision to be), and his espousal of a fluid, mobile city for ever "on the way" in the life and practices of its citizens, parallels in significant ways Augustine's City of God as somewhere on pilgrimage towards the eternal Kingdom of God until the end times. It is not unreasonable to see in de Certeau a mixture of an Augustinian eschatological horizon, suspicious of any notion of the ultimate fulfillment of human desire within contingent time and space, and a sociopolitical concern to transgress all "programmed and regulated operations in the city."[40] De Certeau's statement in the same essay that "the Concept-city is decaying" embraces an Augustinian antipathy to idolizing the "the city" as an idea. As for Augustine, so for de Certeau, the human city is always a provisional reality that can only, at its best, prefigure the mysterious Heavenly City. Hence his suspicions of Le Corbusier's utopian visions where the city itself becomes the ultimate goal of human desire, a kind of secularized salvation realized through social engineering or highly regulated urban planning. However, it is clear that de Certeau does not reject or underestimate the importance of the everyday city – quite the contrary. What he rejects is only what are, to his mind, idolatrous ways of turning the everyday city into a definitive, yet limited, vision of human aspiration and potential fulfillment.

Notes

English translations are cited wherever available.

1 For a corrective to this understanding of de Certeau, see Ian Buchanan, *Michel de Certeau: Cultural theorist*, London: Sage, 2000.
2 See Graham Ward, "Michel de Certeau's 'Spiritual Spaces'," in Ian Buchanan (ed.), *Michel de Certeau – In the Plural*, special edition of *The South Atlantic Quarterly*, Spring 2001, 100(2), pp. 501–517.

3   See "The weakness of believing: from the body to writing, a Christian transit," in Graham Ward (ed.), *The Certeau Reader*, Oxford: Blackwell, 2000, pp. 214–243, reference is to p. 234. This 1977 essay was originally published in *Esprit*.

4   See "The weakness of believing," *passim*.

5   See Introduction to *The Certeau Reader*, pp. 1–14.

6   See her recent biographical essay on the French Jesuit website: www.jesuites. com/2012/05/de-certeau/#more-7175.

7   *The First and General Examen which should be proposed to all who request admission into the Society of Jesus*, 7 in George Ganss (trans. and ed.), *The Constitutions of the Society of Jesus*, St Louis: The Institute of Jesuit Sources, 1970, pp. 79–80. See also *Formula of the Institute*, 4 in Ganss, p. 68 and *Constitutions*, 529 and 603 in Ganss, pp. 239 and 268. Standard references are given as *Constitutions* followed by paragraph number.

8   *Monumenta Historica Societatis Jesu, Monumenta Nadal*, V numbers 195 and 773.

9   *The Certeau Reader*, p. 236.

10 On the impact of Surin on de Certeau, see his reference to "my guardian" in *The Mystic Fable*, Volume 1, *The Sixteenth and Seventeenth Centuries*, Chicago: University of Chicago Press, 1992, p. 2 and numerous references throughout the book.

11 For the text of the lecture/essay, "How Is Christianity thinkable today?" see Graham Ward (ed.), *The Postmodern God: A Theological Reader*, Oxford: Blackwell, 1997, pp. 142–155, reference is p. 151. This was a 1971 lecture at the American Jesuit St Louis University.

12 See Ganss (ed.), *Constitutions of the Society of Jesus*, p. 129.

13 See Michel de Certeau, "Mystic speech," in *Heterologies: Discourse on the Other*, Minneapolis: University of Minnesota Press, 1995, Chapter 6, pp. 81 and 82.

14 Michel de Certeau, *The Practice of Everyday Life*, Berkeley: University of California Press, 1988, p. ix.

15 Ganss, *Constitutions*, paragraph 136, p. 121.

16 Luce Giard, "Introduction to Volume 1: History of a research project," in Michel de Certeau, Luce Giard and Pierre Mayol, *The Practice of Everyday Life*, Volume 2, *Living and Cooking*, Minneapolis: University of Minnesota Press, 1998, pp. xiii–xxxiii.

17 Luce Giard "The Question of Believing," in *New Blackfriars* 77(909), November 1996, Special Issue on Michel de Certeau, p. 478.

18 For an English translation, see Maurice Giuliani, "The Ignatian exercises in daily life," in *The Way Supplement*, 49, Spring 1984, pp. 88–94.

19 Philippe Lécrivan, SJ, "Theologie et sciences de l'autre, la mystique ignatienne dans les 'approches' de Michel de Certeau SJ," link on www.jesuites.com/ 2012/01/certeau.

20 "L'universalisme ignatien, mystique et mission," *Christus*, 13(50), 1966, pp. 173–83.

21 de Certeau *et al.*, *The Practice of Everyday Life*, Volume 2, p. 263 n 5.

22 de Certeau, *The Mystic Fable*, especially Introduction, pp. 1–26.

23 Catholic Social Teaching is a tradition of critical yet constructive engagement with social realities which grew into an official body of teachings.

24 Michel de Certeau's thinking about cities is to be found especially in "Walking in the city" and "Spatial stories" in his *The Practice of Everyday Life*, 1988; also Part 1: Living, especially "Ghosts in the city," in de Certeau *et al.*, *The Practice of Everyday Life*, Volume 2, pp. 133–144; also "The imaginary of the city" and other isolated comments in *Culture in the Plural*, Minneapolis: University of Minnesota Press, 2001.

25 *The Practice of Everyday Life*, 1988, p. xi.

26 See comments in Buchanan, *Michel de Certeau – In the Plural*, Chapter 1, especially p. 20.

27 For sharp criticisms of the kind of Cartesian "rhetoric of interiority" that imbued Le Corbusier see, e.g., Walter A. Davis, *Inwardness and Existence*, Madison: University of Wisconsin Press, 1989; also Fergus Kerr, "The modern philosophy of the self," in *Theology after Wittgenstein*, London: SPCK, 1997, Chapter 1.

28 For a detailed study of Le Corbusier's theories of self and society see Simon Richards, *Le Corbusier and the Concept of the Self*, New Haven, CT: Yale University Press, 2003.

29 de Certeau, *The Practice of Everyday Life*, 1988, p. 115.

30 de Certeau, *The Practice of Everyday Life*, 1988, pp. 122–30.

31 Paul Ricoeur, *Time and Narrative*, Volume 1, Chicago: University of Chicago Press, 1984, p. 75.

32 *The Practice of Everyday Life*, 1988, pp. 122–30.

33 "Spatial stories," in *The Practice of Everyday Life*, 1988, Chapter IX.

34 See de Certeau's essay, "Ghosts in the city," in *The Practice of Everyday Life*, Volume 2 – originally "Les revenants de la ville," *Traverses*, 40, 1987, pp. 75–85.

35 de Certeau, "Walking in the City," in *The Practice of Everyday Life*, 1988, pp. 91–110.

36 "Walking in the City," p. 92.

37 "Walking in the City," p. 96.

38 "Indeterminate," p. 203 in *The Practice of Everyday Life*, 1988.

39 See Michel de Certeau, *The Capture of Speech and Other Political Writings*, Minneapolis: University of Minnesota Press, 1997, p. 11.

40 "Walking in the City," p. 95.

PART TWO

Theological Reflection and the City

CHAPTER 6

Place and the Sacred

In the Introduction I noted the fact that, both as human communities and as built environments, cities enable or disable people's sense of place identity. A sense of "place" is one of the categories of human experience with the greatest impact on how we understand the world and situate ourselves within it. Consciously or not, we all have a worldview in terms of which we live and identify ourselves. Thus, the "world" that surrounds us, including the city, is not simply raw data but something that evokes meaning. "Place" is more than a mere division of physical space or a social construction of secondary importance. In terms of wider human perception, "the world" does not exist as a straightforward given. It is experienced differently depending on perspective. Phenomenologists such as Martin Heidegger, Gaston Bachelard and Edward Casey therefore re-embrace a conviction that "place," the tangible, specific, and relational, is prior to our general perceptions of the world. We come to know reality in terms of our experience of specific places.[1]

What does "place" mean? It involves far more than geography. Rather "place" is location with particular significance because of its connection with the people who live "there" rather than somewhere else, or because it evokes something of significance, for example the historical memories of a long-standing community. "Place" thus involves a dialectical relationship between physical environments, including cities, and human narratives. A sense of

The Spiritual City: Theology, Spirituality, and the Urban, First Edition. Philip Sheldrake.
© 2014 Philip Sheldrake. Published 2014 by John Wiley & Sons, Ltd.

"place" is also bound up with moral and social values. "To know your place" implies a sense of identity in relation to a wider social framework of people. To be "in the right place" is to be at home or to be related to what is natural to us. To be "out of place" signifies the opposite. In the words of a modern urban architect, "we need to think about where we are and what is unique and special about our surroundings so that we can better understand ourselves and how we relate to others."[2] The biblical scholar Walter Brueggemann underscores the importance of spatial connections in human life. It is here that we most deeply encounter the meaning of existence. Importantly, for Brueggemann, to have a sense of place also embodies social and moral commitments.

> Place is space which has historical meanings, where some things have happened which are now remembered and which provide continuity and identity across generations. Place is space in which important words have been spoken which have established identity, defined vocation and envisioned destiny. Place is space in which vows have been exchanged, promises have been made, and demands have been issued. Place is indeed a protest against an unpromising pursuit of space. It is a declaration that our humanness cannot be found in escape, detachment, absence of commitment, and undefined freedom... Whereas pursuit of space may be a flight from history, a yearning for a place is a decision to enter history with an identifiable people in an identifiable pilgrimage.[3]

Place and Social Crisis

Since the Second World War, people living in cities in Western countries have, in many ways, lost their sense of place identity, because urban existence has increasingly been driven largely by economic rather than communitarian considerations. Thus, the importance of a sense of "place" embedded in a "locality," or "neighborhood" has been de-emphasized for the sake of values such as mobility, centralization, or economic rationalization. In different contexts, this rationalization has produced contradictory impulses: the centralization of what was once devolved and the dispersal to multiple sites of what was once a multidimensional localized mixture of home, work, and leisure. In a "dramatically delocalized world," what does "local" mean any more? It "seems to have lost its ontological moorings."[4]

The fate of once-vibrant former industrial towns has been a sad example of the loss of place-identity. For example, the string of urban centers along the River Tees in northeast England, running from Middlesbrough to Redcar, were all "company towns." In other words they were dominated by a few major companies in the steel or shipbuilding industries in which the towns became world leaders (for instance, providing the steel for Sydney Harbour Bridge). During the nineteenth and early twentieth centuries some of the places grew from small rural villages into industrial towns, and others, such as Dormanstown, were entirely new creations built by the steel factories for their workers. The companies employed most of the local workforce, built much of the housing stock, provided the social and sporting facilities, and were the focus of a strong sense of identity and local pride. The closure of the shipyards in the 1980s and the massive contraction of the local steel industry caused serious unemployment, attendant social problems, and a loss of place identity. The newer chemical and digital industries, the development of Teesport, the tenth-largest port in Western Europe, and some residual small-scale steel manufacturing have not underpinned a sense of local identity in the same way as the older industries. They do not dominate people's lives in the same way or employ as many people.

As we saw in the Introduction, on another note, the social geographer Anne Buttimer deplores the deleterious effects of an overemphasis on mobility.[5] Indeed, mobility is now understood to be a freedom bought by money and education. Remaining in the same place has come to symbolize a lack of choice, an entrapment, which is the lot of the poor, the elderly and people with disabilities. In an increasingly placeless culture we become not merely mobile people but also, implicitly, removable and replaceable. Thus, just as the vibrant steel towns on the River Tees once attracted workers from all over the country, their populations have now seriously contracted as skilled workers, those people who went to university, or those with enough money, moved elsewhere. In the more desolate housing estates, the people who did not move away have sometimes been unemployed for several generations.

Place, Belonging and Commitment

It is this sense of placelessness that makes the contemporary Western quest for meaning so concerned with roots. According to Brueggemann, "There are no meanings apart from roots."[6] Our longing for place is more than biological or aesthetic. Simone Weil suggested that the hunger for roots is fundamental to our deepest identity:

> To be rooted is perhaps the most important and least recognized need of the human soul. It is one of the hardest to define. A human being has roots by virtue of his real, active and natural participation in the life of a community which preserves in living shape certain particular expectations for the future. This participation is a natural one, the sense that it is automatically brought about by place, conditions of birth, profession and social surround-ings. Every human being needs to have multiple roots. It is necessary for him to draw well-nigh the whole of his moral intellectual and spiritual life by way of the environment of which he forms a natural part.[7]

We also seek authentic "place" in other ways. Although, as I suggested in the Introduction, there can be an unhelpful and unbalanced empha-sis on "the local," meaning the readily familiar, some sense of "being at home" seems vital if human identities are not to be fragmented. *The Poetics of Space*, by the French philosopher Gaston Bachelard, is one of the most influential books on the notion of "home." "For our house is our corner of the world. As has often been said, it is our first universe, a real cosmos in every sense of the word." However, home is more than simply where we originate or where our family lives. "All really inhabited space bears the essence of the notion of home."[8] The concepts of roots and home represent critical truths about our spatial experi-ence. First, "home" represents our need for a location where we can pass through the stages of life and develop our fullest "self." Second, we need a place where we belong to a community. Third, we need a place that offers a fruitful relationship with the natural elements and with the rhythms of the seasons. Finally, we need a place that offers access to the sacred (however we understand that term), and perhaps, crucially, relates us to life itself as sacred.[9]

"Belonging" involves both our connection to specific places and also our existence within networks of stable relationships. In European towns and cities until relatively recently, the local parish was the boundary of many people's worlds. A parish was not simply a religious concept; it was also a geographical and social reality that was coterminous with a city neighborhood, an urban borough or even a small town. The boundaries of the parish tended to dominate human associations. This sense of place was intense. The next parish, borough or town was "other" and foreign territory. People felt spiritually and humanly dislocated when they moved, voluntarily or not, beyond their familiar boundaries. The notion of a local parish determined not only the behavior of people who lived within it but also how they thought and felt, or did *not* feel. A recorded anecdote from past centuries notes that one man remained completely unmoved when a whole church full of people wept over a particular sermon. When asked why he alone had not cried, he looked surprised and replied, "But I'm from another parish."[10]

Place and Commitment

"Place" thus has a great deal to do with our commitment to human contexts and also being accepted within them. Some recent writing on the psychology of place speaks of "participation" as a key element in being effectively placed. A true "place," as opposed to a mere "location," invites active participation in the environment. "Environment," in the fullest sense, implies a range of relationships both between people and between the natural context and human beings. The psychologist David Canter suggests a threefold model of place:

> A place is the result of relationships between actions, conceptions and physical attributes. It follows that we have not fully identified the place until we know a) what behavior is associated with, or it is anticipated will be housed in, a given locus; b) what the physical parameters of that setting are; and c) the descriptions, or conceptions, which people hold of that behavior in that physical environment.[11]

Place and Memory

The importance of "remembering" also needs to be recovered and affirmed as critical to human existence. Christian theology offers a "high" view of memory, tradition, and human narrative, especially shared narrative, as vitally important for human flourishing. As we saw in Chapter 5, Michel de Certeau writes both of the dangers inherent in erasing the urban past and also of the role of everyday urban narratives – the stories people tell each other on the streets – in actually creating a city. Memory is redemptive in that only by handling the past constructively are we able effectively to shape the present and name a future that we may aspire to.

Places are profoundly associated with human memories, whether individual or collective, localized in our urban environments.[12] In his monumental book, *Landscape and Memory*, Simon Schama reminds us that human memory about landscapes, whether natural or urban, has a more powerful effect on us than the physical contours in isolation.[13] However, memory embedded in a place involves more than any single personal story. There are deeper narrative currents that embrace all those people who have ever lived there. Even as we make our contemporary stories a thread in that place's meaning, we have to come to terms with the many layers of story that already exist there. To put matters theologically, the Christian doctrine of incarnation proclaims that God is not revealed solely in the immediacy of raw nature but is also mediated through the cultural and contextual overlays in our environments, including painful and challenging ones. A hermeneutics of place progressively reveals ever more complex interpretations in the ongoing conversation between environment, memory, and the actions of particular people at any given moment. "All human experience is narrative in the way we imaginatively reconstruct it… and every encounter of the sacred is rooted in a place, a socio-spatial context that is rich in myth and symbol."[14] Thus, there can be no sense of place without narrative.

The French Christian philosopher Paul Ricoeur, mentioned briefly in the last chapter, has been greatly preoccupied with the importance of memory and narrative to human identity and with reconstructing a viable "historical consciousness." This, he argues, is vital to our individual and collective identities – and, implicitly, to our spiritual wellbeing. "[T]ime becomes human time to the extent that it is organized after the manner of a narrative; narrative, in turn, is meaningful to the extent that it portrays the features of temporal existence."[15] Ricoeur recognizes that humans cannot live without narratives. If we reject the possibility of narratives that mediate meaning, the result may be profoundly oppressive. The reason is that without narrative we risk two things. First, we undermine a key element of human solidarity because, as we noted in the last chapter in reference to the urban writings of Michel de Certeau, people bond together by sharing stories. Second, without memories we are trapped in the immediacy of the present and reduce a key incentive for changing the urban status quo, as well as an important means of bringing this about.[16] Rather than abolish narratives we need to ask, "Whose narrative has been told?" "Who is allowed a place in the story of this city?"

Ricoeur revives memory and history as more than disconnected and objectified "events" emptied of existential human engagement. Instead, a sense of history implies engagement, commitment and ultimately responsibility. These added facets of commitment and responsibility are a powerful reminder that history is not merely about a dead past but also about a living present and a possible future. A historical consciousness opens us to possible action rather than to passive acceptance of "the way things are." Ricoeur's concern to recover what we might call a "narrative of the oppressed" reminds us that "place" is always a contested rather than a simple reality and our human engagement with it is therefore a political issue in the broad sense.

Place and Particularity

All this suggests that a theological attempt to reconstruct an effective narrative of place, with room for the unheard or marginalized, needs to begin with serious attention to the value and importance of "the particular" – particular people, particular narratives, particular contexts. The problem with the Modernist thinking that has dominated Western culture over the last couple of hundred years is that its impulse is to stress the "objective" rather than the particular or the vernacular, the "universal" or disengaged rather than the personal and the contextual. The connection with certain abstract tendencies in some versions of theology is obvious. One might assume that a religion based on the doctrine of the Incarnation would have been consistent in according a fundamental importance to human history and to material existence. However, if the stories of Christianity's origin suggest an affirmation of history, there has always also been a siren voice suggesting that what is really important exists in an elevated and purified eternal realm on the far side of time and place.

In seeking a theological vocabulary that enables us to engage with "particularity," it may be helpful to look once again at one of the great figures of medieval philosophy and theology, the Scottish Franciscan John Duns Scotus. Scotus flourished towards the end of the thirteenth century at Oxford and Paris, and maybe at Cambridge as well. Academic interpretations of Duns Scotus, known as the *doctor subtilis* or "subtle doctor," have tended to be somewhat inconclusive and uncertain. This helps to explain why he has received less attention than another medieval theologian, Thomas Aquinas. However, it is now widely agreed that an important key to Scotus's thought and originality is his theology of particularity and individuality. At the heart of Scotus's view of the particular lies a distinctive and particularly rich understanding of the Christian doctrine of the Incarnation. For Scotus, the Incarnation is God's greatest work and cannot be explained by anything other than God's own fundamental reality and eternal intention. In other words, creation and redemption are a single dynamic. The Incarnation is "the highest good in the whole of creation" and "was immediately foreseen from all eternity by God as a good proximate to the end."[17] By "the end" Scotus means God's fundamental purpose for creation. For Scotus, this purpose is ultimately the "deification" of humanity, and indeed of creation as a whole. Deification implies a sharing in God's own life. This life is so fruitful that it inherently and constantly overflows and finds its expression in the particularities of the created order.

Duns Scotus offers a theologically positive view of what is specific and individual, even the smallest of details. This includes places and people. In his theology of Incarnation Scotus taught that everything, without exception, is rooted in the very purpose of creation. This purpose is Jesus Christ. By implication, all things exist not only to be themselves and to "do" themselves. They are also to "do Christ." Thus, each individual or particular thing is more than an example or symbol of something more universal and more valuable. That would make specific things, individual people, and particular places dispensable – perhaps useful but ultimately disposable. On this basis, one thing might be substituted for another if it proved to be a better symbol. There would be no unique value in any individual or particular thing or person. In affirming the sacred quality of all particular things, Scotus departs from the better known medieval scholastic theory of analogy, whereby true being exists only in God and everything else is derivative, pointing only indirectly toward true being. In contrast, Duns Scotus suggests that all things, precisely *in their particularity*, participate directly in the life of God the Creator. Because everything participates directly in God, each thing is a uniquely important expression of God's beauty as a whole.

If we think of a "place," such as a given city, in relation to Scotus, to the category "city" is added an individualizing form or final perfection. This makes a certain city *this* rather than that. Scotus gave the individualizing form the name of "thisness" or *haecceitas* in the belief that an individual thing is immediately knowable by the intellect aided by the senses. The first act of our human knowledge is therefore to recognize, even if only vaguely, the individual, the concrete, the particular glimpse of "thisness." Only by knowledge of the particular and the concrete are our minds able to arrive, by a process of abstraction and by comparing what is "like this, but not this," at the knowledge of the general, for example a "place" or a "city." As Scotus suggests in his treatise *De Anima*, we first need to know the "singular" or "particular" before we can abstract "universals." Scotus raised "the particular" from being merely an exemplification of a certain category. For Scotus, what is particular and individual is primarily itself, even if it is related to similar but other realities. It follows as a corollary that what is particular and specific is actually more perfect precisely because it is unique. Indeed, creation is predetermined to singularity.[18] *Haecceitas* is utterly specific and is to be found only in this and that particular. This concept of absolute particularity, as opposed to the greater perfection of what transcends particularity or achieves a certain abstract universality, accords somewhat with one aspect of contemporary postmodern sensibilities.[19] This is certainly highly relevant to our ability to take seriously the unique and particular reality of each city and each community.

While Scotus's principle of individuation and his epistemology attached great importance to individuality, this is not in the later, post-Enlightenment, sense of isolated individualism. For example, every particular person has a unique contribution to make to community or "common nature." Each particular person, place and context is to be understood as standing within a unique set of relationships. God's love for creation and humanity may be thought of as truly universal precisely because it is also particular and excludes nothing and no one as dispensable or irrelevant.

It is notable that Franciscan scholars emphasize that Duns Scotus's concept of the perfection of "the particular" was influenced above all by the Canticle of Creation of Francis of Assisi.[20] Consequently, it is interesting to ask what the Canticle really means. The problem is that it is possible to reduce it to a purely romantic love of nature. However, the underlying meaning of the Canticle is both more complex and more challenging. The key is that all our fellow creatures (whether animate or inanimate) are our brothers and sisters and reflect to us the face of Christ. St Francis experienced every specific element of the created order, not merely "Creation" as an abstract whole, as coming from the same source – the goodness of God-as-Trinity revealed in the Incarnate Son. The corollary is that each created particularity is an aspect of revelation. People may come to know God through each element of the created order, even a grain of sand. The foundation of Francis's respect for all created things is the fact that the One through whom everything was created has come among us as a human being.

The majority of verses in the Canticle speak of the cosmic solidarity of all elements of creation. Thus,

> Let everything you have made
> Be a song of praise to you,
> Above all, His Excellency the Sun (our brother);
> Through him you flood our days with light.
> He is so beautiful, so radiant, so splendid,
> O Most High, he reminds us of you.

However, this uplifting doctrine of cosmic solidarity conceals a much sharper and prophetic edge. Francis does not simply celebrate God's goodness expressed in God's gift of all elements of the natural world. Verses 10–11 of the Canticle celebrate the peace that comes from mutual pardon or reconciliation. It is generally thought that these verses were written as part of a campaign to settle a conflict between the city authorities and the bishop of Assisi.

> Be praised, my Lord,
> Through those who forgive for your love,
> Through those who are weak,
> In pain, in struggle,
> Who endure with peace,

For you will make them Kings and Queens,
O Lord Most High.[21]

Thus the solidarity of all things in Christ makes the created world a "reconciled space." There is no room in this vision of the world for violence, contention or a rejection of the "other." The Canticle suggests that for Christians, life is based not on the "me" as isolated subject but on an "I" in its fundamental condition as a "brother" or "sister" to what is other than myself. However, there is also the question of what Francis understood by the "other." The "other" for Francis had a very particular meaning.

Behind the text of the Canticle, and underlying Francis's whole theology of creation and incarnation, is another narrative. This is the story of the transformation of his consciousness brought about by an early encounter with a leper which we noted broadly in Chapter 3. In the first three verses of *The Testament*, dictated shortly before his death in 1226, Francis of Assisi actually identified the first moment of his spiritual life with his encounter with the leper.

> 1. The Lord granted me, Brother Francis, to begin to do penance in this way: While I was in sin, it seemed very bitter to me to see lepers. 2. And the Lord Himself led me among them and I had mercy upon them. 3. And when I left them that which seemed bitter to me was changed into sweetness of soul and body; and afterwards I lingered a little and left the world.[22]

The meeting with the leper was not merely a passing encounter with an example of human suffering but was also, in the medieval context, a challenge to Francis to embrace the excluded "other" both physically and morally. Lepers came to symbolize the sinful side of human existence onto which medieval people projected their fears and suspicions. As moral outcasts banished from society, lepers joined other marginalized categories of people in the human city: the criminals, the mad, the excommunicated, and the Jews. In many respects, lepers were not only perceived as wretched and dangerous but they were also symbols of the corrupt nature of fleshliness in general, and therefore scandalous. There was more than a hint that leprosy was a divine punishment.[23]

Through his encounter with the leper, Francis of Assisi came to understand that participation in human suffering, as well as the experience of marginalization and rejection, were at the heart of

God's incarnation as revealed in the face of the crucified Christ. If Duns Scotus's theology of "particularity" is a kind of exposition of the spirituality of the Canticle of Francis, then *haecceitas*, thisness, necessarily involves a sense of God's place among the rejected people of this world. "Thisness" expresses the absolute inclusivity of a God that embraces all things without exception.

The image of a leper becomes for Francis, and implicitly for Duns Scotus, a paradigm for our understanding of creation, incarnation, and also of discipleship. By entering the world of the concrete, specific, and particular, and by taking on our human nature, God in Jesus Christ is committed to, and thus redeems, all humanity including what is "other" as well as all the places where humans dwell.

The Sacred and Place

The theology of particularity outlined above forces us to rethink the nature of "the sacred," where and how it is expressed, and what its role and value might be in urban environments. To begin with, the concept of "sacred" is not a simple given but is an intellectual construct whose meaning has varied considerably throughout history and across cultures. Definitions of "the sacred" are dependent on the theoretical assumptions that dominate particular contexts.[24] As we saw in Chapter 4, many conventional interpretations of the sacred, at least implicitly, reflect the approach of the twentieth-century historian of religion, Mircea Eliade. Importantly, Eliade tends to collapse together the distinct concepts of "profane" and "secular." For Eliade, the "profane" embraces everything that lies outside what is explicitly dedicated to the sacred. This includes the *saeculum*, the "here and now," everyday reality, which is interpreted as existing in "a wholly desacralized cosmos."[25] This desacralization of material and mundane reality is characteristic of the intellectual presuppositions of Modernity.

A rather different Christian way of viewing the world as sacred understands it, despite some ambivalence, as the gift of God's creation and as a revelation of divine presence. As a result, "the sacred" is not removed from the world or from history onto some other spiritual plane. No part of the world should be viewed as inherently opposed to the sacred, although the world may be profaned by human sinfulness. "The sacred" stands for what is inviolable or of intrinsic rather than instrumental worth, and this remains not only a viable concept but an important one even in post-religious Western cultures. "The sacred" is articulated in a variety of ways, of which the built environment is one example. However, in multicultural, plural Western cities, while the articulations of "the sacred" will include traditional religious buildings, it will undoubtedly extend beyond them.

The Function of Sacred Space

First of all, as we saw in Chapter 3, the great churches and cathedrals of the past explicitly expressed in their architecture and decoration a quite specific image of reality. Religious buildings are, if you like, "texts" in the sense that we can read their sign systems and interpret their meaning. Because church buildings were originally intended to be acts of worship in themselves, as well as spaces for ritual, it is not unreasonable to say that their architecture is directly at the service of theology and spirituality. Religious architecture is a bearer of specific ideas and symbols – not least images of God (for example the reference to the Trinity in the three-level elevation of Gothic churches – arches, triforium, and clerestory) and understandings of human existence.

In urban environments we cannot separate functional, ethical, and spiritual questions. If a city is to be more than merely efficient, it needs to embrace some sacred quality – above all, it must affirm and promote the sacredness of people and the human capacity for transcendence. In an earlier age, the great churches fulfilled that function in Western cities. A church building was at the same time an image of God and a symbol of the ideals of the citizens set in the heart of the city.

The American philosopher Arnold Berleant suggests that the great churches of older Western cities were guides to an "urban ecology" that contrasts with the monotony of the modern city, thus helping to transform it from a place where our humanity is threatened into a place where it is continually reinforced and enhanced. At best, the great city churches center the city and offer communion with something that lies deeper than the need for an ordered public life. This kind of center is not purely functional but also evocative. If we leave for a moment the religious language that we must inevitably use of an explicitly Christian symbol, it is possible to speak more generally of a church building somehow speaking of "the condition of the world." In this way, city landscapes were given focus by the "sacred spaces" of churches and cathedrals.

These buildings operate spiritually on several levels. They counter a purely functional reading of the city by evoking a kind of meta-physical environment, offering a treasury of spiritual meaning and acting as symbols in stone of the ideals of a city. Perhaps most impor-tant of all, city churches are frequently repositories for the cumulative memory of the city and the constantly renewed hopes of the com-munity, structurally through monuments, and more subtly through an intangible atmosphere engendered by generations of pilgrims and visitors. Churches evoke a sense of urban place that is at odds with understandings of a city as simply an impersonal, smoothly running machine.

Is Sacred Space Important?

Does sacred space remain important in today's cities? What difference does the idea of "the sacred" make to city life? It encapsulates a vision of ultimate value in human existence. "The sacred," by introducing a critical note of otherness, grounds what is centrally important about existence in something more than the mere enhancement of "the self." Sadly, contemporary cities too frequently lack a centered quality because we have built nothing into them that is precious to us. It is not unusual to regard the modern city as a purely functional environment. Yet even function involves more than simply practical organization. The issue of space is more than an impersonal problem of engineering. The question of city space has a great deal to do with the creation of perceptions. The height of massive commercial buildings such as Canary Wharf Tower in London's Docklands development is not the same kind of elevating moral and spiritual presence as a city cathedral: it tends to speak of the impersonal power of size and economics. As we explore the future of cities, the value of a sense of "the sacred" is its capacity to evoke reverence for the wider good. A church or other religious building is a kind of paradigm: it points to the fact that, at its best, our sense of place is a sense of the sacred – what is sacred to one-self, to the city community, and sacred in relation to the higher order of things, however that is understood.

What Counts as Sacred Space Today?

Growing numbers of people sense that there is a "spiritual deficit" not adequately addressed by conventional political and planning agendas. An interesting question is what might be a significant role for sacred spaces in today's radically plural, multicultural city. What makes a contemporary sacred space, how do such spaces function, and what might be their role?

In our so-called secular society, it seems that "the sacred" has not so much disappeared as been dispersed into many forms and structures in wider culture. If we believe that expressions of the sacred extend in contemporary cities beyond religious buildings, what kinds of places qualify? This elicits a range of responses. Although for some people protected domestic spaces are particularly sacred, it is interesting that many common responses point to various forms of public place. Two that are regularly mentioned in discussions are natural places such as parks, lakes, or rivers, and art galleries or museums. In the case of the first, when I spoke to an audience in the northern English city of Newcastle I asked them what one thing summed up the city without which it would lose its heart, the overwhelming response was not the iconic St James' Park football stadium but the river. "The River Tyne is Newcastle's soul." More broadly, the open spaces of urban parks and gardens evoke deep feelings of connection to nature or a sense of the numinous and equally enhance the human spirit. Yet, as places also for recreation and play, public parks counter the association of "the sacred" exclusively with solemnity and seriousness. For other people, galleries and museums, especially national ones attached to important and evocative public spaces, such as the National Gallery on London's Trafalgar Square, have a particular capacity to be "sacred." Whatever form it takes, a sacred space is likely to contain powerful symbols of a community's creativity, aspirations, and quest for self-transcendence. It will be a kind of sanctuary from the pace of city life – a space for silence, for thinking, even for a kind of healing.

Because the sacred also has resonances of reverence and awe, it is important to think about what makes buildings "awesome" in a constructive sense. It surely implies more than sheer amazement at design innovation or at the overwhelming presence of buildings that materially dominate the skyline. "Awesome" also reflects motive and purpose. Genuine reverence and awe are more likely in relation to structures that reinforce the overall value of people and of shared public life rather than merely project the profiles of socioeconomic elites. In this context it is interesting to reflect on debates about the contemporary genre of "iconic buildings." These have replaced the symbolic landmarks of past centuries that had a power to persuade or that enshrined reminders of the foundational values of a society.[26]

People's reactions to iconic buildings are ambivalent. On the positive side, thoughtful architects suggest that, apart from being impressively designed and highly visible, iconic structures should once again act as collective symbols that animate a place and articulate its true nature. Two prominent architectural thinkers make interesting comments. Laurie Peake suggests that an authentic iconic building has a material spirituality because it embodies a kind of ascetic self-denial. "This may be seen as their principal role, a selfless denial of their own significance for the betterment of their context.[27] They are a "symbol of aspiration, rising above the dreary mediocrity of buildings measured by profit margins and speed of construction" and they function as a landmark, "giving us security on the horizon in a fast moving world."[28] Charles Jencks further suggests that an iconic building, just like religious icons, has "a trace of sanctity about it, the aura of a saint. By definition it is an object to be worshipped, however fitfully."[29]

However critical questions remain. In practice, do contemporary so-called iconic buildings, particularly if they are not public spaces, merely treat people in ways that suggest a fundamentally contemptuous culture? In a world of critical financial crises this has a sharp edge when what are described as modern icons are often commercial buildings or investment banks – for example, Norman Foster's prize-winning Swiss Re building for Credit Suisse in the City of London. As Charles Jencks sharply comments, if religion or other meta-narratives are no longer central to the life of a city, are we left simply with money, size, and power as the new "universals" to be worshipped?

In contrast to many contemporary iconic buildings, it is critical to their interpretation that churches have always historically been places not merely of religious worship but of social connection and of community definition. It is worth recalling that in earlier ages there was a greater permeability between religious spaces and the streets, the sacred and the everyday. In the Middle Ages, as we saw in Chapter 3, church buildings were often the only significant public spaces and were therefore multiuse, with markets in the nave, hosting community feasts, providing meeting spaces for the craft guilds, and even in some places acting as a kind of hospital. In contemporary terms, the famous church of St Martin-in-the-Fields sits on one of London's iconic public spaces, Trafalgar Square. It continues to offer multipurpose spaces as a creative take on the older tradition. Regular religious worship mingles with less defined opportunities for quiet and meditation: there are regular music concerts and art exhibitions, there is café hospitality in the crypt and, above all, St Martin's has a major center for the homeless with multiple facilities. This mixture offers a contemporary example of the role that may be played by accessible and nonexclusive sacred space in a major public square in a cosmopolitan world city.

In contemporary Western cities all kinds of people, including the socially disadvantaged, regularly enter churches from the city streets in order to find physical warmth, mental solace, or something more spiritual that they cannot quite define. These should not be thought of merely as "visitors" in ways that suggest that the real and sole meaning of the building is as a place of Christian liturgy. Worship remains central to such buildings, but there is a danger of an over-purified notion of the integrity of a church building that does not embrace spiritually or socially different people with their varied needs. Sacred spaces in today's cities need to regain a sense of being public spaces that, while in some sense set apart from the rush of the streets, need to be accessible, hospitable, and inclusive in spirit. Clearly these values of accessibility, hospitality, and inclusivity must find expression in how such sacred spaces are designed.

In addition, at different points in time, certain architectural styles were given priority in the portrayal of sacredness. As we saw in Chapter 3, Gothic had particular theological and spiritual resonance during the European Middle Ages. Equally, during the nineteenth century, Victorian thinkers also thought that the Gothic style was more spiritual in the case of churches and generally elevating in the case of public buildings. In our contemporary age, Minimalism appears to have become the new "design spirituality." This portrays a Zen-like higher life, marked by pure, light spaces and relatively few objects. The British architect John Pawson is a noted apostle of Minimalism, and has also achieved prominence as the designer of the striking Cistercian monastery of Novy Dvur in Bohemia. Pawson denies promoting a new spiritual asceticism but he wants his designs to connect with a vision of what is most profound in human existence.[30] There may be some question-marks about over-emphasizing Minimalism in that its spaces of stillness sometimes appear to mimic the priority of inward-looking spaces over effective public space in the work of Le Corbusier which has already been noted in Chapter 5. Indeed, Le Corbusier is one of Pawson's heroes. Nevertheless, there can be no doubt that Minimalism consciously relates aesthetics both to a notion of "the spiritual" and to an ethic of simplicity and ecological sensibility in a world of excess. In the context of the design of urban sacred spaces, it may also be argued that Minimalism also represents the potential of a kind of "material silence" in response to one of the spiritual problems of our contemporary cities – restlessness and the desperate quest for distraction.

The City as Sacred Space

The urban planner Leonie Sandercock's concept of "cities of spirit" was briefly noted in the Introduction. While a secular humanist, she is clear that sacred or spiritual values continue to be vitally importance in human life whether one is religious or not. As she puts it, "the completely profane world, the wholly desacralized cosmos, is a recent deviation in the history of the human spirit."[31] She believes that the resacralization of the human city is a social and political necessity. However, she is clear that we cannot simply recover the sacred spaces of past ages. We need to think creatively about ways to nurture what she calls "the presence of spirit" in the city. In this regard she shares with Thomas Merton, Michel de Certeau, and Jane Jacobs (who we shall discuss in the next chapter) a sense that we must recreate cities as centers of human spontaneity, creativity, and festival. Like de Certeau, Sandercock questions the work of those "rational planners" who seek to control how people use public space. In similar ways to the idea of "tactics" in the urban writings of Michel de Certeau she suggests that ordinary people will insist on finding creative ways to reappropriate city space in order "to fulfill their desires as well as their needs."[32]

Notes

English translations are cited wherever available.

1   See Martin Heidegger, *Poetry, Language, Thought*, New York: Harper & Row, 1975; Gaston Bachelard, *The Poetics of Space*, Boston: Beacon Press, 1994; Edward S. Casey "How to get from space to place in a fairly short stretch of time:

Phenomenological prolegomena," in Steven Field and Keith H. Basso (eds.), *Senses of Place*, Santa Fe: School of American Research Press, 1996.

2 Donlyn Lyndon and Charles W. Moore, *Chambers for a Memory Palace*, Cambridge, MA: MIT Press, 1994, p. xii.

3 Walter Brueggemann, *The Land: Place as Gift, Promise and Challenge in Biblical Faith*, Philadelphia: Fortress, 1977, p. 5.

4 Arjun Appadurai, *Modernity at Large: Cultural Dimensions of Globalisation*, Minneapolis: University of Minnesota Press, 1998, pp. 29, 178.

5 Anne Buttimer, "Home, reach and the sense of place," in Anne Buttimer and David Seaman (eds.), *The Human Sense of Space and Place*, London: Croom Helm, 1980, p. 174.

6 Brueggemann, *The Land*, 4.

7 Simone Weil, *The Need for Roots*, Arthur Willis (trans.), London and New York: Routledge, 1997, p. 41.

8 Bachelard, *The Poetics of Space*, pp. 4, 5.

9 See the comments by architect Robert Mugerauer in his *Interpretations on Behalf of Place: Environmental Displacements and Alternative Responses*, Albany: State University of New York Press, 1994, especially Chapter 10.

10 A.J. Gurevich, *Medieval Popular Culture: Problems of Belief and Perception*, Janos B. Bak and Paul A. Hollingsworth (trans.), Cambridge: Cambridge University Press, 1990, p. 79.

11 David Canter, *The Psychology of Place*, London: The Architectural Press, 1977, pp. 9–10, 158–59.

12 See Bachelard, p. 7.

13 Simon Schama, *Landscape and Memory*, London: HarperCollins, 1995.

14 Belden Lane, "Galesville and Sinai: the researcher as participant in the study of spirituality and sacred space," *Christian Spirituality Bulletin* 2, no. 1 (Spring 1994): p. 19.

15 Paul Ricoeur, *Time and Narrative*, Volume 1, Kathleen McLaughlin and David Pellauer (trans.), Chicago: University of Chicago Press, 1984, p. 3.

16 *Time and Narrative*, Volume 1, p. 75.

17 Cited by Allan Wolter in D. McElrath (ed.), *Franciscan Christology*, New York: Franciscan Institute, 1980, pp. 141, 153.

18 *Opus Oxoniense*, II, 3, 6, 2.

19 See Umberto Eco, *Art and Beauty in the Middle Ages*, New Haven, CT: Yale University Press, 1986, pp. 85–88.

20 For example, see Michael Blastic, "Franciscan spirituality," in Michael Downey (ed.), *The New Dictionary of Catholic Spirituality*, Collegeville, MN: The Liturgical Press, 1993, p. 416.

21 New translation by Sister Frances Teresa, *Living the Incarnation: Praying with Francis and Clare of Assisi*, London: Darton, Longman & Todd, 1993, p. 129.

22 Translation in Regis Armstrong and Ignatius Brady (eds.), *Francis and Clare: The Complete Works*, New York: Paulist Press, 1982, p. 154.

23 See for example, Bronislaw Geremek, "The marginal man," in Jacques Le Goff (ed.), *The Medieval* World, London: Collins & Brown, 1990, especially pp. 367–9; and R.I. Moore, *The Formation of a Persecuting Society*, Oxford: Blackwell, 1994, pp. 45–63.

24 See T. Fitzgerald, *The Ideology of Religious Studies*, Oxford: Oxford University Press 2000.

25 M. Eliade, *The Sacred and the Profane: The Nature of Religion*, New York: Harcourt Brace Jovanovich, 1987, p. 13.

26 See for example, L. Peake, "Smashing icons," in *Will Alsop's SuperCity*, Manchester: Urbis 2005, pp. 39–49, and C. Jencks, "The iconic building is here to stay," *City* 10(1), April 2006, pp. 3–20.

27 Peake, "Smashing icons," p. 41.

28 Peake, "Smashing icons," p. 49.

29 Jencks, "The iconic building is here to stay," p. 4.

30 See John Pawson, *Minimum*, London and New York: Phaidon Press, 2006.

31 Leonie Sandercock, *Cosmopolius II: Mongrel Cities in the 21st Century*, London and New York: Continuum, 2003, p. 225.

32 Sandercock, *Cosmopolius II*, p. 226.

CHAPTER 7

The Art of Community

As we noted earlier, the city historian Joel Kotkin robustly contends that without some kind of "shared belief system it would be exceedingly difficult to envision a viable urban future."[1] As Kotkin suggests, whatever the historical or social contexts, and whatever forms it takes, human community necessarily involves the quest for shared values and beliefs. This implies that creating community is a demanding commitment, even perhaps a vocation, as Richard Sennett notes.[2]

A number of urban thinkers suggest that "the term community is on many lips today."[3] In this context, the word "community" is frequently closely associated with a notion of localism and of neighborhood. This preoccupation is a reflection of the fact that there is a widespread perception that a belief in common values and a sense of shared responsibility has deteriorated in our contemporary cities. However, one significant problem with much of the language of community in urban thinking and planning is that it lacks a sense of definition or a clear ethical basis. As we shall see, other commentators point out certain difficulties with adopting exclusively a "neighborhood" or "community of place" model without qualification. This chapter will suggest that the Christian understanding of community has some implicit values to contribute to reflection on cities. Christian approaches to community are intended to be a paradigm for human community in general rather than simply to underpin an introspective, Church-centered, theology.

The Spiritual City: Theology, Spirituality, and the Urban, First Edition. Philip Sheldrake.
© 2014 Philip Sheldrake. Published 2014 by John Wiley & Sons, Ltd.

Urban Theory and Community

Several eminent urban writers in recent decades offer a vision of community in the "good city." Jane Jacobs (1916–2006), the American-born, but later Canadian, urban writer and activist, is arguably one of the most provocative and influential city thinkers of the second half of the twentieth century. She is most widely known for her classic book *The Death and Life of Great American Cities* which is a powerful critique of the kind of urban regeneration that dominated North American and European cities in the 1950s and 1960s.[4] Although she did not explicitly employ the word "community" in relation to her urban values, Jacobs essentially fought for the priority of the creative realities of human community as opposed to abstract and politicized urban planning. For example, apart from her influential writings, Jacobs organized grass-roots opposition to urban renewal projects that would have destroyed, or at least neutralized, local neighborhoods. She was instrumental in preventing two major urban highways in the United States (Lower Manhattan Expressway) and Canada (Spadina Expressway) that would have cut through neighborhoods and, she believed, would have helped to undermine urban community.

Jacobs strongly opposed the prevailing regeneration philosophy of the 1960s in the light of which older (and frequently poorer) neighborhoods were pulled down to create uncluttered, purified but sterile and unnatural urban space. In that sense, Jacobs echoed the concerns of Michel de Certeau described in Chapter 5. She defended what she thought of as the messy but creative reality of city living and was opposed to any kind of abstract urban aesthetic.

> When we deal with cities we are dealing with life at its most complex and intense. Because this is so, there is a basic esthetic limitation on what can be done with cities: *A city cannot be a work of art.*[5]

Jacobs rejoiced in the diversity and dynamism of the older mixed-use neighborhoods whose energy she believed arose from maintaining urban density. In her way of seeing things, if you crowd people and human activities together, the result is a vibrant and joyous urban confusion. The "good neighborhood" was characterized, apart from mixed use and density, by a clearly defined center and an identifiable edge or boundary. In other words, it was a limited space determined by the distances people can comfortably walk, by different kinds of housing in close proximity and by a network of interconnected streets with civic and other public buildings appropriately placed.[6] Not for her the "very nice towns" (her own words) of the Garden City movement which to her mind encouraged docility and a lack of action. In Jacobs' notion that a city should not merely help people to survive but encourage people to dream, it is possible to detect parallels to the kind of "spirituality of the streets" promoted in different ways in the city writings of Michel de Certeau and Thomas Merton that we have already reviewed.

The contemporary urban planner and thinker Leonie Sandercock promotes, alongside the need for a well-balanced economy and environmental sustainability, the importance for urban community of such values as a concern for social justice, inclusiveness, and altruistic citizenship. Greed needs to be moderated by the virtue of generosity. Private ambitions need to be balanced with civic ambition. Care for others should be promoted as much as, or even more than, care for self. We also need to think of the potential needs of future generations and not merely of our immediate "wants." In similar ways to the urban thinking of Michel de Certeau, city communities are shaped by memory and so this needs to be valued alongside the inevitability of change. Finally, the "good city" greets the stranger and welcomes the newcomer.

As an urban planner, Sandercock offers a sharp critique of common approaches to the notion of "urban regeneration." "Regeneration" is today's favorite word to express the renewal of urban community, and has largely replaced previous keywords such as reconstruction and redevelopment. On the face of it, the concept appears to be more than mere pragmatism. Indeed, its origins lie in religious and, indeed, explicitly Christian thinking. However, Sandercock is clear that "regeneration" needs to transcend statistical and target-driven accounts of what makes a good city in favor of addressing the deeper questions. Sadly, as she suggests, conventional regeneration strategies tend to coalesce around the four key principles of success in economics, infrastructure, governance, and culture. These relate to physical resources, wealth-creation, sustainability, and political structures. It is not that these principles are unimportant: it is simply that they do not engage the deeper but less quantifiable questions related to the human face of a city – the quality of life it enables, well-being, happiness, and whatever the inhabitants identify as the "soul of a city."[7] Obviously the latter is highly symbolic, and what constitutes "soul" will be particular to each place. Sometimes it will be a particular building, whether religious or not, sometimes it will be a historical monument or other symbol of a city's memories. However, as we saw in the last chapter, it will often be a natural feature – for example a large central park or a river that runs through the city.

Interestingly, Sandercock notes how the use of "culture" in regeneration projects has become increasingly common. Hence, there is intense competition among European cities to win the prize of being named as "European City of Culture" for a future year. The assumption is that cultural events attract tourism, raise the public profile of a city, redress dreary stereotypes especially in postindustrial or rust-belt cities, buoy up the local economy, and attract new long-term residents of a distinctive kind. The latter point underlines the prevalence of the theory that it is the growth of a "creative class" that lies at the root of economically successful cities. However, if we leave aside the dangers of instrumentalizing "culture" and thus evacuating it of its depth and spiritual power, the use of cultural regeneration in the context of reflections specifically about urban community renewal raises a number of critical questions: Does the embedded local community really benefit from living in a culturally-enriched city? How easy it is for the wider community really to take ownership of such an arts-driven notion of "culture"? Finally, are the fruits of any resulting wealth creation in previously economically problematic towns and cities equitably distributed throughout the local community?[8] The experience of some socially challenged, post-industrial English cities with new arts and music centers (for example MIMA – Middlesbrough Institute of Modern Art – in Middlesbrough or the Sage Centre in Gateshead) has been ambiguous, and not everyone who lives in them is yet convinced. It is worth noting that while the work of Charles Landry pioneered the connections between culture and city transformation, he uses the concept of "a culture of creativity" more broadly than simply promoting the arts. Rather, creativity refers to the overall response of city organizations to dramatic social and economic change.[9]

Remaining specifically for the moment with the wider theme of community, the social theorist and human geographer David Harvey seeks to combat the commodification of city community by the marketing of a notion of the "quality of life" and by making freedom of choice a social icon. In this way a possessive individualism becomes the template for human social community. "Citizenship" is reduced to "lifestyle." Against this trend, Harvey promotes the values of participation and empowerment present in what is known as "community organizing." This originated in 1930s and 1940s Chicago and is defined as grass-roots organizing that mobilizes communities to further their own proper interests. The concept is particularly associated with Saul Alinsky (1909–72), who sought to involve churches, trade unions, and neighborhood organizations. Alinsky argued against the power difference between an elite political class and the locals, and supported bottom-up and informal empowerment. Harvey also defends a cooperative culture and underlines the values of fostering resilience, a sense of belonging, and collective solidarity. He promotes the virtue of "civility," the appropriate use of power, versus "incivility," the misuse of power. Harvey's definition of community includes the further urban virtues of mutual respect, caring, neighborliness, and the cultivation of some kind of spiritual–moral discourse as the basis for cultivating community virtues.[10] This notion of urban virtue will be developed in Chapter 9.

The eminent Catalan urban theorist Manuel Castells offers three "types" in relation to human identity and socialization in cities.[11] First, "legitimizing identity" is promoted by dominant groups to encourage participation in approved community institutions and social processes. However, "resistance identity" counters this, as people build processes of resistance and survival that counter the dominant institutions. This concept echoes some aspects of Michel de Certeau's emphasis, as outlined in Chapter 5, where the "tactics" of the powerless run counter to the strategies of the powerful. The downside of Castells' version of this form of identity is that it is essentially defensive. This will be mentioned again when we further explore the concept of regeneration at the end of the chapter. Finally, "project identity" involves moving beyond this polarization to build a new identity to transform society. Such community-orientated movements draw people together to work for a different way of life. Castells emphasizes that the boundaries between the three "types" are not impermeable. There are hybrids. Equally, specific urban communities are fluid in nature and change over time and so they may in fact turn Castells' "types" into something closer to stages of development rather than alternative frameworks.

In a British context, the so-called "Third Way" promoted by the New Labour government under Prime Minister Tony Blair (1997–2007) placed a great deal of emphasis on "community" and social co-responsibility.

This concept of "community" is arguably essentially functionalist rather than idealistic. It was intended to counter both consumerist individualism and unbalanced "State-ism." The language was fairly traditional: it included shared moral values, cohesion, strong families where social obligations are learned, and place-bound community, with an emphasis on locality, neighborhood and its institutions including the social, geographical and religious concept of "the parish." There was some recognition by politicians and policy-makers that faith communities did add a value to urban renewal and regeneration processes, that is, "the needs and concerns of the actual people living in particular areas" who wish to be drawn into the discussion. However, in reference to this approach there is also a need to be careful about how the notion of "community" is actually used, particularly when associated with policy-makers and politicians. It can sometimes become no more than a warm and fuzzy concept. It can also reflect an uncritical nostalgia for a vanished and often romanticized solidarity in the past. It can also be reduced to whatever stands between us and social disorder. Finally, it may encourage an idealized homogeneity in contrast to the contemporary realities of diversity and plurality and also may privilege unity over difference.[12]

Finally, the urban writing of a theologian like Tim Gorringe underlines the contrast in social definitions of community between the primacy of "community as territory" and "community as shared values." The "village" model of community is often idealized because it appears to provide defined patterns of friendliness and cooperation. This leads to another contrast between ancient "rooted" communities prior to the Industrial Revolution and their replacement by the anonymous city of teeming slums and smoke-belching factories combated by such people as the American pastor, Dana Webster Bartlett who was mentioned in Chapter 4. Thus, the village came to stand for mutuality, trust, and neighborliness, and the city came to mean individual self-interest and relationships based solely on contract. However, this is too simplistic. In reality, the classic "village," at least in British terms, was often (and still is) riven with social class and deference, frequently supplemented by suppressed and rebellious anger. As a "school of morality," the village could also make quite ruthless impositions. The traditional nostalgia for "community" unfortunately often implies the elimination of difference and the absence of any sense of plurality.[13] In other words, as Richard Sennett suggests, such conventional notions of "community" are often built upon the fear of challenge or of real participation in the public realm – which is a context of mixture, ambiguity, confrontation, and even conflict.[14]

Models of Christian Engagement

In thinking about how religion, and particularly Christianity, can engage with public issues, we should recall Augustine's image of two cities. He suggests that these overlap and mingle in contingent time and space. This image expresses the provisionality of living between two horizons, the here and now and the "not yet." The Christian is called to participate as a citizen in a world that is God's creation yet is not to be totally assimilated into the here and now.[15]

When we turn to the question of whether, and how, Christian theology may contribute to a constructive reflection about social and civic issues such as urban community, there are broadly two models – a collaborative model and a prophetic–critical model. The work of José Casanova offers a very helpful survey of the different roles that religion may play on the public stage in a postsecular environment. Apart from being a detailed critique of modern secularization theory and its attempt to privatize religion, Casanova also challenges religion itself by asserting that faith-based contributions to public life are conditional on faith communities being able to live with and operate within a culture of pluralism. In terms of reflections about community, Christian theology may have a legitimate voice if it can respond constructively to "difference." In these terms, Casanova's own preference is clearly for some form of collaborative model, although liberation theology reminds us that this may not be appropriate in contexts of structural injustice and oppression.[16]

In stark contrast, the so-called "postliberal" theology of such Christian theologians as George Lindbeck, Stanley Hauerwas, and the Radical Orthodoxy group appears to be opposed to anything that might be described as accommodation between Christian life and theology and "secular rea-son" or Modernist culture. It seems that, unlike Casanova or the Jesuit social ethicist David Hollenbach, who will be discussed in Chapter 9, such thinkers are not confident about the possibility of achieving a "common wisdom" in the public sphere.[17] Consequently the Church is to be seen as a community that stands over against, even actively contends against, wider culture. It is indeed a context where a vision of the good life and ideal human community is portrayed. In the Church, virtue is cultivated, the meaning of human existence is defined and the exemplary practice of life is shaped by worship and the sacraments. The ultimate transformation of human community (regeneration) is both portrayed *and* enabled by the power of God in Jesus Christ. However, the ecclesiology, or theology of the Church, is not one of the Church as a servant of society and a witness to what is meant to be true of human community at large. Rather, in a particularly stark interpretation of the theology of Augustine, the Church is a wholly alternative public realm and is the only authentic human community. Because of this, it does not seek to translate its wisdom into language that is intelligible to the wider world beyond its boundaries. Nor does the Church seek to influence secular discourse.

However, in reference specifically to cities, the theologian Graham Ward, while associated with Radical Orthodoxy, is knowledgeable about urban theory, takes it seriously and makes a substantial contribution to urban theology. On the positive side, Ward clearly believes that the Church is not simply a detached utopian world but offers a worldview, not least of community, that actively reminds the human city of its own vocation. In that sense, human cities may actually be seen to have a vocation. On the other hand, Ward's view of the human city does appear to be unremittingly bleak. The dominance of cyberculture produces rootlessness, while consumerism falsely promises an ultimate satisfaction and happiness that cannot be delivered in practice. Indeed, nothing is lasting. The human city as portrayed in Ward lacks contextual grounding. As the basis for theological reflection, there is no significant reference to the existential realities of actual cities. In this sense, the book is definitely not an exercise in contextual–practical theology.[18]

Those who adopt a "hard" prophetic edge may best be described in terms of contestation. However, in practice, the two approaches, the collaborative and the prophetic–critical, need to be held in creative tension rather than be unhelpfully and inaccurately polarized.

Theological Themes

When we turn to some key theological themes that enable deeper reflection on "community," it is important to state that I do not see theological discourse as exclusive in the sense of being concerned merely with shaping Christian self-understanding or the Church community in its distinctiveness. This applies even to overtly Church-engaged theology such as ecclesiology and sacramental theology. In the first case, underpinning the varied "models" of the Church is a kenotic or self-giving theology. The Church is the prolongation of the *missio Dei*, that is, God's engagement with the human condition in terms of redemption as manifested in the life and teachings of Jesus Christ. As such, in the spirit of the New Testament Letter to the Philippians (2:6–11) the Church exists to pour itself out in service of a world that God has redeemed. As we shall see in the next chapter, in the case of the Eucharist, the central and community-defining ritual of Christianity, the liturgy is a social drama that expresses and promotes a vision of human existence as a whole rather than solely of an inward looking, self-protected community of faith.

Such an approach is implied by the whole tradition of Catholic Social Teaching that began with Pope Leo XIII in the late nineteenth century, and a parallel tradition of Anglican social thought that began with the nineteenth-century theologian F.D. Maurice.[19] Both social traditions involve conversations between Christian values and the public realm. Depending on the context, such conversations may be either collabora-tive or prophetic or a mixture of the two. For example, in 1971, Pope Paul VI wrote an Apostolic Letter, *Octogesima Adveniens*, to mark the eightieth anniversary of Pope Leo XIII's initial social encyclical, *Rerum Novarum*. While the latter was provoked by the social consequences of the nineteenth-century industrial revolution and its associated urbani-zation in Europe and North America, Pope Paul VI was concerned about the social consequences of the irreversible process of unplanned urbani-zation in the developing world brought about by rapid industrialization. His approach was both constructive and robust. The particular concern was for the millions of poor farmers who were fleeing the land for the big cities in the hope of a better life. All too frequently they became isolated from their families and original village networks and often ended up homeless, discriminated against by urban social inequalities, lonely, and exploited. Exactly the same concerns appeared 20 years later, in *Centisimus Annus*, an encyclical to mark the centenary of *Rerum Novarum* by the then pope, John Paul II.[20]

In terms of a theology of community, certain themes seem to offer particular richness: the Trinitarian understanding of God, the understanding of community arising from this and embodied in the Christian church as the carrier of the vision of a new humanity, and a richer understanding of regeneration.

God-as-Trinity

It may seem strange to suggest that Christianity may have something to contribute to reflections about urban community by focusing on Christian language about God. However, at the core of a Christian understanding of human identity lies the affirmation that people are created "in the image of God." The Christian understanding of God-as-Trinity is a frail attempt in human language to touch upon the complexity and ultimately inexpressible nature of a transcendent God. It is not a purely abstract doctrine. On the contrary, this way of imaging God has far-reaching and challenging implications for every dimension of life – not merely Christian life but human life in general. The underlying affirmation is that the one God who lies at the heart of existence is a mysterious communion of "persons" united in love. The classic language used is the Greek word *perichoresis* or mutual interrelationship. God is not to be thought of as absolutely simple but as "being-in-communion." God's relational quality is fundamental.

The American theologian, the late Catherine LaCugna, wrote a significant book in the retrieval of Trinity theology as a form of practical theology. "The doctrine of God is ultimately a practical doctrine with radical consequences for Christian [and I would add "human"] life."[21] The doctrine of the Trinity in the West, sadly, became in large measure disconnected from the theology of redemption and of human existence (that is, what is called theological anthropology) until relatively recently. The consequence was a separation between doctrine and "practical" theology of any kind, not least spirituality. The theological frameworks employed both in post-Reformation Roman Catholicism and within the Churches of the Reformation suffered from the same problem. In contrast to this Trinitarian void, the 1980s and 1990s witnessed an extraordinary re-assessment of the doctrine of the Trinity. The Trinity once again became the centre of theological debate. The complex reasons for this recovery of interest are beyond our consideration in this book.

The foundation for much contemporary thinking about the Trinity lies in some version of German theologian Karl Rahner's dictum that "the 'economic' Trinity is the 'immanent' Trinity and the 'immanent' Trinity is the 'economic' Trinity."[22] To put it in simpler terms, the inner life of God is to be understood not as essentially other than, but as inherently bound up with, the "work of God" – how God acts in the context of redemption. Many of the attempts to draw out the practical implications of Trinitarian belief, for example the work of LaCugna quoted above, often base themselves on the theology of Rahner. While Rahner's approach to the Trinity has found wide acceptance, it has sometimes been criticized for appearing to suggest that there is no more to God than God's activity in human history. This kind of reductionism that compromises God's absolute freedom in the process of self-revelation is not Rahner's viewpoint, even though his dictum may need to be nuanced slightly. However, his dictum acts effectively to exclude all abstract speculation about the "being" of God apart from God's action in creation and in the redemption of human failure. The absolute freedom of God cannot imply the utter arbitrariness of God's action. This would suggest a kind of divine dysfunctionality where there was no congruence between what God does and what God is. God can only be free to do what God essentially *is*. However, this is not the same as suggesting that God is no more than the processes of human history.

It is worth recalling that Karl Rahner's theology owes a great deal to the spirituality of the *Spiritual Exercises* of Ignatius Loyola, the founder of the Jesuit order to which Rahner belonged. So, in Ignatius's meditation "Contemplation on the Incarnation," what he refers to as "the Three Divine Persons" look on the world and on humanity "in Their eternity" and resolve from that eternal perspective that "the Second Person" should become human "to save the human race."[23] So, according to Ignatian thought, in God's Trinitarian existence, creation, Incarnation, and redemption form a single process. More crucially, this process is an outworking of who God is. God's "being" is identical with Trinitarian mutual communion but also with a three-dimensional dynamic of loving action towards humanity.

If we wish to understand the doctrine of the Trinity, with its newly recovered dynamism, we need to understand it to be more than merely one Christian teaching among many. In reality, to affirm God-as-Trinity touches every aspect of Christian belief, attitudes, and living. There have been a variety of proposals concerning how a Trinitarian theology of God has implications for both Christian life and for our understanding of human identity more generally. To some extent these themes group around the idea of "relationality" and its implications for social ethics as well as for a theology of Church community and for human community in general.

The concept of "relationality" has become a popular focus for contemporary reflections on God-as-Trinity. The problem is that such a concept is capable of being reduced to a rather simplistic equation: "The nature of God is social therefore human life is social." Despite the dangers of reductionism, the concepts of relationship and community offer especially fruitful connections between Christian belief, spirituality, and social ethics. To put it in other ways, while a great deal of Christian theology has been concerned with understanding personal salvation, the theology of God-as-Trinity reminds us that to be truly personal is necessarily also to be interpersonal. Relatedness stands in sharp contrast to inherited images of God as essentially distinct from the world, disassociated from the boundaries of time and space, and disengaged from human events. In a relational model, the doctrine of God-as-Trinity reveals a different understanding both of the nature of God and of human personhood created in the image of God. The fundamental truth of existence is that to be human is to be rooted in mutual self-giving love. To exist consists of being-in-relationship.

One approach to the implications of a relational model of God is that it has strongly political and ethical overtones. The German Protestant theologian, Jürgen Moltmann, suggests that the cardinal point of the doctrine of God-as-Trinity is that no divine person is more significant than any other. Moltmann again points to the traditional image of mutual interrelationship (*perichoresis*). He argues that, as a consequence of our theology of God, "superiority" and "subordination" have no place in the social order either.[24]

Both liberation theology and feminist theology have also contributed to the social model of the Trinity. Not surprisingly, both approaches share with Moltmann a strong antipathy to hierarchies. An equality of relations within God is the basis for nonhierarchical relationships more generally. This is not merely by way of example but also expresses God's concrete action within human society.[25] In relation to human equality, the Brazilian theologian Leonardo Boff moves beyond a purely exemplary approach to God's social nature. To be "social" is the very goal of our existence, collectively as well as individually. The purpose of human history is to become "society" in a true sense. Thus, our duty is to protest against all structures of domination that inhibit this fundamental vocation of humanity.[26]

Other contemporary theologians understand God as "persons-in-communion." Attempts to develop a "communion" model for God's nature owe a great debt to the work of the Greek Orthodox theologian, Metropolitan John Zizioulas, who in turn bases himself upon the fourth-century theologians known as the Cappadocian Fathers.[27] According to this communion–*koinonia* model, God is not to be thought of as absolutely simple or as perfect self-sufficiency but as "being-in-communion." In other words, communion makes things be, and nothing exists without it. God's unity consists in the free and loving interrelationship of persons. This understanding of God is particularly rich in possibilities for a theology and spirituality of human personhood and social community. "A person" is not a self-contained category. Both individuality and interrelationship are structured into the very nature of what it is to be human.

The contemporary emphasis on community, love, and relationship at the heart of God clearly points to the practical and ethical consequences of affirming God-as-Trinity. Yet we need to avoid the danger of approaching the theology of Trinity merely in terms of relevance. The validity and strength of the doctrine does not consist simply in sanctioning contemporary social ethics or a spirituality of social justice, however vital and admirable these may be. In the end, the doctrine of God-as-Trinity is necessarily distinct from our needs or preferences. In other words, it is not an extrapolation from contingent human values such as "community" or "equality." We only come to know something of the nature of God because of God's own self-revelation in creation, in the life and work of Jesus Christ and in the gift of God's Spirit within each of us.

Christianity and Community

Consequently, in terms of a Christian theological vision of human existence, every human community is to be made up of people united by bonds of communion and mutual love. Just as Christians confess God as a Trinity of "persons in communion," a *koinonia* in Greek, so too the Kingdom of God as preached by Jesus Christ envisions the ultimate reconciliation and communion of all people in the all-embracing Spirit of God. Thus, diverse community is intrinsic to human existence.

In the last 50 years there has been renewed reflection on the ancient Christian concept of communion/*koinonia* as a way of describing the Christian community but also the wider human community "in the image of God." The concept does not appear to have been used by Jesus himself and first makes its appearance in the New Testament in Paul's first Letter to the Corinthians. The term was translated into Latin as *communio* and is frequently translated into English as "communion," "fellowship," "participation in," or "sharing in." Etymologically, its meaning is grounded in the Greek root *koinōn*, meaning "common and shared" – indeed "everyday" or "commonplace" as opposed to special.

Koinonia has a rich semantic field of meaning in Paul's writing in reference, particularly, to the life of the Christian community. Here, there is a dual dimension to the usage of *koinonia*. It describes both the fellowship of Christians with God in Christ and the Spirit, and also their fellowship with other believers. Modern theology and spirituality have taken a renewed interest in the concept of *koinonia*. It has been particularly influential in renewed theologies of the Church. However, as we have seen, another fruitful line of development, with much wider social implications, explores the conviction of early Christian writers that *koinonia*/communion describes not only the Christian believer's relationship with God-as-Trinity but also the interdependent relationship within God the source of all things. God is not a self-contained divine solitary but has been revealed in Jesus Christ as one who does not merely *enter into* relationships of one kind or another but rather as a God who is, in the divine existence, perfect relationship. From this perspective, God is also the key to understanding the nature, demands, and possibilities of authentic human personhood, created "in the image of God." The implications of this are immense. Community and sociality are at the core of any adequate understanding of human life along with the corollaries of mutual dependence, mutual self-giving, and solidarity.

Much of Western philosophy, ancient and modern, has been based on an ontology, or theory of "being," that analyzes "being" as encountered in the individual soul or, following René Descartes, in the individual mind. However, if the source of all being, God, is perfect relationality and society, and if, according to the Christian understanding of creation, all that exists proceeds from the creative outpouring of God's own existence, then an unbalanced emphasis on individuality must give way to society as the core of existence. "Personhood" is an inherently social category. This line of development places the concept of *koinonia/* communion at the forefront of any contemporary theological reflection on human community as a whole. Authentic human existence is now to be understood not in terms of self-sufficiency, but in being-for-others. Humans are made for society. One's spirituality is realized not only in one's relationship to God but also relating to other persons and to the cosmos as a whole.

A crucial corollary of the concept of *koinonia* both in relation to God and to human life is that our nature of "being in communion" is inherently related to diversity. Further, the notion of diversity is necessarily related to an essential equality. There is no God-given hierarchy of personal worth or value. In the Christian vision of a new creation and of a redeemed humanity, "there is no longer Jew or Greek, there is no longer slave or free, there is no longer male or female" (Letter to the Galatians 3:28). Apart from promoting the value of the quality of all classes and races, this image also calls into question any overemphasis on localisms and familiar neighborhoods – that is, the known, the knowable, and the manageable. The image of the Christian community, and by extension all of redeemed humanity, as a single body is a powerful image in the Christian scriptures. This extends to the notion that we should treat with great care what seems weakest, and that if one member of the body suffers so all the others suffer with it. This is most powerfully and unequivocally expressed in the First Letter to the Corinthians 12:12–26.

Regeneration and Redemption

Finally, the concepts of "new creation" and "redemption" take us back to the contemporary use of the word "regeneration" for the renewal of urban communities. In terms of human community, it seems important to recapture the underlying spiritual dimension of the notion of "regeneration," a word which has explicitly Christian roots in the notion not merely of healing but of new birth or a new creation wrought by God. However, in practice, in the context of so much urban planning, "regeneration" is often a socially and politically driven term.

It comes across as less pragmatic than the earlier concepts of "reconstruction" and "redevelopment" because it speaks of the revitalization of urban community life. However, the weakness of the concept in terms of urban policy and planning is that it seems to imply that only *some* people, *some* communities, *some* neighborhoods or towns are to be defined as unregenerate. Equally, regeneration tends to emphasize the two poles of either a moral crusade to promote an individualized "reform of the self" in favor of "personal responsibility" and being an "active citizen," or a quasi-spiritual emphasis on the notion of "individual happiness" as the major goal of human existence and therefore of "the good city."[28]

However, if we return to the Christian concept of "spiritual regeneration" we may be able to express something that applies equally but differently to everyone. Every human person and every human community needs redemption in that, alongside an inbuilt impulse towards "the good," or God, also lies an in-built freedom that may undergird a tendency to choose selfishly. How might a Christian vision of human transformation contribute to debates about social regeneration? A Christian view of all reality is that it is "sacramental" – that is, it is potentially a revelation of the divine. Everything is of profound value. However, at the same time, our experience of reality speaks of human loss and the necessary re-ordering of what is disordered and damaged. At its best, "regeneration" is linked to the Christian concept of redemption – but not in the sense of being freed from individual slavery to sin, or being the object of God's judgment. Rather, contemporary reflections on this classic Christian theme focus more strongly on liberation from the "structural sins" of human enslavement to poverty, racial prejudice, gender inequality, and so on. Redemption thus implies a trajectory of hope, rebirth, and the challenge of profound transformation for everyone in the city.

Is it possible therefore to understand "the city" as a potential sacrament of redemption – a space for the healing of the human condition? In one sense, the answer is yes. However, this needs to be balanced by a suspicion of any promise of premature, utopian completion or of an arrival at the perfect society. Christian theology has a strongly "eschatological" dimension. This means that human existence is understood to be on a perpetual journey towards an ultimately undefinable transcendent horizon. Thus part of Michel de Certeau's critique of Modernist urban planning, discussed in Chapter 5, seems to be precisely a theological discomfort with any utopian model of the city as the *complete* realization in the here and now of all human aspirations.

Conclusion

This brief exploration of Christian understandings of community raises some fundamental questions. Is "community" simply a more satisfactory expression of city life that we should aim for as an ideal? Or, more fundamentally, is community inherent to human identity, and are we by nature orientated towards "the other"? In other words, if we are social and communal by our very nature, as opposed to merely by arbitrary choice, we cannot fully flourish without community. Christianity suggests that the second interpretation is the case, based on its understanding of the nature of God and of humanity as created in the image of God. In this vision of existence, relationality, *koinonia*, and communion lie at the very heart of God and therefore of human life.

Having said this, human community in a fully-developed sense is not something that is simply automatic and unconscious. It demands our commitment, a quest for shared values, and a measure of self-sacrifice. In Augustine, community demands moral action, value-driven aspiration, a commitment to the service of others and collaboration to make the city an expression of the highest good. Monasticism suggests that the deepest call is to honor everyone and not merely those to whom we owe a duty, those who are like us, or those from whom we can gain some benefit. The reception of strangers and hospitality to otherness are critical values. In the medieval thought of Thomas Aquinas, community is fundamental to the human vocation in order to make the "good life" realizable. Following his hero Aristotle, Aquinas believed that we can only develop social virtues by real interaction with others in mixed groups. After the Reformation, the Lutheran tradition strongly promoted justice and equality and a common human responsibility for both the natural and the social environments. The post-Reformation Ignatian spiritual tradition highlighted the quest we undertake together for "the more universal good" and the importance of "edification" in the city – that is, a continual renewal of existing urban situations. Finally, Michel de Certeau sought to highlight the importance of "indeterminacy" in city life and urban design. This both resists the totalizing systems of top-down planning that leaves no room for otherness and also promotes the value of the everyday practices of human encounter and shared stories on the streets that continually bring a city into existence.

Notes

English translations are cited wherever available.

1   Joel Kotkin, *The City: A Global History*, New York: Random House, 2006, p. 159.
2   See Richard Sennett, *Together: The Rituals, Pleasures and Politics of Cooperation*, London and New York: Allen Lane, 2012, Chapter 9.
3   Dick Atkinson, *The Common Sense of Community*, Demos Paper 11, London, 1994, p. 1.
4   Jane Jacobs, *The Death and Life of Great American Cities*, New York: Random House Modern Library Edition, 1993 [1961].
5   Jacobs, *The Death and Life of Great American Cities*, p. 485 and see as a whole Chapter 19 "Visual Order: Its Limitations and Possibilities."
6   Jacobs, *Death and Life*, Chapters 6 and 15.
7   Leonie Sandercock, "Spirituality and the urban professions: the paradox at the heart of planning," *Planning Theory & Practice*, 7 (11), 2006, especially pp. 65–7.
8   For some reflections on these questions, see for example Chapter 6 "Cities of culture," pp. 99–114, in Elaine Graham and Stephen Lowe, *What Makes a Good City? Public Theology and the Urban Church*, London: Darton, Longman & Todd, 2009.
9   See Charles Landry, *The Creative City: A Toolkit for Urban Innovators*, London: Routledge, 2008.
10   David Harvey, "The Right to the City," *New Left Review*, 53, 2008, pp. 23–40.
11   Manuel Castells, *The Power of Identity, The Information Age: Economy, Society and Culture*, Volume 2, Oxford: Blackwell, 1997.
12   See Robert Furbey and Marie Macey, "Religion and urban regeneration: a place for faith," *Policy & Politics*, 33(1), 2005, pp. 95–116, especially pp. 97–8 and 100–104.
13   See T.J. Gorringe, "Constructing community," Chapter 7 in *A Theology of the Built Environment: Justice, Empowerment, Redemption*, Cambridge: Cambridge University Press, 2002, pp. 166–70.
14   Richard Sennett, *The Uses of Disorder*, New York: Norton, 1990, pp. 42, 108, 163.
15   On Catholic social teaching and its implications for a Christian contribution to debates about society and human community, see the comprehensive and authoritative multiauthor collection of essays and commentaries on the major documents: Kenneth R. Himes, ed., *Modern Catholic Social Teaching: Commentaries and Interpretations*, Washington, DC: Georgetown University

Press, 2005. For some specific discussion of the theme of "community" in Catholic social teaching, see Judith A. Merkle, *From the Heart of the Church: The Catholic Social Tradition*, Collegeville, MN: Liturgical Press, 2004, pp. 241–65.

16 José Casanova, *Public Religions in the Modern World*, Chicago: University of Chicago Press, 1994.

17 For example, see Stanley Hauerwas, *After Christendom? How the Church is to Behave if Freedom, Justice and a Christian Nation are Bad Ideas*, Nashville, TN: Abingdon Press, 1991; also John Milbank, *Theology and Social Theory*, Oxford: Blackwell, 1990.

18 Graham Ward, *Cities of God*, London: Routledge, 2000.

19 See for example, Jeremy Morris, *F. D. Maurice and the Crisis of Christian Authority*, Oxford: Oxford University Press, 2005, especially Chapter 5 "The Church in society."

20 For references, see Michael Hornsby-Smith, *An Introduction to Catholic Social Thought*, Cambridge: Cambridge University Press, 2006, pp. 192 and 227–8 for *Octogesima Adveniens*, and p. 101 for *Centisimus Annus*.

21 Catherine LaCugna, *God for Us: The Trinity and Christian Life*, San Francisco: HarperCollins, 1993, p. 1.

22 Karl Rahner, *The Trinity*, London: Burns & Oates, 1970, p. 22.

23 See *The Spiritual Exercises*, paragraph 102, in Joseph Munitiz and Philip Endean (eds.), *Saint Ignatius of Loyola, Personal Writings*, London: Penguin Classics, 2004.

24 See Jürgen Moltmann, *History and the Triune God: Contributions to Trinitarian Theology*, London: SCM Press/ New York: Crossroad, 1992.

25 See for example, Elisabeth A. Johnson, *She Who Is: The Mystery of God in Feminist Theological Discourse*, New York: Crossroad, 1996, Chapter 10.

26 Leonardo Boff, *Trinity and Society*, New York: Orbis Books, 1982.

27 John Zizioulas, *Being as Communion*, Crestwood: St Vladimir's Seminary Press, 1985.

28 See Robert Furbey, "Urban regeneration: reflections on a metaphor," *Critical Social Policy*, 19(4), 1999, pp. 419–45.

CHAPTER 8

Reconciliation and Hospitality

The last chapter reminded us that to nurture a sense of community in today's plural cities inevitably confronts us with the strongest contemporary challenge in the public realm – that is, how to deal with inclusivity and diversity, "otherness" and alienation as critical social and spiritual issues. Overall, our spiritual visions for the city need to be robust enough to confront the shadow side of human existence and behavior. The word spirituality, so much in vogue these days, implies a vision of what our human existence is intended to be and in what ways our daily lives need to be transformed. It follows that spirituality should ideally offer us a language to confront such structural evils as power dominance, violence, injustice or social exclusion. To put it in more overtly theological language, spirituality must include a narrative of "redemption" – the hope we are called to affirm, and the process of change or conversion to which humans are called upon to commit themselves. In this sense, a robust Christian version of spirituality will not simply offer an inspirational framework for thinking about human cities. It will also "interrupt" or confront the everyday city by effectively acting as a civic critique built upon religious–spiritual values. One important value is that of reconciliation, expressed in this chapter by the complementary themes of "catholicity" and "hospitality."

This chapter is essentially a manifesto for keeping faith with the vital importance of human reconciliation in our cities at a time when siren

The Spiritual City: Theology, Spirituality, and the Urban, First Edition. Philip Sheldrake.
© 2014 Philip Sheldrake. Published 2014 by John Wiley & Sons, Ltd.

voices suggest that this is a hopeless task. Reconciling difference is not the same as promoting an artificial "sameness." Reconciliation, properly understood, actually underlines the importance of a creative heterogeneity, so that a city community celebrates variety as opposed to the deadening homogeneity as portrayed, for example, by Italo Calvino's literary image of the city of Trude.[1]

What does it mean to reconcile otherness? How is human reconciliation to be achieved? Many people suggest that what is needed in today's cities is protection from all that threatens us by creating high walls or fences – whether metaphorical ones or the physical ones that provide security-protected "gated communities" in cities world-wide. Against this, I hold strongly the view that the complicated and challenging commitment to human reconciliation is central to human flourishing and is also a vital Christian contribution to the wider world at the start of the twenty-first century. As the South African theologian John de Gruchy suggested in his Cambridge Hulsean Lectures, the doctrine of reconciliation is "the inspiration and focus of all doctrines of the Christian faith."[2]

The Words We Use

The words we use are critical. So what does the word "reconciliation" imply? It is important to have a realistic understanding of the challenge, the knowledge we need, the actions we should take and the likely process. A basic issue is whether reconciliation is the same as political models of conflict resolution. While I accept that conflict resolution is involved, reconciliation embraces more than strategies for changing social systems. Several words are often treated incorrectly as interchangeable: reconciliation, conciliation, and accommodation. "Conciliation" is associated with pacifying or placating our neighbors from whom we are estranged. This lowers the temperature but does not necessarily promote deep change. For example, many local processes of conflict resolution aim to conciliate but fail to transform people at the deepest level. This leaves long-standing problems that will inevitably re-emerge in other guises. "Accommodation" or tolerance enables us to establish pragmatic arrangements, achieves a compromise but promotes a kind of parallelism. Here we learn to live alongside the "other" but avoid the kind of significant interchange that might mutually change us. Certain versions of multiculturalism in Western cities have faced this criticism.[3] Pragmatic arrangements and compromise may initially be necessary in the world of *realpolitik*, but on their own they do not ultimately go far enough. Neither side needs to learn from the other or to be changed by the encounter. In contrast the notion of reconciliation goes a great deal deeper because it suggests harmony and concord. Interestingly the *Oxford English Dictionary* defines reconciliation not merely as the restoration of harmony but also as "the reconsecration of desecrated places." If you like, all those people whose lives are marginalized by what other people do or say in contexts of conflict are "desecrated places" because their unique value and identity as sacred and as images of God is denied.

How far can we deal with reconciliation in a universal way? While the word has a general definition, its reality is always in terms of particular times, places, and complexities. Simple translations from one place to another are impossible. We can learn from other cities and other neighborhoods but, in the end, the challenge is ours alone. Equally, situations of conflict and separation are never reducible to one level of analysis. It is therefore unhelpful to juxtapose competing and reductionist explanations. For example, different groups blame contemporary urban divisions solely on continuing class conflicts or on misplaced social engineering by politicized urban planning. A proper appreciation of the history of cities for example soon reveals a complexity of social, political, economic, cultural, and ethnic divisions. In some cities religion has been, or is, used to promote social discrimination and marginalization in various forms of religious and ethnic ghettoes.

Costly Reconciliation

First of all, reconciliation implies a complex balance between structural change and spiritual harmony.[4] No change of emotional climate can take place without structural change, yet structural change alone cannot guarantee reconciliation. Secondly, the process of reconciliation is evolutionary.[5] A knowledge of history and of contemporary reconciliation processes suggest that long-term and deeply rooted reconciliation cannot be achieved without mutual repentance and the discovery of common ground. It is important to avoid quick or "cheap reconciliation" without truth-telling and justice. To appreciate the full complexity of reconciliation, a number of difficult questions need to be faced at the outset of a process to which protagonists are likely to have different instinctive responses. First, what exactly is to be reconciled? Are there two equally valid but opposing viewpoints, or are there issues of moral right and wrong? If the latter is the case, neutrality and consensus-building alone would be unethical and politically misplaced. Second, what is "justice" in this situation? All parties may agree that justice is important but see its reality very differently depending on their place in the prevailing social power system. Third, is violence endemic in the current social and political frameworks? Is readjustment sufficient or must a whole system be dismantled? Fourth, what is the true nature of the conflict? Is it political, social, cultural, ethnic, religious, or a mixture of all of these? Conflict always involves issues of power, and so reconciliation implies a gradual redistribution of power in all sectors of life. This cannot just be theoretical.

This leads me to the critical thought that genuine reconciliation can only be *between equals*. A sharp question for protagonists on all sides of a social conflict is whether they are capable of thinking of those from whom they are separated as their equals, humanly, morally, and spiritually. The uncomfortable reality is that reconciliation results from making equal space for "the other." This is different from tolerance, which may simply promote a series of parallel, yet carefully protected, spaces. This is a structural and social issue but it is also a theological and spiritual one because it touches upon our understandings of human identity. At the heart of reconciliation lies an initial belief that everyone is diminished by the situation we seek to change. So, the quest is for new ways of collaboration and integration that will empower everyone. Historically, it is worth recalling that changes in relationship between groups rely on two long-term factors: the gradual equalization of status, leading to the creation of a common cultural discourse.

Excluding Otherness

Reconciliation demands that everyone has to modify their view of the world and to risk the way they identify themselves, because a sense of identity is too often achieved "over against" another group. We tend to handle "otherness" by different strategies of exclusion. In terms of physical space, we continue to create ghettoes which are often shaped architecturally (for example by gated communities) or by planning. We only have to think of the desolate estates of postwar "social housing" in English cities, or the peripheral low-cost housing projects of the 1960s, the *banlieues*, around Paris. Morally or socially we demonize others – we fear those who are different in class or color and seek to eliminate them from our lives. Our desire is that they go away or remain invisible. I recall my experience a few years ago of living in a market town in the north of England where, to my surprise, I encountered no people from non-European ethnic groups on the streets despite the presence of an Indian restaurant and a Chinese take-away. When I mentioned this to a local vicar, I was told that such groups were present in the town but they had learnt that it was better to remain invisible.

Alternatively we colonize those who are different – we think of them as inferior and to be pitied. They become objects of our charity or our attempts to control them. Frequently, we generalize about others by taking care not to see them as individuals, but only as a type. Our desire is to keep control of the situation and not to have to deal with the challenge of personal encounters. A common strategy is to trivialize – we ignore disturbing differences and domesticate the strangeness by allowing some others to become honorary members of our club. Our desire is not to be challenged by their presence but to be affirmed as good people for allowing them to join us. Another version is to homogenize the situation – we say that there is no real difference at all. In a well-meaning way, we make premature pleas for tolerance and closure. Finally, we may ignore others – we simply make "the other" disappear by not acknowledging them at all.

Fear and Loathing

Underlying the various strategies for excluding "otherness" is some element of fear and loathing. This is manifestly the case in acute contexts of conflict, but is more subtly present in urban contexts, for example where divisions have given way to tolerance but not to reconciliation. Sadly, this has often been the case in varied forms of multiculturalism promoted in Western cities which have not addressed the deeper questions involved in renegotiating a sense of "the common good." Racism, often allied to religious–cultural suspicion, lurks just below the surface, ready to re-emerge in situations of social or economic pressure or in response to isolated violence by religious extremists or by disaffected socioeconomic groups. Fear is one of the most powerful currents in our contemporary world. Ongoing religious or ethnic divisions, as well as the notorious global "war on terror" since the events of 9/11, suggest how fear, and its close associate anger, shape our responses and cripple our ability to respond effectively to the deeper needs of fellow citizens. The overwhelming imperative then becomes the satisfaction of emotional needs posed by fear and anger. We tend to rush towards emotionally satisfying but superficial actions. Politically we create places to detain and then expel illegal immigrants or marginalize certain voices without addressing the deeper challenges. Fear and anger are among the greatest spiritual blocks to effective collective discernment and to making good choices.

Fear and unacknowledged anger tend to promote evasion, hiding, and paralysis. This works in three ways. First, fear and anger provide a narrative structure to answer the question of why we are in a mess. This needs a clear plot and a plausible cast of goodies and baddies. The story-line must be big enough to provide a convincing description of our fear, which usually means that the threat is greatly inflated. Such narratives offer emotional reassurance on several levels. They affirm that it is understandable that we are afraid; that we are on the side of good versus evil; that good (meaning our perception of good) will prevail. Second, anger and fear respond to our desire for uncompromising clarity. When we are fearful, we want to know who is on our own side and we want loyalty to be unconditional rather than complex. Everyone is assigned a label. "We stand for what is just and right. They need to change their ways (or repent). You need to be tougher and exercise proper authority." Nowadays, there is a growing tendency to escape into willful ignorance – people do not want to understand otherness if understanding is not straightforward. Third, fear and anger prompt a desire to bond with the apparently like-minded. There is much talk of forging alliances and of shared values. However, the quest for meaningful identity in such an over-simple sense is always at risk of buckling under the weight of too many hidden contradictions.

Spaces

Reconciliation involves "making space" for the other, not least in terms of our social and historical narratives. As we saw in Chapter 5, Michel de Certeau underlines the importance of stories in creating a city. Our city narratives are never neutral, value-free or "true" in some simple way. They are partial in that they are built on what is included and excluded in our map of life. A critical question for every human community is what kind of stories do we foster or live by? Do they offer a justification for maintaining barriers of separation?

Every human division leaves its scars. A process of reconciliation must make space for memory. The Latin word *memoria* has connotations of mindfulness. This relates both to attentiveness (to people, contexts, and my own reality) and to the vision of "catholicity" or "embracing the whole" that will be discussed in a moment. Such a vision is opposed to either a comforting forgetfulness or a highly partial view of history. In the context of urban renewal, what historical narrative for a place is promoted? All versions of history are partial, both in the sense that they are not complete and in the sense that they tend to favor certain groups over others. So a critical question in our urban environments is, what kind of historical sense have we created and do we foster? There is often a tendency to rehearse a particular version of social or local history as the justification for maintaining barriers of separation. In his powerful novel *Looking on Darkness*, the South African writer André Brink focuses on the recollections of a so-called "Cape Coloured" actor, Joseph Malan, as he awaits execution. He is proud that his family have a story, a remembered history, because so many non-whites do not. Yet the Malan history scarcely intersects with "official" public history "as if we've always existed apart from it." "It surrounds our story but forms no part of it. For my tale is not history, but, at most, the shadow-side of history."[6]

Reconciliation does not mean forgetting but remembering in a new way, in a new context where we learn how to create a new, common history and how to remember *together* rather than continue to trade memories in the same way that we trade blows. Making space for a new history moves people beyond the selectivities based on tribalism or sectarianism. The new history should liberate by relativizing cherished myths and allowing the recovery of forgotten voices. Space for memory enables communities as a whole to begin to come to terms with the truth of the past. To have to speak and to have to listen is profoundly transforming. Reconciliation involves the healing of memories particularly of belittlement, rejection, and denial. Part of a process of healing is to realize the incompleteness of any one story when isolated from the other stories. So a space for memory also implicitly celebrates diversity. This involves a process of seeking a shared vocabulary which ultimately cannot be imposed but which arises from shared life and shared experience.

A Christian Response

There are specifically Christian characteristics to reflections about reconciliation. It is not simply a political or psychological word with some incidental theological-spiritual gloss. Protestant approaches tend to emphasize reconciliation between God and humanity as a result of Jesus's death on the cross (see Romans 5:6–11) and Catholic approaches tend to emphasize how the love of God poured out upon us as a result of the divine–human reconciliation creates a new humanity in which the walls of division between people are broken down (see 2 Corinthians 5:17–20 and 6:1). In fact, both dimensions need to be held in tension. Interhuman reconciliation is not simply a matter of giving each person their due but is really to give God *God's* due, by building a world that God's all-embracing forgiveness demands.

Catholicity and God

A key word in relation to reconciliation is "catholicity," which implies achieving full humanity in the image of God.[7] Catholicity is not narrowly religious in origin. The word itself derives from the Greek *katholikos*, which means "general" or "universal." It is generally thought that the word has its roots in an adverb *kath' holou*. This means "on the whole," or "generally speaking," or "in general." This adverb is connected with *kata holos*, "in respect of the whole," or "what is not partial." At its roots, to be "catholic" is the opposite of what is narrowly confined to a limited or exclusive group of people, whether in a religious sense or in the more general social or ethnic sense. Thus St Augustine in his *Epistle* 49, n3, contrasts a catholic community with any group that wishes to separate itself off from the general mass of people.

Theologically speaking, the way we describe human community is founded upon a particular understanding of God. Only God is "catholic" in the fullest sense of embracing the "mystery of the whole." What do we learn about catholicity if we begin with God? This is a complex question that I have already touched upon briefly in the last chapter. To think of God in terms of Trinity speaks of a *koinonia* or communion of mutually co-inherent relationships in which the unique personhood of each is substantiated in mutuality. The letters of St Paul promote the theme that the communion between believers brought about by the Spirit of Christ is to share in the very life of God (1 Corinthians 1:9; 2 Corinthians 13:13).

In other words, the implication for human existence of affirming God-as-Trinity is that God's presence in every person is the source of and the goal of the inner dynamics of human identity. The indwelling of God underpins the uniqueness of our particular identities yet at the same time subverts our tendency to self-enclosure by orientating us to "the other." We might say that a Trinitarian anthropology suggests an inherently transgressive rather than hard-boundaried and individualistic understanding of human identity.[8] "Catholicity" implies that we become fully human only by giving space to everyone to whom God gives space.

Becoming Catholic People

The notion of "catholicity" concerns how we "perform" our lives in the human city. God's own catholicity is manifested in time and space through God's "Incarnation" in the person and teachings of Jesus Christ. In the person of Jesus Christ, "the whole fullness of divinity dwells bodily, and you have come to fullness in him who is the head of every ruler and authority" (Colossians 2:9–10). So, for Christians, the key to our human capacity for inclusivity is to participate in God's "catholic" nature in and through following the way of Jesus Christ.[9] However, to live within the "whole story" of Jesus Christ implies coming to grips with a narrative of human ambiguity, incompleteness, and failure. In Christian perspective, human existence is at the same time "graced" (a gift of a loving creator God) and yet also flawed because of our human capacity for self-seeking, which is the heart of what we mean by "sin." Thus, an important dimension of God's relationship to humanity, not least through God's presence and action in the person and teachings of Jesus Christ, is referred to as "redemption." The central Christian ritual of the Eucharist speaks powerfully of this divine process of redeeming human sinfulness, reordering the disordered, healing what is broken, reconciling what is alienated.

Thus, becoming catholic people is a process of hope, the hope of transformation that is not achieved through human efforts alone and whose completion is beyond time and space. The whole truth of life revealed in Jesus Christ is always in process of being realized in us. So, a fundamental quality of this vision of existence is expectancy. Expectancy implies knowing that there is always more to life and becoming ever more receptive to "the more" that we need. In terms of life in plural cities, this receptivity is perhaps most sharply expressed in and through an engagement with individuals and groups who are unlike us – other, strange, unnerving, and even distasteful.

The Demands of Hospitality

In 2006 a British Church-sponsored, ecumenical, interfaith Commission on Urban Life and Faith published a report, *Faithful Cities*.[10] Among other things, the report suggested that a critical spiritual and moral issue in the modern city was the need to move beyond the dominant catchword of liberal societies, "tolerance." Tolerance is a passive notion that suggests the magnanimity of the powerful towards those who are less favored. It can also result on various forms of social parallelism. The report promotes the more challenging biblical theme of "hospitality." This implies a real relationship with those who are different and the risk that we may be moved out of our comfort zone and be changed in an encounter with "the other." Hospitality is also an important element of the virtue of "catholicity."

Interestingly, the emphasis in both Hebrew and Christian scriptures is on hospitality to the stranger. Many texts in the Hebrew bible make it clear that receiving the stranger as if they were our close kin is God's command. An important foundation is for the people of Israel to persistently remember their ancestors' own situation while living as strangers in Egypt (Deuteronomy 10:19). Part of the narrative of Abraham suggests that his hospitality to the three strangers is actually hospitality to God (Genesis 18). In the gospels, Jesus is frequently portrayed as the wanderer without a home (for example, Matthew 8:20) or dependent on the hospitality of others (for example, Luke 9:58) or, in the Gospel of John, as the stranger in our midst (for example, John 8:14 and 25ff). An important feature of Jesus's own practice was to push his followers away from familiar places into situations they found disturbing. In the Gospel of Mark 6:45, he forces his reluctant disciples into the boat to cross the lake of Galilee to gentile Bethsaida. In Luke 8:26–39, he healed the demoniac on the east side of the lake in the land of the Gerasenes. In the Gospel of Matthew, Jesus crosses into the land of Tyre and Sidon to heal the daughter of a Syro-Phoenician woman and to commend her faith. In Mark 8:1–10 he fed a multitude on the eastern or non-Jewish side of the lake. "Ever dragging his disciples away from the familiarity of home, he declares present the power of the kingdom [of God] in the alien landscapes of another land."[11] Finally, hospitality to the stranger is presented as the vision of the Kingdom of God – and, indeed, has a bearing on our eternal destiny in the portrayal of the final judgment in the Gospel of Matthew, chapter 25.

The Christian narrative of redemption describes the nature and destiny of humanity. It speaks of alienation from God, from creation, and from other humans, but also of how God overcomes this alienation. The suffering and death of Jesus Christ offers a new concept of reconciling love that risks everything, accepts death and rejection, and so enables the transformation of the unjust. Yet reconciliation is not yet experienced in its completeness – the evil of human division remains a reality. For now there is an assurance, a confident hope that God will finally establish justice and peace. The Christian community, as the prolongation of the mission of God, is called upon to embody in its own life a narrative of reconciliation for the benefit of all.

Christian approaches to reconciliation also challenge the notion that difference should be viewed purely as part of the human predicament. Trinitarian theology speaks powerfully of a God in whom difference is the very foundation of existence. The Letter to the Ephesians also suggests that the Christian community is called to be the carrier of a vision of a new humanity in which Jew and Gentile are reconciled as members of one body. The walls of enmity are broken down, and those far off, even our historic enemies, are made near (Ephesians 2:11–22).

Spirituality of Reconciliation: The Rule of St Benedict

In the final part of this chapter, I have selected two Christian resources for what might be called a spirituality of reconciliation. The first is the monastic Rule of St Benedict; the second is the Christian ritual of the Eucharist.

As we saw briefly in Chapter 2, part of the historical witness of Christian monasticism as an "alternative city" was a new vision of human solidarity expressed especially in the approach to strangers. The literature associated with the fourth- and fifth-century Egyptian desert fathers and mothers offers numerous examples of charity and hospitality as a central rule of life.

> A brother went to see an anchorite and as he was leaving said to him, "Forgive me, abba, for having taken you away from your rule." But the other answered him, "My rule is to refresh you and send you away in peace."[12]

The monastic spirituality of the Rule of St Benedict has a great deal to offer in terms of the Christian vocation of promoting reconciliation in a renewed city.[13] There are two critical words. First, the opening word of the Rule is the imperative "Listen!" – *Obsculta*! This sets the tone for the whole Rule and its approach to the Christian life. At the heart of reconciliation lies a commitment to listening. For this we need to learn silence, to cultivate attentiveness, so that we become capable of receiving what we do not have from what we are not, in other words, from "the other." Silence counteracts the human tendency to rush to angry judgment and to destructive words. The Rule, of course, is full of scriptural quotations and resonances, and a broad analysis of the Bible shows that "listening" or "hearing" takes precedence over activity. Listening or attentiveness is associated with true wisdom and this, in turn, is connected not only with our relationship to God but to the notion of obedience – obedience to the Rule but, by implication, to the human community and its life together. Listen contemplatively to your brethren (or more broadly to your fellow humans) for here God speaks. This is, to quote from the Rule, the "school of the Lord's service," a school of discernment and wisdom. Listening implies giving oneself wholeheartedly rather than conditionally to a common enterprise. And, finally, listening implies being silent in order to learn or to be taught. Chapter 6 of the Rule, On Silence, *De Taciturnitate*, reinforces this. Interestingly, the word used for silence is *taciturnitas* rather than *silentium*. That is to say that silence, literally "to be taciturn," consists not merely in the absence of noise or in being quiet but in being sparing about what one asserts. This is the opposite of being domineering, and involves keeping one's mouth firmly closed so that the evil thoughts or the lies in our hearts may not issue forth. In this discipline, we may slowly be converted to a gracious heart.

The spiritual quality of silence is closely related to reconciliation because it implies a refusal to engage in any kind of polemic which the Rule considers to be unchristian. The Rule goes on to say that acceptable speech in community should always be modest and reasonable. Other medieval monastic texts talk of silence as a necessary preparation for any speech that is meaningful rather than ill-thought-out in terms of its consequences.[14] Do not rush to speak or to assert, the texts suggest – above all, avoid speaking out of anger. However, of course there is a wrong kind of silence – that is, refraining from speaking out in contexts of injustice and oppression. By implication all *good* speech is informed by contemplation – of God first of all but also, by extension, by a contemplative attentiveness to the human "other." The point is that silence and listening are part of the process of good and fair communication.

Human reconciliation is also closely related to another key Christian virtue taught by the Rule – that is, the virtue of hospitality. This offers a critical stance in relation to the normal ordering of any city or society. Rule Chapter 53 states that all guests who arrive are to be received as Christ – *Omnes supervenientes hospites tamquam Christus suscipiantur*. But it is important to notice that the Rule goes on to say "for he himself will say, I was the stranger and you took me in." In other words, Christ is in the stranger. This implies a deeper theology or spirituality of hospitality than merely giving food and board to a passing visitor. Commentators have always noted the word *omnes*, "all." This portrays an inclusivity linked particularly to *strangeness*, or we might say "otherness," in contrast to those who are "like us." *Supervenientes*, "those who arrive," underlines the point even more strongly. It literally means those who "turn up unexpectedly." However, this is not a question merely of those who did not warn us that they were coming but those who are a surprise to us in a deeper and more disturbing sense. Close to the surface of the text is the understanding that Christians are not to be choosey about whom they keep company with. The word *hospites* is a nicely ambiguous word that can legitimately be translated as "strangers" as well as the more straightforward "guests." The former sense is reinforced by the reference to Matthew 25:35, "I was a stranger and you took me in." Finally, the word *suscipiantur* literally means "to be received," but its deeper sense is "to be *cherished*." Thus, the stranger turns into someone who, while different from us, we learn to value as closely as if they were one of our own kin or tribe. It is interesting that the Rule makes clear that the poor are particularly to be cherished. "Great care and concern are to be shown in receiving poor people and pilgrims, because in them more particularly Christ is received; our very awe of the rich guarantees them special respect." (Rule, Chapter 53, 15). Hospitality is personal and face-to-face even though it is surrounded by rituals. In the Rule, hospitality is actually a blending of the inside and the outside worlds. In other words, it creates a "between place." In this liminal space, those who are "other" are encountered and the socially ingrained differences of any particular time and place are transcended, even if only momentarily.

Spirituality of Reconciliation: The Eucharist

Christians classically enact their theology and spirituality of community in celebrations of the Eucharist. Unfortunately some approaches to a theology and spirituality of the Eucharist concentrate on building up the community of the Church in and for itself. In this case, the Eucharist ends up as the celebration of the spiritual equivalent of the secure "gated communities" we increasingly find in upscale areas of large global cities such as London, Paris, and New York, and nowadays New Delhi. This is what the Bolivian theologian Victor Codina, in his reflections on the Eucharist, refers to as "drawing room communitarianism" whose harmony is not marred by any solidarity with the poor.

It is perfectly possible, as Codina hints, to limit reconciliation to a magic circle of those people whose social and cultural worlds overlap to a reasonable degree.[15] However, this dilutes the *risk* of celebrating the Eucharist. To live in the spirit of the Eucharist outside the church doors and in the streets commits us to cross the boundaries of fear and prejudice in an embrace of strangers in the public square in whom we are challenged to recognize the real presence of God.

I would suggest that the meaning of the Eucharist offers a critical center for a Christian spirituality of reconciliation. In the Eucharistic ritual of taking bread and wine, blessing them and sharing them is, according to Christian belief, made present the transformative power unlocked by Jesus's death, resurrection, and union with God. The Christian community, as the "body of Christ" in the world, is called to live out the dynamic of Jesus Christ – that is to sacrifice itself for the life of the entire world. The all-embracing "catholicity" of God is ritually expressed in the community of believers filled with the Spirit of the risen Jesus and shaped by the Eucharist. The Eucharist is not simply a practice of religious piety but is the enactment of the special identity of the Christian community for the sake of wider humanity. As such the Eucharist is an *ethical* practice, although not simply in the superficial sense that it provides an opportunity for a didactic form of moral teaching.[16] The link between ethics and the Eucharist is intrinsic rather than extrinsic.[17] Ethics embodies a way of being in the world that is appropriated and sustained fundamentally in worship, especially in celebrations of the Eucharist. Conversely, the Eucharistic enactment of God's all-embracing love necessarily opens the community up to appropriate ways of living in the world.

As we have seen in Chapter 6, a sacramental understanding of material reality and human existence also demands a reordering of the existential situations in which we live. To live sacramentally involves setting aside a flawed condition in favor of something that is offered to us by God's grace for "where we habitually are is not, after all, a neutral place but a place of loss and need" which needs to be transformed.[18] Part of this damaged reality consists of our flawed identities – whether these suggest that we are people of power or diminish us as people of no worth. The transforming dynamic of the Eucharist demands that the presumed identity of everyone should be radically reconstructed. This necessitates honest recognition of what is wrong as well as a process of painful dispossession and fearless surrender as a precondition of reconciliation.

To enter the "sacred space" of the Eucharist implies becoming open to a radical transformation of our human existence. It is no longer to be centered on the individual ego or on safe gatherings of the like-minded but is to be discovered in becoming "people for the others." Every time the Eucharist is celebrated in the human city it introduces a transformative power that is transcendent rather than simply policy-driven. It also makes a powerful statement about human identity for those who are prepared to see. All those who participate in celebrations of the Eucharist are called upon to commit themselves to crossing the boundaries of fear, of prejudice, and of injustice in a prophetic embrace of other people. There are no exceptions to those in whom we are challenged to discover the real presence of a God who has entered into and is committed to the human condition. In the words of a famous ecumenical statement about the Eucharist produced by the World Council of Churches:

> Reconciled in the Eucharist, the members of the body of Christ are called to be servants of reconciliation among men and women and witnesses of the joy of resurrection. As Jesus went out to publicans and sinners and had table-fellowship with them during his earthly ministry, so Christians are called in the Eucharist to be in solidarity with the outcast and to become signs of the love of Christ who lived and sacrificed himself for all and now gives himself in the Eucharist.[19]

We have already touched briefly upon the power and importance of memory. The Eucharist is very much a landscape of memory – including ambiguous or conflicting memories. Beyond the immediate participants, there are wider and deeper narrative currents in all Eucharistic celebrations. The central narrative, that is, the revelation of God's salvation in Jesus Christ, enables all human stories to have an equal place and yet at the same time reconfigures them. The Eucharistic narrative makes space for a new history that tells a different human story beyond the selectivity of tribalism, classism, or sectarianism. It invites us to undertake the radical business of creating human solidarity and changing the status quo in the human city. According to its own logic, the Eucharist, despite our human attempts to regulate and control it, engages a power beyond the ritual enactments themselves that offers an entry point into another transcendent dimension. This dimension embraces the oppressed, the marginalized and the excluded.

The Eucharistic action speaks of a radically catholic "place" in the world of space and time. The redemptive narrative of the Eucharist tells a different story from one shaped by human divisions. There is, therefore, a perpetual and uncomfortable tension between this ritual practice that engages God's reconciling and redeeming power and the many efforts of Christians to resist the logic of human reconciliation. Christian disciples are bound into solidarity with those they have not chosen or whose presence they have not negotiated and indeed would not choose of their own free will. Consequently, the new community, the new world, proclaimed in the Eucharist is deeply subversive of a humanly constructed social order.[20]

The Eucharist does not simply bind individuals to God in a vertical relationship or bind people to each other in another kind of purely social construction. We are bound to one another "in Christ." And Jesus Christ, the head of the body, is to be found persistently on the margins among those who are the least in the kingdom of this world. The margins include those who are other, foreign, strange, dangerous, subversive – even socially, morally, or religiously distasteful in our eyes. Yet the Eucharist insists that humans find solidarity where they least expect it and, indeed, least want to find it. In Chapter 3 we recalled the story in the final Testament of Francis of Assisi of his encounter with the despised and distasteful leper. By means of this experience Francis moved from a romantic understanding of God's presence in creation to embrace a God who was uncomfortably present in the excluded "other."

The most challenging dimension of the Eucharist is the question of recognition. Christians over the centuries have tussled with what is meant by the notion of Christ being "really present" in the Eucharist. However, a more critical question is who we recognize as our brothers and sisters in Christ, and who we are able to respond to in the real presence of Jesus Christ. The heart of the Eucharistic notion of real presence, however one understands this, is *God's* critical recognition of us. A spirituality shaped by the Eucharist involves a belief that human identities are determined by God and God's affirming and life-giving gaze rather than by our limited presuppositions. In so far as the Eucharist is understood as shaping the identity of the community of believers, all are incorporated solely because of God's recognition. The demands on those who practice the Eucharist are consequently more powerful than any notion of solidarity based solely on a social theory, however inclusive or just it seeks to be.[21]

An affirmation of the "real presence" of Christ in the Eucharist also stands in judgment on all our exclusions and negative assessments of other people. A most challenging question for Christians who take part in the Eucharist is who and what they receive with Christ. In receiving the presence and power of Jesus Christ the Christian disciple receives at the same time all who are part of the "body of Christ" in the sense used by Paul in his New Testament letters. We find ourselves in communion not merely in some romantic way with God, the whole court of heaven, and the communion of saints who safely visit us from elsewhere. We also find ourselves, if we dare to face it, in communion with the truly catholic "mystery of the whole" in present time and space. We know from the gospel narratives of the Last Supper that the "catholicity" of Jesus's act of incorporation included not only disciples like Peter, who would deny him, but Judas, who went on to betray him. In Christ, the revelation of the transcendent God, all those people whom we prefer to exclude from a relationship with us in the public world are already uncomfortable ghosts at our Eucharistic celebrations.

As we saw in Chapter 3, in medieval European cities the Eucharist was in a variety of ways a public event, a public drama. Clearly, in our contemporary radically plural cities a Christian ritual cannot function as a public event in the same way. Yet the essence of the Eucharist remains public rather than private or sectarian. The theological core of the Eucharist refuses to limit its relevance merely to a church audience. So, can the Eucharist be authentically a "space for the world" in the midst of the human city? For the Eucharist to be celebrated in virtually empty city churches raises challenging questions for Christian mission. However, there is a strange yet powerful dynamic implied by, for example, the presence of small contemplative communities of Christians living in the midst of today's inner cities. Such groups by their simple presence and accessibility to their neighbors, including their regular celebrations of the Eucharist, not only seek to speak of God's loving hospitality to their neighbors. They also stand for the faithful presence of a divine, redemptive and reconciling power that offers hope and transcendent possibility in the midst of human pain and social ambiguities.

Conclusion

The vocation of proclaiming human reconciliation is not incidental to Christian life but lies at its heart. Being "in communion" with anyone at all is a risky commitment to others enabled by the power of God's unconditional love for humankind. This commitment is expressed by our struggles to stay together in our difference, even in our disputes, within a single "common house."

Any attempt at human reconciliation demands sound discernment as much as political or social negotiation but a climate of anger and despair inhibits the spiritual freedom needed for this. The long Christian tradition of discernment (*diakrisis*), or practical wisdom, teaches a process of prayerful and critical reflection on human experience as the basis for making good choices and undertaking fruitful action. To be capable of such discernment, we must have enough inner freedom to recognize for what they are the various forces and emotions that influence us. This demands considerable spiritual and psychological maturity. In the words of a contemporary writer on the theology of discernment,

> Spiritual discernment has arisen naturally and most necessarily for such a common life, because it reflects the pressure of a living truth – refusing partiality and bias, pushing beyond individual understanding, opening the discerning community to the creative, self-sharing life from which all truth springs.[22]

This theme of practical wisdom and discernment will be developed further in the next chapter on urban virtues.

In summary, a challenging question for everyone seeking human reconciliation in the human city is, what kind of energy underpinned the divisions of the past and what energies are released in resistance to, or commitment to, the quest for reconciliation? Whatever one's views on the presenting political, social, religious, or ethical issues in situations of conflict, the dark and dangerous energies are those that suggest that this reconciliation is impossible, is a lesser value, or is even positively dangerous.

Notes

English translations are cited wherever available.

1   See Italo Calvino, *Invisible Cities*, London: Random House, 2001.
2   John de Gruchy, *Reconciliation: Restoring Justice*, London: SCM Press, 2002, p. 44.
3   See the comments of the former British Chief Rabbi, Dr Jonathan Sachs, in his *The Home We Build Together: Recreating Society*, London and New York: Continuum, 2007, Chapters 17 and 20.
4   On the process of reconciliation, see especially Robert J. Schreiter, *The Ministry of Reconciliation: Spirituality and Strategies*, Maryknoll, NY: Orbis Books, 1998, and *Reconciliation: Mission and Ministry in a Changing Social Order*, Cambridge, MA: Boston Theological Institute Series, 2000.
5   On process, I am grateful for the insights of Schreiter, *Ministry of Reconciliation*.
6   André Brink, *Looking on Darkness*, London: Vintage, 1982, especially p. 48.
7   For a fuller development of what follows, see Philip Sheldrake, "Practising Catholic 'place' – The Eucharist," *Horizons: The Journal of the College Theology Society*, 28(2), Fall 2001, pp. 163–82.
8   See Colin Gunton, *The Promise of Trinitarian Theology*, Edinburgh: T & T Clark, 1997, pp. 112ff; and also his *The One, The Three and The Many*, Cambridge: Cambridge University Press, 1995, p. 164.
9   For an expanded treatment of "catholic persons" see P. Sheldrake, "On becoming catholic people: hopes and challenges," in Paul Murray (ed.), *Catholic Learning: Explorations in Receptive Ecumenism*, Oxford: Oxford University Press, 2008.
10 *Faithful Cities: A Call to Celebration, Vision and Justice*, London: Church House Publishing, 2006.
11 Belden Lane, *The Solace of Fierce Landscapes: Exploring Desert and Mountain Spirituality*, Oxford: Oxford University Press, 1998, p. 46.
12 Benedicta Ward, *The Wisdom of the Desert Fathers*, Fairacres Publications, 48, Oxford: SLG Press 1986 edition, no. 151.
13 There are several good editions of the Rule of St Benedict with translations and scholarly commentaries. One of the best is Terrence C. Kardong OSB (ed.), *Benedict's Rule: A Translation and Commentary*, Collegeville, MN: The Liturgical Press, 1996.
14 On the different interpretations of silence in monastic writers and among those leading the canonical life, see Caroline Walker Bynum, *Jesus as Mother: Studies in the Spirituality of the High Middle Ages*, Berkeley: University of California Press, 1984, Chapter 1.

15 Victor Codina, "Sacraments," in Jon Sobrino and Ignacio Ellacuria (eds.), *Systematic Theology: Perspectives from Liberation Theology*, London: SCM Press, 1996, pp. 218–219.

16 The link between the enactment of identity and the ethical nature of the Eucharist is discussed by the Catholic moral theologian, the late William Spohn, in *Go and Do Likewise: Jesus and Ethics*, London and New York: Continuum, 1999, pp. 175–84.

17 On this point, see Donald E. Saliers, "Liturgy and ethics: some new beginnings," in Ronald Hamel and Kenneth Himes (eds.), *Introduction to Christian Ethics: A Reader*, New York: Paulist Press, 1989, pp. 175–86.

18 Rowan Williams, *On Christian Theology*, Oxford: Blackwell, 2000, pp. 209–10.

19 *Baptism, Eucharist and Ministry*, Faith and Order Paper 111, Geneva: World Council of Churches, 1982, paragraph 24.

20 See Williams, *On Christian Theology*, Chapter 14 "Sacraments of the new society."

21 Williams, *On Christian Theology*, pp. 212–214.

22 See Mark McIntosh, *Discernment and Truth: The Spirituality and Theology of Knowledge*, New York: Crossroad, 2004, p. 255.

CHAPTER 9

Urban Virtues

In the previous chapter we reflected on the vital importance of "reconciliation" within urban communities and that this implies far more than mere tolerance but embraces the radically challenging virtues of hospitality and solidarity. In a variety of ways, such an approach raises the broader question of urban virtue and virtues. Interestingly, in English the virtue of "civility," being cultured, refined and polite, ultimately derives from city life. You might say that, by definition, cities are meant to "civilize" us by teaching us the arts of cooperation and creative living. In this chapter we will explore what urban virtues are and, in particular, what urban virtues stand out as critical in the early part of the twenty-first century.

As a starting point, Joseph Grange comments in his book *The City as Urban Cosmology* that a city is a gathering place where diverse people come together to share their lives and gifts as well as their heritage of symbols.[1] Because people increasingly settle in large cities to expand their social and economic opportunities, cities have become places of expectation, whether realistically speaking or not. In large cities, the population is continuously shifting year by year. Because of this fluidity and mobility, people in cities must persistently form new bonds of community.

The heart of successful city living is communication whose goal is what Grange refers to as "urbanity."[2] Classically, "urbanity" implies

The Spiritual City: Theology, Spirituality, and the Urban, First Edition. Philip Sheldrake.
© 2014 Philip Sheldrake. Published 2014 by John Wiley & Sons, Ltd.

being elegant, sophisticated, suave and courteous. However, for Grange "urbanity" implies something much sharper. This may be thought of as one of the foundational urban virtues. To achieve this virtue, city dwellers need to acknowledge both rights and duties and freely to subordinate certain aspects of self-interest to create a culture of mutuality.[3] Such a perspective parallels the long tradition of Roman Catholic Social Teaching and the documents of the Second Vatican Council, for example Pope John XXIII's encyclical letter *Pacem in Terris* (section 53) and Council document "The Church in the modern world" (*Gaudium et Spes*, section 73). As we saw in Chapter 7, a significant theological underpinning for notions of human community is the inner life of God-as-Trinity – the mutual exchange within God in whose image humanity is created. If we reread Grange's "urbanity" from a theological perspective it takes on a quasi-sacramental meaning. That is to say, city-dwellers undertake the vocation of living together in a way that reflects the love and beauty of God's inner life. In a sense, every city is a potential embodiment of God's presence in which the inhabitants confront the daily challenge of promoting justice against injustice, beauty against ugliness and love versus social indifference.

Building upon the broad notion of social solidarity, the American urban philosopher and ethicist Eduardo Mendieta, who also studied theology, writes about the societal need for the virtue of "frugality" in response to the problematical nature of globalization and a growing culture of consumption.[4] We exist in an interdependent world, shaped by the persistent encounter of strangers. The "other" is no longer able to be kept at a distance, beyond the well-defended boundaries of the *ecumene*, that is, those "like us." Mendieta detects a sometimes pragmatic and sometimes principled shift from a default position of rejection of alterity, otherness, to the language of tolerance and solidarity. This change in social realities demands a shift in how we think of social virtue. Mendieta himself argues that true virtue does not arise from inhabiting purified or protected spaces. Rather, the greatest human moral codes emerged from contexts of pluralism.

> Such codes arose precisely because individuals were thrown into the proximity of each other and were thus confronted with each other's vulnerability and injurability. The injunction to take care of the poor, the indigent, the orphan, the widow, the invalid, could only arise out of the urban experience of the contiguity with the injurable flesh of the stranger.[5]

This "turn to solidarity" has profound consequences – not least that we recognize that the challenge is not simply to extend our culture of choice and material luxury to those who currently do not benefit from it. Rather we need to come to terms with the fact that there has to be a radical, systemic change. Hence, Mendieta's urban virtue of frugality implies that we develop a global culture that does not simply enable everyone else to live like the "haves." Frugality asks of everyone that they live at a level that allows access for all to the basic human rights of adequate food and drink, health, education and a decent environment. Mendieta notes the power of religious images and practice such as the voluntary pursuit of poverty as a practice of holiness by such people as St Francis of Assisi.

On a related but different note, in *Civic Spirit: The Big Idea for a New Political Era*, the British writer Charles Leadbeater argues, like Grange, for the social effectiveness of the principle of "mutuality," which balances diversity with the reconciliation of competing claims. Leadbeater thinks in political and pragmatic rather than philosophical or religious terms. Ethics is, in the end, what "works best." At the heart of mutuality is the notion of reciprocity – to claim rights also implies accepting obligations. Interestingly, Leadbeater suggests that mutuality embraces reconciliation, although his conception of reconciliation, while demanding more than mutual understanding, is nevertheless essentially a process of negotiating priorities in relation to material and social resources. This falls somewhat short of the more demanding process of conversion outlined in the last chapter. However, Leadbeater also focuses on "belonging" – the need to generate a sense of trust based on a shared sense of identity. In the end, "mutuality" demands what Leadbeater calls "renunciation." This specifically implies letting go of the absolute claims of individual choice. Leadbeater recognizes that this is a considerable challenge. "Persuading people to be self-denying is a delicate and time-consuming process. It requires us to value restraint as a virtue as much as choice – a counterintuitive view in consumer society."[6]

In reference to the connections between urban design, architecture and virtue, the eminent British architect, Richard Rogers, in his 1995 BBC Reith Lectures (later published as *Cities for a Small Planet*), highlighted seven key values that may be thought of as spiritual.[7] The good city should be "just" – that is, somewhere that expresses social and economic equity. Physically, design needs to make adequate and inclusive space for appropriate places for food, housing, education, and healthcare. Second, we should promote the importance of the "beautiful city." There should be architecture and design to "stir the soul," that is, nourish us both materially and aesthetically. Cities should be "creative," offering what he calls "open-minded space" that people may explore and psychologically "expand." The good city should be "ecological." That is to say that it minimizes the ecological footprint, balances nature with the built environment and encourage efficient building. For a city to be humane, it should facilitate "easy contact." Public space needs to be readily accessible to encourage social mixing and to foster community. Equally, a good city is "compact" and "polycentric." This is both an ecological principle (it protects the countryside against urban sprawl) and a "contact" principle (it integrates local neighborhoods and maximizes community proximity). Finally, the good city is "diverse." That is, its design should consciously speak of difference and "otherness" being valued.

These values are especially evident in Rogers' promotion of "open-minded space."[8] This has spiritual resonances. Such space (for example the piazza or public square) is person-centered. Its function is left open rather than predetermined by planners or politicians. It does not prioritize efficiency but human participation. Consequently, it is accessible physically, intellectually and spiritually. "Open-minded space" evokes inclusivity, encourages diversity and enables creativity and play as opposed to control and constraint. Like Michel de Certeau and Richard Sennett, Rogers believes in the social value of ambiguity and indeterminacy, the human ability to transcend imposed, static order. Rogers grew up in Florence and writes of the purposeful Italian custom of *passeggiata* – casual "wandering about in public" – that leaves room for surprise and celebrates people's social personae.

On a similar theme, the contemporary human geographer Ash Amin also underlines that the physical and social dynamics of public space still play a major role in shaping urban virtue. However, more than Rogers, Amin emphasizes the radical multiplicity of today's cities and that the everyday virtue of what he calls "conviviality" arises from a direct experience of multiplicity, an instinctive or reflexive routine of response to this and the consequent daily negotiations of difference.[9]

Christian Theology and Urban Virtue

If we turn explicitly to theology, we will find that the concept of the "common good" is a particularly powerful theme that runs through Christian thought over the centuries, particularly in Roman Catholic Social Teaching. The virtue of pursuing this common good and its relationship to discernment and the art of choosing well, especially in the spiritual wisdom of the sixteenth-century Catholic reformer Ignatius Loyola, will be the focus of the remainder of the chapter. In the development of Catholic Social Teaching, why and how did a strong emphasis on the link between spirituality and social justice come into being? After all, social inequalities and oppression were hardly new phenomena in the nineteenth and twentieth centuries. However, a self-consciously social version of Christian teaching is relatively new. A series of radical economic and social readjustments took place in the Western world during the nineteenth century as a result partly of the aftermath of the French Revolution followed by further social unrest (for example the so-called 1848 revolution) which impacted on several Western states, partly of the Industrial Revolution, and partly from the new nationalisms which gave birth to the Germany Empire and to the Kingdom of Italy.

By the end of the century the response to these challenges, in particular under Pope Leo XIII (1878–1903), was the beginning of a tradition of the critical yet constructive engagement with social realities which grew into the official body of teachings that became known as "Catholic Social Teaching." As its basis there have appeared a number of significant encyclicals and other papal documents that continue to the present day. The foundational encyclical *Rerum Novarum* by Pope Leo XIII in 1891, subtitled "The Condition of the Working Classes," was written explicitly in the light of the harsh conditions of Europe's urban poor. It took a clear stand against laissez-faire capitalism and the priority of "market forces" which the pope described as the cause of "the misery and wretchedness pressing so heavily and unjustly... on the vast majority of the working classes." In urban terms, Pope Leo generally supported the right to private property but also saw it as the duty of the state to protect the interests of the poor. The fortieth anniversary of the encyclical in

1931 was marked by a further foundational encyclical, *Quadragesimo Anno*, by Pope Pius XI. This appeared at a time of acute economic and political turmoil. The tone was if anything stronger and more concrete than *Rerum Novarum*, particularly in relation to the need for social-structural as well as moral change. While rejecting socialism as a full-scale political creed, Pius XI nevertheless made some comparisons between the values of socialism and those of Christian tradition. Specifically, he argued that certain kinds of property, related to general or public welfare, should be reserved to the state. Behind both encyclicals lay the concept of the "common good" to which we shall return later. Finally, and interestingly, *Quadragesimo Anno* explicitly highlights the spiritual tradition of Ignatius Loyola as "a most precious means of personal and social reform" and as a tool for the renewal of society.

In today's cities, we continue to live in contexts of great social and economic inequality. There are no simple answers. However, the Ignatian spiritual tradition, particularly its teaching on discernment, has powerful things to say. To begin with, there are two aspects to discernment. First, and vitally, discernment relates not merely to what goes on in prayer or meditation but also to the practice of everyday life. At the climax of the spiritual process outlined by Ignatius's Spiritual Exercises, the key value is a capacity to "find God in all things." This implies more than how we are to read our interior "spiritual" experiences. Rather, it embraces a response to God's action in the processes and challenges of the everyday world.[10] Second, the long Christian tradition of discernment that lies behind the spiritual teachings of St Ignatius Loyola is not merely a matter of personal choices but presupposes a social understanding of human existence and applies to communities, institutions and society as well as to individuals. Thinking of our own contexts, it seems clear to me that this alternative wisdom tradition offers something important as a response to contemporary social crises. I will return to this later.

The word discernment in English means "to distinguish between things" or "to recognize something." In the Christian tradition of discernment this implies the wisdom to recognize the difference between courses of action that are life-directing and ones that are potentially destructive and out of harmony with our deepest self and with our relationship with God. Discernment of spirits is meant to form a spiritual and ethical backdrop to our lives as a whole and to the ways they are orientated, whereby we instinctively recognize our deepest truth and respond to God's self-communication in daily existence. As a form of wisdom, discernment invites us to a *critical* reflection on human experience – critical because such experience is fundamentally ambiguous. Faced with choices, whether overtly moral or not, we are subjected to contradictory influences from inside and outside. Some of these incline us to what is authentic or morally good (what Ignatius Loyola called consolation), others to what is inauthentic or morally flawed (what he called desolation). However, it is not always easy to distinguish between the two. I will return to this later.

Origins

The English word "discernment" derives from the Greek *diakrisis*. This has its roots in ancient philosophy, in the scriptures, and in Christian tradition. I want to begin briefly with the Greek philosopher Aristotle because the wisdom implied by Christian discernment, not least in Ignatius Loyola, stretches back via Cicero's *discretio* to Aristotle's ethics, specifically his third kind of knowledge, *phronesis* or "practical wisdom."

In Aristotle there are three kinds of knowledge: *epistome* (theoretical knowledge), *techne* (the application of theory), and then *phronesis* – practical wisdom or prudent judgment. For Aristotle, practical wisdom or prudence is not abstract but derives from intuition, imagination, emotional engagement, and desire. Interestingly, Aristotle saw it as applicable particularly to our existence in society and to promoting the "common good." Aristotle suggests that this kind of wisdom actually grows *in and through* our immersion in everyday human contexts.

The key text is the *Nicomachaean Ethics*. When Aristotle talks about ethics – and discernment is certainly ethical in the broadest sense – it is not simply a question of identifying good and bad actions. Aristotle is clear that human beings, of their nature, need relationships with others. What is distinctive about being human is that our true fulfillment places demands upon us that do not necessarily equate with purely individual satisfaction. Two books of the *Ethics* (IX: 8 and 9) discuss human relationships. These contrast mere self-seeking with true self-love, which is related to the quest for real friendship or true society. A fulfilled life is not merely pleasurable but is also "noble" because it involves some degree of self-giving.[11]

Practical wisdom also relates to a broadly-based sense of how to live a fulfilled life. What is crucial is that practical wisdom is neither a matter of slavishly applying rules nor merely of acquiring certain skills.[12] There are pointers here as to how we should understand Christian "discernment," not least as developed in the *Spiritual Exercises*.[13] Practical wisdom demands that we reflect about our overall purpose because a virtuous life involves decisions and choices that should be made for clear reasons in alignment with our sense of purpose. This reflection embraces our affectivity as much as our reason – the "emotional" as well as rational responses of a virtuous person. A balanced emotional sensitivity is an important element in what goes to make up good decision-making. It is instructive to compare this with St Ignatius's teaching on attending to our desires as the basis of true discernment. For St Ignatius, "consolation" involves what he calls "the good spirit" guiding us via life-enhancing desires rather than superficial "wants." Equally, Aristotle's "practical wisdom" is related to the achievement of *eudaimonia*, which can be translated as "happiness" or "fulfillment." However, like Ignatius Loyola's concept of "consolation," Aristotle's "happiness" is not the same as mere enjoyment. Rather, it is a way of thoughtfully living out a virtuous life within society, within the city.

True virtues are certainly habitual (see *Nicomachaean Ethics*, II, 5) but they are habitual dispositions to react to situations by having appropriate feeling-responses. In Aristotle, feelings are broader than raw emotion, are partly cognitive and involve some kind of belief. This is very different from instinct. Consequently, feelings may be subject to rational guidance. Importantly, among Aristotle's list of feelings (in II, 5) is "desire." We can learn to shape desire. Thus, (in III, 10–11) Aristotle writes of "moderation" which balances our desires because, like all emotions, it can be unbalanced.

So, how is desire to be shaped? Apart from a good childhood upbringing and moral education, Aristotle (in *Ethics* II, 1) suggests training our emotional responses by engaging in appropriate actions even if at first we do not feel inclined to. This resembles the notion of *agere contra* in Ignatius's Spiritual Exercises – consciously acting against instincts that are self-regarding or unbalanced. Such instincts are what Ignatius means by "disordered attachments." They are indicators of a lack of spiritual freedom. The process of the Spiritual Exercises is divided into what Ignatius calls four "weeks" – that is, progressive phases of a movement towards inner spiritual freedom and the capacity to respond wholeheartedly to the call of God. In his First Week Rules for Discernment (that is, advice addressed to people at the outset of their spiritual journey), Rule 6, paragraph 319, we read "Although in desolation we must make no changes in our former decisions, it is however very helpful to make an intense effort to change oneself in a sense opposed to this desolation e.g. by more insistence on prayer and meditation..." The notion of "going against" our instincts also appears at the beginning of the Second Week of the Exercises in the key contemplation, The Call of the King, Part II, The Call of Christ (Exercises, paragraph 97). The desired response to Christ's call demands that Christian disciples go "against their sensuality and their carnal and worldly love." However, it is clear that for Ignatius this is not a matter simply of a decision driven by sheer willpower. In Ignatius's language, we need "the grace," the power of God. So, in a later contemplation in the same "week" on the Three Kinds of Persons (in the note to paragraph 157), when we still feel attachments to riches and are not indifferent or free we should pray that we be chosen by God for actual poverty – that is, to be put in a concrete situation that goes against our instincts. As Aristotle puts it (*Ethics* II, 1, 1103b 21–25), "In a word, habits are born of similar activities so we have to engage in behavior of the relevant kinds, since the habits formed will follow upon the various ways we behave."

Discernment in Christian Tradition

I now want to turn briefly to the scriptural and other religious origins of Christian discernment. The Hebrew Scriptures implicitly speak of discernment in Moses' exhortation to the people of Israel "to choose life" (Deuteronomy 13:15–20). "Wisdom" (see Wisdom 8:9 or Proverbs 6:7) is described in terms of a power that makes it possible for humans to order their lives in accordance with God's desire. The New Testament shows an early Church preoccupied with the need to test out the influences that affected the community. For Paul, discernment is a gift of the Spirit (1 Corinthians 12:10) and, like all genuine spiritual gifts, should be tested in terms of whether it builds up unity and a desire for the common good in the Christian community (1 Corinthians 12:7 and 12f). The Pauline letters suggest criteria for discriminating between "the works of the flesh" and the works of the Spirit of God (e.g. Galatians 5:16–26; 1 Corinthians 3:3). The First Letter of John is often cited in works on discernment – "test the spirits to see if they are of God" (1 John 4:1).

From the fourth century CE onward, discernment (*diakrisis*) is a key value in early Egyptian monasticism. How are we to lead the ascetic life? Echoing Aristotle, the important word is "balance," for which discernment is the guiding principle. As St Antony the Great is said to have asserted, "Some have afflicted their bodies with asceticism, but they lack discernment, and so they are far from God." However, balance is also linked to humility – a loss of self-preoccupation and the compulsion to be seen as a spiritual giant. Importantly, among the signs of discernment in this monastic tradition are the social virtues of compassion, charity, and attentiveness to others.

One of the earliest Western monastic writers is John Cassian (late fourth and early fifth centuries CE). His famous *Conferences* reflect first-hand experience of desert monasticism but also an awareness of Greek philosophy. His approach to *diakrisis* (or in Latin *discretio*) again preaches moderation or balance – the virtue which measures everything else and avoids the excesses of other apparently spiritual values. However, Cassian also offers a more explicit portrayal of the relational character of discernment. Discernment is "discretion" – behaving in a way that avoids causing offense and deciding responsibly as a *social* act. In Cassian there is a fundamental contrast between those people who prefer to be governed by their individual understanding of, for example, the life of prayer, and those who attend to the counsels of the brethren. In Cassian, discernment is related to *communal wisdom*.[14]

In subsequent spiritual and theological reflection on the life of virtue, for example in the Rule of St Benedict, in texts of mystical theology such as Bernard of Clairvaux and Richard of St Victor, or in philosophical theology such as Thomas Aquinas in the thirteenth century or Jean Gerson in the fifteenth century, discernment becomes "practical prudence." This has a double meaning: first, discernment regulates all other moral or intellectual virtues; second, the ability to distinguish good and bad influences is dependent on humility and is ordered both at the love of God and at the common good.

Ignatian Discernment

In Ignatian spirituality the various elements of the discernment tradition come together. I should add that we know little about Ignatius's sources for his teaching on discernment. However, it seems likely that, apart from his own experience, he learned something about the longer tradition while studying theology in Paris. In the reflection entitled "Principle and Foundation" at the very beginning of the Spiritual Exercises (Exx 23) the foundation of discernment is freedom from disordered attachments so that we judge and choose in the light of our true purpose. The core principle is what has become known in Latin as *tantum quantum*, literally "in as much as." Material things are to be used only in as much as they enable us to "pursue the end for which we are created." In other words, you use only what you need. Less is more effective than more. At the heart of this counter-intuitive spiritual vision is the virtue of balance or proportionality, which runs counter to the excesses of market capitalism or the culture of endless choice. Ignatius understood well that the purpose of life is so to shape our characters that we are able to live productively and in peace with ourselves and others. For this to be the case, everyone is called to make difficult choices on a daily basis. These will concern the things we use, the people we associate with, the values we embrace, the projects we take on, and the attitudes which direct our thinking, judging, and decisions.

Within the dynamic of the Spiritual Exercises, and the spirituality that arises from them, the gift of discernment, or right choice, becomes the means by which we come to know ourselves and to recognize the movement of God's Spirit. For example in the spiritual practice known as the daily "Examen" (Exx 43–44), or prayer of attentive awareness to God's communication within everyday events, discernment is the guiding light. The desired climax of the process of the Exercises, expressed in the "Contemplation to Attain Love" at the very end of the text, is the gift by which we come to choose connaturally with God by dwelling "in Christ."

In Ignatius Loyola, discernment works in a kind of sequence. First, a contemplative cultivation of spiritual insight leads to, second, a skill to distinguish between good and bad "spirits," resulting in, third, an ability to determine true balance in the spiritual life and the exercise of virtue. This is actually what St Ignatius means by "detachment."

Thus, for Ignatius, discernment arises from a contemplative attentiveness to God that gradually enables deepened awareness. For that reason, discernment and contemplative prayer go hand in hand. The ability to judge and choose wisely is practiced through various meditative exercises that focus on contemplating Jesus's life in the gospels and through the daily practice of spiritual attentiveness, known as the Examen. The process of formal meditation or contemplation in the Exercises, recalling the scriptural story, composition of place, asking for what we desire, meditating or contemplating and the final intimate conversation with God or colloquy, are a spiritual discipline through which we become increasingly imbued with God's presence and thereby have our powers of judgment refined.

Desire, Discernment and Choice

As Ignatius recognized, desire is what powers our spiritualities. However, as in Aristotle, the question is how we focus our desire. At the heart of Christian spirituality is the sense that humanity has a longing that, as Augustine affirmed, can only be satisfied in God. Ignatius's teaching on discernment in the Spiritual Exercises emphasizes the need for "detachment" in favor of seeking "the more" which is, ultimately, God. These words may sound austere and moralistic but are actually concerned with reaching a healthy inner freedom. Such freedom cannot be artificially constructed. It is God's gift to which we have to be open.

For each of us, certain desires have the potential to shape our most serious choices and therefore to give direction to our lives. These are what Ignatius calls "great desires." Discernment enables us, first, to be aware of the full range of desires that we experience. From this starting point we are slowly led to understand how our desires vary in quality.

As already noted, one of the most helpful elements of Ignatius's teaching on discernment is his understanding of the two basic kinds of motivation that he calls consolation and desolation (Exx 313–336). For Ignatius, it is much less helpful to search for the origins of our desires than to focus on the direction in which they are leading us. Certain ways of desiring, if we follow them through, tend towards a dispersal of our spiritual energy or a fragmentation of our attention. Other desires promise a greater concentration of energy and a harmonious centeredness. What is confusing is that the less healthy desires are sometimes initially more attractive because they make us feel happy or good. In other words, the direction and potential of our desires is not always immediately self-evident.

According to Ignatius, the basic characteristics of consolation are an increase of love for God as well as a deepening of human love, an increase of hope and faith, an interior joy, an attraction towards the spiritual, a deep tranquility and peace. It is vitally important to remember that when Ignatius mentions consolation, he is not talking about the immediately pleasurable. "Interior joy" or "deep peace" may practically-speaking be deeply uncomfortable and challenging.

In contrast to consolation, desolation is not necessarily immediately unpleasant. It may sometimes feel attractive. So, Ignatius suggests that for those who have made some progress in their spiritual journey, "it is characteristic of the bad angel [or spirit] to assume the form of an angel of light to enter the devoted soul in her own way and to leave with his own profit; that is, he proposes good and holy thoughts well adapted to such a just soul, and then little by little succeeds in getting what he wants, drawing the soul into his hidden snares and his perverted purposes" (Exx 332). However, such experiences or influences, on deeper reflection, ultimately reveal themselves as destructive.

Throughout the Spiritual Exercises, Ignatius Loyola returns again and again to the subject of desire, which is always ordered towards a deeper and healthier way of choosing. For Ignatius, the spiritual journey is fundamentally away from fragmentation and towards harmony. It is a movement from the surface of life and experience to the center – the center of our true selves and also the core of life's deeper meaning, the truth of the world in which we are embedded. Equally, the spiritual journey is from spiritual imprisonment towards inner freedom. Again, in Ignatius' terms, the whole point of our "spiritual activities" is to be gradually rid of what he calls "disordered affections" (Exx 1). This movement is away from dysfunction and being driven by an overwhelming neediness that entraps us. This is what both Aristotle and Cassian meant by "balance" and what Ignatius implies by the word "indifference" (Exx 23).

Individual, Personal or Social?

Interestingly, Christian discernment has frequently been interpreted as essentially an individual process. Yet, as we have seen from Aristotle, its longer history suggests otherwise. Equally John Cassian, in the second of his monastic *Conferences*, discusses *discretio* in terms of the truth-bearing inspiration of God at work within a *community*.[15] In fact, in its foundations, Christian discernment preserves people from self-obsessed desire by relating a practice of collective wisdom to the common life of a Trinitarian God. In Cassian, discernment describes the capacity to keep one's own desires in balance by reference to communal wisdom and mutual affection.

Equally, we should not read Ignatian discernment in purely individualistic terms. Hugo Rahner, the brother of Karl Rahner, is clear in his theological study of St Ignatius that discernment is not a matter of pure subjectivity. Rather, the nature of both consolation and desolation were understood by Ignatius to be illuminated by a person's growing capacity through scriptural prayer to respond with the mind of Christ.[16] The contemporary theologian Mark McIntosh in his book on discernment notes that the wider tradition of discernment has clear "relational signs." Thus, in 1 Corinthians, Paul is clear that a critical sign of healthy progress in the Christian "life in God" is mutual up-building – the quest for the "common good" beyond my own sense of well-being and satisfaction. Does our life-practice relativize distinctions between people that tend to encourage envy, hatred, fear, competitiveness, and oppression? If we take Paul's writings seriously, the shaping of life in God's Spirit *together* rather than in isolation is a major criterion in distinguishing between what St Ignatius Loyola calls "the good spirit" and "the bad spirit."[17]

As we saw earlier, Pope Pius XI's 1931 encyclical *Quadragesimo Anno*, which helped shape Catholic Social Teaching and which appeared at a time of acute economic and political turmoil, explicitly highlights the Ignatian Exercises as a tool for the renewal of society. Pedro Arrupe, the Superior General of the Jesuits from 1965 to 1983, explicitly linked Ignatian spirituality to the promotion of social justice. This emerged particularly in the Fourth Decree of the Thirty-Second General Congregation (equivalent to a general chapter) of the Society of Jesus in 1975. The Decree was entitled, "Our Mission Today: The Service of

Faith and The Promotion of Justice." Perhaps not surprisingly in the aftermath of this important governing meeting, more and more Jesuits as well as other men and women associated with the Ignatian spiritual tradition began to work with the poor and to contribute substantially to a spirituality of social justice. This is strikingly present in the writings of the Jesuit theologians in Central and Latin America, Juan Luis Segundo, Jon Sobrino, and Ignacio Ellacuría (who was one of the Jesuits martyred in El Salvador in 1989).

Ignatius's teaching on discernment is radically self-forgetting. True spiritual wisdom, as well as the ability to choose well, is embodied in service of our neighbor – who may, as in the parable of the Good Samaritan (Luke 10:29–37), be the despised outsider. To put it another way, the kind of practical wisdom implied by Ignatian discernment promotes a *relational* approach to life as we are drawn more deeply into the inner life of God-as-Trinity. The Contemplation on the Incarnation at the beginning of the Second Week of the Exercises invites us to contemplate the Trinity as the starting point for seeing and understanding human life and "the world" through God's compassionate eyes.

Two other key meditations of the "Second Week" have powerful social implications. For example, the issue of discernment presented in the meditation on the Two Standards (Exx 136–148) is not to choose between what is self-evidently good and what is obviously evil but between what initially appears to be good in the abstract and what is *really* good in the concrete circumstances of life. In this meditation, Ignatius uses the imagery of two contrasting cities, Jerusalem and Babylon, and a narrative of forms of leadership – that of Christ and that of Lucifer as they invite humanity to follow their divergent ways. Through this imagery, Ignatius poses two very different ways of working for the Kingdom of God – the way of power or the way of love. Christians face a temptation to use seemingly good things such as wealth and power to follow Jesus Christ and to serve others, but the ultimate word spoken by Jesus is that of vulnerable risky service rendered only out of love. Those who wish to follow Jesus Christ must choose the way of love and "humility" that risks suffering and the cross.

Another meditation, on "Three Ways of Being Humble" (Exx 165–68), is part of the preparation for what Ignatius calls "an election" – that is, choosing a way of life that is single-heartedly concerned with what he calls "the purpose for which I am created" (that is, who I truly am) and with "desiring to serve God" (that is, my sense of ultimate purpose). In modern understanding, "being humble" is not always positive because it implies either something false or self-demeaning. However, for Ignatius "humility" is the opposite of the prevailing sin of his own aristocratic class, *hidalguía*, "pride" in being "the son of a somebody" – having an inherited status and dismissing other people as insignificant. In the end, humility is to take on the mind and heart of Jesus Christ. Interestingly, Ignatius describes the third way of being humble as "the most perfect." This moves beyond duty. Here, our desire is simply to imitate Jesus Christ who, according to the gospels, came to serve others rather than to be served.

Discernment, The Common Good and Making the Good City

As we saw, the remote foundations of the Christian tradition of discernment in Aristotle's "practical wisdom" are essentially social. "Practical wisdom" is applicable especially to the public realm (which Aristotle associated with cities) and to a quest for what he called "the common good." At the heart of Aristotle's practical wisdom is how to discern what the fitting goals are to enable a "good life." One key is that the truly good life is orientated towards what is shared with others. What is truly good for me is inseparable from what is good for you, and what is good for both of us is associated with what is good for all. This is "the common good" – not merely a pragmatic arrangement but expressing something essential about human life. Thus, in the *Nicomachaean Ethics* (1094b): "the attainment of the good for one person alone is, to be sure, a source of satisfaction; yet to secure it for a nation and for cities is nobler and more divine."

Aristotle's "more divine" is echoed strongly in Christian history. The great thirteenth-century theologian Thomas Aquinas, in his *Summa Contra Gentiles* (III, 17), writes that "the supreme good, namely God, is the common good, since the good of all things depends on God." Aquinas wrote both about cities and about the inherently social nature of human life. For Aquinas, the city is the most complete of human communities, and community is vital to human flourishing. As we have seen, the purpose of "politics" according to Aquinas is to be a practical philosophy for promoting goodness in human affairs.[18]

Following Aristotle's notion of cities as creative of the virtues, Aquinas noted that cities persist for the sake of "the good life." This embraced the human virtues of courage, temperance, liberality, greatness of soul, and companionable modesty. These are only learned by social interaction. Indeed, Aquinas thought it unnatural for humans to live outside community.[19]

While studying theology in Paris, Ignatius Loyola would have encountered the work of Aquinas in lectures at the Dominican Convent of Saint-Jacques. However, in Ignatian discernment, Aquinas's "the common good" is extended to embrace "the greater good" or "the more universal good." In Ignatius's *Formula of the Institute*, the document that lays out his founding vision for the Jesuit order, the greater glory of God (*ad maiorem Dei gloriam*) is the primary goal, but God's glory is inherently linked to the reality of the common good. Ignatius' vision goes beyond Aristotle's city state or Aquinas's medieval kingdoms to embrace a wider motivational horizon derived from the expanded geographical reach of the so-called European "age of discovery" in the sixteenth century. Hence "the more universal good," a phrase that appears repeatedly in the Jesuit *Constitutions* (e.g. paragraphs 618 and 623), acts as the dominant criterion for collective discernment and decision-making.

I want now to suggest that "the common good" and the Ignatian "more universal good" are particularly challenging to the way that we think generally about contemporary society and, more specifically, about how to discern what is needed to advance "the good life" in the expanding and radically diverse contexts of contemporary cities.

As we noted in the Introduction, the meaning and future of cities globally is one of the most critical spiritual as well as economic and social issues of our age. Urban environments are where, for the majority of humanity, the practice of everyday life takes place, either constructively or destructively. We are also dealing increasingly with mega-cities where social and economic divisions are, if anything, heightened. In this context, we desperately need to relate city-making to some vision of the human spirit and to what is needed for the "good life" to flourish for the majority of the population rather than for the elite few.

Clearly it would be naïve to refer uncritically to pre-modern approaches to city community which, in the times of both Aristotle and Aquinas, was compact and local. Yet as we have already noted it is vital to construct some kind of compelling moral and spiritual vision for cities – both as social communities and as built environments – and to recover a sense that a city can be sacred to its inhabitants. A key question is what are cities *for*? They no longer have strictly practical roles for defense or as a focus for economic systems. If cities are to have "meaning" for people rather than being merely oppressive and irreversible, this must be to fulfill the wider possibilities of human life. There needs to be greater reflection on the civilizing possibilities of cities. They have a capacity to focus a range of physical, intellectual, and creative energies precisely because they combine differences of age, ethnicity, culture, gender, and religion.

Indeed, the city is quintessentially the public realm. It is not nowadays regarded as a spiritual reality because "the spiritual" is associated less with "the street" or neighborhood and more readily with interiority, the private realm or self-chosen community networks. As an environment of strangers who are unacquainted with each other or who occupy different cultural worlds, the public realm was until recently interpreted by social commentators as fundamentally barren. Life within it was a-social and human encounters were presumed to be incidental and unreflective. For this reason, as well as the increasing multicultural diversity of larger cities, shared values, and a genuinely common purpose were not deemed possible. This has begun to change. Some British politicians, for example, have preached the Big Society, and policy-makers are talking again about new localisms and about what makes "the good neighborhood." A number of writers are reflecting, sometimes from a spiritual viewpoint, on new understandings of "the good city" – creative communities built upon negotiation and compromise as positive virtues.[20]

In this context, a contemporary American Jesuit social ethicist, David Hollenbach, offers interesting insights based partly on the Ignatian tradition that complement the work of Michel de Certeau discussed in Chapter 5. Like de Certeau, Hollenbach is suspicious of attempts to define universalistic utopian models of the good life. The contemporary diverse city is always provisional, in process of becoming, and necessarily the product of multiple negotiations on the street corner.

Hollenbach poses some down-to-earth questions. In this he shares many of the same values as well as the realism of such leading contemporary urban thinkers as Ash Amin.[21] The sheer size and radically plural nature of today's cities make a sense of "commonality" or the achievement of solidarity much more elusive than before. So, is it even possible to recover a sense of "the common good"? Can people of different backgrounds identify aspects of "the good life" that they agree are desirable? Some people nowadays sense in any reference to the "common good" a pressure to assimilate difference and "otherness" into the established ethos of dominant groups. "Why can't *they* be more like *us*?" They suggest that passive tolerance of irreconcilable differences is the best we can hope for. However, Hollenbach believes that we can go beyond passive tolerance. He offers an explicit and challenging exposition of the validity, in contexts of diversity, of seeking "the common good" and, referring to Ignatian spirituality, "the more universal good." This has to come about not through top-down imposition but by persistent negotiation. As Hollenbach makes clear, such negotiation is not a quick fix. It may be a difficult concept for those who still believe that what constitutes "the common good" is, or should be, more definitive and self-evident. However, what matters more than the prospect of a guaranteed, successful conclusion is the solidarity that grows from our commitment to *a process* of making meaning, creating values and negotiating a common ethical and spiritual vocabulary. This process may in fact be open-ended.

> This common pursuit of a shared vision of the good life can be called intellectual solidarity... for it calls for serious thinking by citizens about what their distinctive understandings of "the good" imply for a society made up of people with many different traditions. It is a form of solidarity, because it can only occur in an active dialogue of mutual listening and speaking across the boundaries of religion and culture. Indeed, dialogue that seeks to understand those with different visions of the good life is already a form of solidarity even when disagreement continues to exist.[22]

David Hollenbach's concept of a profound solidarity produced in the ongoing process of social negotiation, based on mutual respect, listening, and interchange, is a striking example of the potential public and communal application of the Ignatian tradition of discernment as a social virtue. This process has rich potential in relation to the creation of effective urban community in our contemporary contexts, not least because it powerfully counters the dominance in political and social culture of the sins of factionalism and self-interest and more effectively underpins the quest for truly social virtues in the human city.

Notes

English translations are cited wherever available.

1 See Joseph Grange, *The City as Urban Cosmology*, Albany: State University of New York Press, 1999.
2 Grange, *The City as Urban Cosmology*, p. 195.
3 Grange, *The City as Urban Cosmology*, pp. 200–201.
4 Eduardo Mendieta, "Invisible cities: A phenomenology of globalisation from below," *City* 5(1), 2001, pp. 1–25.
5 Mendieta, "Invisible cities," p. 17.
6 Charles Leadbeater, *Civic Spirit: The Big Idea for a New Political Era*, London: Demos, 1997, Demos Arguments 14, p. 30.
7 The Reith Lectures were published as Richard Rogers, *Cities for a Small Planet*, London: Faber, 1997.
8 Richard Rogers, *Cities for a Small Planet*, London: Faber & Faber, 1997, pp. 9–10.
9 Ash Amin, "Collective culture and urban public space," in *City*, 12, 1, April 2008, pp. 5–24.
10 The references to the *Spiritual Exercises* of Ignatius Loyola follow the standard paragraph numbers used in all modern editions. These will be shorted to Exx followed by a paragraph number or numbers. Thus, the Rules for Discernment appear at Exx 313–336.
11 Aristotle, *Nicomachaean Ethics*. See Gerard J. Hughes, *Aristotle on Ethics*, London and New York: Routledge, 2001, p. 179.
12 For a detailed analysis of Aristotle's understanding of *phronesis*, see Hughes, *Aristotle on Ethics*, Chapter 5 "Practical wisdom."
13 This connection had been noted by Cardinal John Henry Newman in his theological reflections on knowledge, especially in the *Grammar of Assent*. See Mark A. McIntosh, *Discernment and Truth: The Spirituality and Theology of Knowledge*, New York: Crossroad, 2004, Chapter 7, also pp. 7 and 16.
14 See Colm Luidheid (ed.), *John Cassian: Conferences*, New York: Paulist Press, 1985.
15 Cited in McIntosh, *Discernment and Truth*, p. 39.
16 Hugo Rahner, *Ignatius the Theologian*, San Francisco: Ignatius Press, 1990, pp. 146 and 154.
17 For insightful comments on these points see McIntosh, *Discernment and Truth*, pp. 116–117.
18 Thomas Aquinas, *Sententia Libri Politicorum. Opera Omnia*, VIII, Paris, 1891, Prologue A 69–70.

19   Thomas Aquinas, *De Regimine Principum*, Chapter 2, in R. W. Dyson (ed.), *Aquinas: Political Writings*, Cambridge: Cambridge University Press, 2002, pp. 8–10.

20   See Kathryn Tanner (ed.), *Spirit in the Cities: Searching for Soul in the Urban Landscape*, Minneapolis: Fortress Press, 2004; also Andrew Walker (ed.), *Spirituality in the City*, London: SPCK, 2005; and Andrew Walker and Aaron Kennedy (eds.), *Discovering the Spirit in the City*, London and New York: Continuum, 2010.

21   See, for example, Ash Amin, "The good city," *Urban Studies*, 2006, 43, 5–6, pp. 1009–1023, especially pp. 1012–13.

22   David Hollenbach, *The Common Good and Christian Ethics*, Cambridge: Cambridge University Press, 2002, pp. 137–138.

Epilogue: A Spiritual Vision of the Human City

The Introduction to this book began with the stark fact that a radical process of urbanization is rapidly spreading across the globe. For the majority of humanity, cities shape identity for better or for worse. Urban environments create a climate of values that define how we understand and then seek to create human community. The radical plurality of contemporary cities, as well as the mobility of people's lives compared with the past, confronts us with complex and often painful challenges. What this book has sought to underline throughout is that purely instrumental or utilitarian responses to the future of cities are not sufficient. We desperately need to develop a compelling urban, moral, and spiritual vision.

It should now be clear that Christianity does not promote a protected subjectivity or a kind of spiritualized interiority as more authentically human. Mixture and diversity in the public square are not to be seen as essentially a threat to our integrity. Equally, Christianity does not retreat from the everyday world in a restless search for an other-worldly future. On the contrary, as this book has sought to illustrate, Christianity across the centuries has offered a provocative urban vision expressed in a variety of ways.

In particular, Christianity persistently reminds us that the quality of community and of our overall engagement with other people is central to being human rather than a purely secondary factor. There is no absolutely private identity. The public realm is not dispensable. Rather, to be fully human embodies a common life and a common task. In urban environments effective community is fundamentally brought into existence by the everyday encounters of people on the streets and the narratives they share rather than by top-down planning or politically-driven policy. In Michel de Certeau's powerful and evocative expression, it is human gestures that remake the city day by day. A critical question, therefore, is how we are to enable our streets and our neighborhoods to be effective places of mutual engagement, often of a casual nature, rather than places of exclusion for some people and of threat for others.

There is an intimate connection between a sense that human life is essentially relational and the Christian understanding of God as a communion of persons in whose image humanity is created. *Koinonia* or mutual communion underpins all existence. However, this Christian vision of human community is not merely comforting. Nor should it provoke a nostalgic search for the protected localisms of a past age. On the contrary, it is a robustly challenging vision precisely because it places such a powerful emphasis in different ways on the virtue of hospitality to strangers – including those who are radically "other" and even distasteful to us. As the monastic Rule of St Benedict suggests, true hospitality consists of more than simply "receiving" the stranger. Strangers are to be *cherished* – that is, valued as if they were one of our own.

For Christian thinkers like Augustine or Thomas Aquinas, both influenced by classical philosophy, no image embodied the fullness of the human condition better than a city. Thus, in Augustine the city becomes a potent image of heaven. At the heart of a true city is something more than buildings or design. This "something" is *civitas* or the potency of civic life. This value is not a straightforward given. It needs to be persistently worked at and recreated through our commitment to it.

This Christian vision of the city as community poses a number of difficult questions. How are people to approach a life of service and how is a city to be a context for self-giving? At the heart of Jesus's teaching is not only the commandment to love God but also the commandment to love our neighbors (our fellow citizens) "as ourselves." So, what is it to love truly in a city? The question lies at the heart of Augustine's understanding of *amicitia* – civic friendship or even "urban love." His notion is extremely challenging in three ways. First, the ideal extends outside our immediate circle to embrace everyone, without exception, who inhabits the place. This transcends social divisions and rank and radically promotes a sense of fundamental human equality. Second, the ideal of love of neighbor moves beyond purely pragmatic arrangements in the direction of creating bonds of real *attachment*. Finally, it promotes the pursuit of the "common good" which is a concept inherited from ancient Greek philosophy and which runs through the history of Christian approaches to the city. Importantly the "common good" balances the quest for shared ideals with honoring individual needs. However, its force is that we ultimately find our own deepest good by seeking the good of the other and that together we should work for the good of the whole. As we have seen, the social ethicist David Hollenbach underlines that the search for the "common good" in radically plural modern cities is not an easy matter. However, it pushes us beyond a purely passive tolerance of irreconcilable difference to commit ourselves to a long-term, even open-ended, process of negotiating a common language of values and vision.

Sacramentality and the City

Underlying such an urban vision is a sense of what is referred to theologically as "sacramentality." This word originates with the Christian definition of a "sacrament" as a material sign of God's action in human lives and as a medium through which divine life is shared with humanity. Christians understand that the fundamental "sacrament" of God's presence and action in the world is Jesus Christ and, by extension, the Christian community which is described as "the Body of Christ." Historically, this community has expressed its belief in God's transformative action in human lives through the practice of certain key rituals known as sacraments, such as baptism or the Eucharist.

The broader notion of "sacramentality" extends this sensibility beyond purely religious rituals. It suggests that all material reality is potentially a sign of God's presence and a context for God's action in relation to humankind. The material world and the everyday thus have an inherent sacredness, as the writings of Duns Scotus remind us. God's presence is active in the space of the entire *world*, not merely inside the Church. This perception receives one of its classic expressions in Western spirituality in the concluding "Contemplation to Attain Love" in the Spiritual Exercises of Ignatius Loyola which we have already cited and which invites us to find God in all things. The divine may be discerned in the human, the particular, the contingent, the material, and the historical. Ignatius Loyola understood God to be present in everything, without exception.

> I will consider how God labors and works for me in all the creatures on the face of the earth; that is, he acts in the manner of one who is laboring. For example, he is working in the heavens, elements, plants, fruits, cattle and all the rest – giving them their existence, conserving them, concurring with their vegetative and sensitive activities, and so forth.[1]

In a comparable but distinctive way, the important twentieth-century Russian Orthodox theologian, Alexander Schmemann wrote powerfully of the world itself as a sacrament.[2] By this he meant that the world only has real meaning if it is seen as a materialization of God's presence. Any understanding of the world that denies its sacredness is a narrative of ultimate emptiness and meaninglessness. Christianity stands for precisely the opposite point of view. We can live in the world "seeing everything in it as the revelation of God, a sign of [God's] presence, the joy of [God's] coming, the call to communion with [God], the hope of fulfillment in [God]."[3] This vision of the sacramentality of the world is not sentimental for we also have to acknowledge that the divine potential of the world is denied, frustrated, distorted, and defaced by selfish human action. Yet, at the heart of the divine presence in all things is the image of the cross. In the suffering and death of Jesus Christ, God is revealed as one who is in solidarity with the conflict and suffering of the world. In addition, God is revealed as a transformative, redemptive power. Hence Alexander Schmemann sees humanity's role as one of offering back to God for healing the failures of the world. In God's power alone is the ultimate hope of our transformation, including the transformation of the human city.[4]

In the light of this extended sacramental sensibility, the human city qua city, in all its diversity, fluidity, and provisionality is nevertheless a "space" of God's freely-chosen self-revelation. God is above all present in "the other," the stranger and the unexpected person, subverting our prejudices and narrow sense of identity. Urban spaces, with their multiple human narratives and memories, are potential contexts for divine revelation and spiritual vision even if they also inevitably speak of the fragility and ultimate decay of the world and of human lives. The city is undoubtedly a "space" of human limitations and finitude. Yet, understood properly, the human city also has the capacity to point us towards eternity – a horizon of ultimacy and completion.[5]

It is important to underline that a sacramental imagination and sensibility in relation to the human city is not a matter of rose-tinted unreality. It is not an unqualified affirmation that the everyday world, in the words of the seventeenth-century poet and Church of England priest Thomas Traherne in his *Centuries of Meditation*, is "a mirror of infinite beauty," "the Temple of Majesty," "the Paradise of God," "the place of Angels and the Gate of Heaven."[6] Our human existence demands that we find our identity within a material context that is full of ambiguity. Because of this engagement with down-to-earth reality, a true sacramental sensibility also demands that we confront the hard ethical questions posed by human selfishness. In other words, we are forced to engage with the realities of human dysfunction and division, with the radical need for transformation in the world and with the challenging call to human reconciliation.

Eschatology and the City

This sense of the ambiguity and incompleteness of the human city brings us to a second concept, that of "eschatology." From a Christian theological perspective, our visions of the city and of human community demand a careful balance between sacramentality and eschatology. Eschatology literally means a word (*logos*) about the "last things" (*eschata*). In traditional language, these "last things" refer to death, judgment, and what lies beyond as the consequence of a selfless life or of a self-centered life. Historically, eschatology has referred both to the destiny of individual people and also to the end of the world for humanity as a whole. In general terms it underlines the incomplete nature in time and space of all human communities, including the city. Yet, at the same time, it also speaks of an ultimate hope of transformation and a transcendent horizon of meaning.

During the second half of the twentieth century, and in the light of biblical perspectives, there was a return among a number of theologians to the central importance of eschatology. For example, the German theologians Jürgen Moltmann and Karl Rahner both suggest that eschatology is not merely one area of theology but should actually infuse the whole of Christian theology.[7] Importantly, modern eschatology emphasizes that there are elements both of continuity and of discontinuity between our present existence and eternal life.

Earlier, I suggested that a balanced eschatology had a specific value in relation to what Christianity may offer by way of a spiritual vision for cities. The late twentieth-century developments in theology make it much clearer what eschatology actually is and is not. It is not a crude form of futurology – that is, a prediction of when and how the present cosmos will end and what will happen to humankind "beyond time." In terms of our vision for cities, eschatology is not an escape clause from the complications of everyday life ("everything will turn out fine in the end, but somewhere else"). Equally, eschatology does not absolve us from our need to be committed in the here and now to an ongoing vision of social transformation. It is a question of balance. A purely future-oriented eschatology leaves us with the sense that life in the everyday city does not describe anything essential about human existence. It is simply an ephemeral shell for our nomadic pilgrimage through this present life towards an idealized "elsewhere." As we saw in the Introduction, this was one of social scientist Richard Sennett's problems with Christianity.[8]

An interesting recent parable of the destructive potential of an unbalanced eschatology appears in Carol Lake's collection of short stories entitled, *Rosehill: Portraits from a Midlands City* set in the inner city of Derby, England.[9] One story, "The Day of Judgement," explores what would happen if the people of Rosehill had to face the Last Day. God arrives in a new Noah's Ark apparently in order to carry off those inhabitants who are judged worthy to some paradise elsewhere. However, to everyone's surprise, God exits the Ark in order to drink with the locals in a popular pub. The Ark sails away to paradise without God on board. Carol Lake's point is that the Ark, which leaves Rosehill to travel onwards towards a far destination, represents the vision of a utopian heaven based on what she calls the "heartlessness of perfection."

> The Ark is on the edge of the horizon now, its destination the heartlessness of perfection. Most of the inmates already know what they are going to find – endless fruit, endless harmony, endless entropy, endless, endless

compassion, black and white in endless inane tableaux of equality. It sails off to a perfect world; the sky has turned into rich primary colors and in the distance the Ark bobs about on a bright blue sea. (p. 119)

Eventually, with God living in the town, it is the streets of Rosehill that gradually over time become intensely beautiful. Carol Lake's city is initially an image of human imperfection and estrangement, and the Ark represents the promise and offer of liberation in a perfect other-worldly elsewhere. However, eventually the city also represents for those who stay and commit themselves to the place (with God now a fellow citizen) the possibility of the heavenly City of God being built in the streets among the previously marginalized inhabitants of a transfigured Rosehill.

While allowing for these possible dangers, a sense of eschatology guards against the naïve utopian dream that we are capable of creating in the here and now a perfectly harmonious city through architectural designs, systematic planning, and political policies. As we saw earlier, this was one of Michel de Certeau's problems with the urban and architectural theories of someone like Le Corbusier. Eschatology also counters any understanding of our present human existence that can be reduced to the immediacy of pleasure, success, and unrestrained consumer choice. Eschatology suggests that life involves more than instant satisfaction. A horizon of transcendence reminds us that the meaning of existence is ultimately beyond our limited capacities to define, however scientifically or technologically attuned we may be.

A positive eschatology also opens up every "present moment," indeed history as a whole, to a horizon of possibility. History and the "present moment" are not thereby reduced in importance, let alone annihilated, but are actually expanded. In a sense, each moment becomes decisive. An eschatological perspective makes chronological time also *kairos* time. Every instant in time is an opportunity, an "end moment" that points us towards ultimate possibility. This focuses our attention on the urgency of what is given to us in the present moment. It makes whatever we do an act of commitment to seek the ultimate. Finally, in overtly theological terms, eschatology expresses a hope that the transformation of humanity and creation, revealed in the life, death, and resurrection of Jesus, will ultimately embrace the final triumph of good over evil, of justice over injustice, and of love over hatred.

In recent decades, the viability of any eschatology has been called into question by the advent of what is known as postmodernity. Postmodernity is fundamentally the state of society that exists in reaction against many of the assumptions of Modernity, originating in the intellectual movement known as the Enlightenment, which has had a massive impact on wider Western culture. In particular, postmodernity stands for a critical reassessment in the late twentieth century of modernity's over-confidence in the power of human reason, in an ordered view of the world, and in the inevitability of progress driven by human effort. This skepticism was the cumulative result of the powerful challenges of two world wars, totalitarianism, Hiroshima and the atomic age, the end of centuries of European empire in Africa and Asia, the extraordinary development of rapid travel and global communication, as well as a tide of social change regarding the status of women and racial minorities. The old certainties crumbled. Because postmodernity, and the related theory of postmodernism, is deeply skeptical about all grand narratives that describe life and its meaning, such an outlook appears to leave little room for an overarching narrative of human transformation.[10]

However, a number of Christian thinkers believe that postmodernity may actually make space for a new kind of religious discourse, including eschatology. For example, postmodern theorists write about a passion for the impossible, how we may seek to represent the unrepresentable and what it means to attempt to speak about what may not be definitively said. These postmodern aspirations have some affinity with both classic mystical discourse and with eschatology, which also seek to imagine the unimaginable and to express the inexpressible in ways that acknowledge the limited nature of all our definitions and question our attempts to shape reality definitively.[11]

Eschatology speaks of some kind of "more" and "beyond" that transcends the contingent and limited here-and-now existence both of individuals and of humanity collectively. In Christianity, there was originally a balance between the social or communal character of a Jewish notion of human destiny (the "resurrection of the dead") and the individual immortality suggested by Greek philosophy (for example Plato). Eventually, the balance between a communal and individual vision in relation to eschatology was lost, giving way to a perspective focused largely on the eternal fate of the individual person.

The implication of the Christian doctrine of the Incarnation, that God entered human history in the person of Jesus Christ, implies that all that is human is touched by God's redemptive action. Eschatology therefore sees the final reign of God as something that redeems the whole world, not merely the Christian community. It also involves humanity collectively and not merely individual people. The trajectory of human existence portrayed by the concept of eschatology also suggests a perpetual human need to recover the essentially social nature of human identity in the spirit of scripture, Augustine, Thomas Aquinas, and the more recent traditions of Christian social teaching. In particular a sense of eschatology provokes us to commit ourselves to counter the prevailing fault of humanity which is to dilute the essential bonds of love, community, or sociality with each other.

Conclusion

The Judaeo-Christian scriptures and Christian theology more generally are sharply realistic about the human history of fragmentation and the need for redemption. This underlines a sense that any final healing of the human condition is beyond our unaided capacities to achieve. Hence, theology defines the redemption of humanity as ultimately God's work. However, this does not absolve us entirely of responsibility. On the one hand we have no independent way of guaranteeing the ultimate completion of the human city. *Civitas* has no final form, no "perfection" that we can precisely define – let alone one that we can conjure up through our planning or public policy. However, on the other hand, Christian tradition provokes us to commit ourselves unreservedly within the human city to the continually challenging and never-ending process of building community and of negotiating the common good. Such a process is always fragile and therefore persistently in need of being reconceived and reconstructed.[12] Yet, Christian theology also expresses a confidence that, within God's providence and love, nothing significant is ultimately lost.[13]

Notes

English translations are cited wherever available.

1 Exercises, paragraph 236. English translation in George Ganss (ed.), *The Spiritual Exercises of Saint Ignatius*, Chicago: Loyola University Press, 1992.
2 Alexander Schmemann, *The World as Sacrament*, English edition London: Darton, Longman & Todd, 1965.
3 Schmemann, *The World as Sacrament*, pp. 140–141.
4 Schmemann, *The World as Sacrament*, p. 16.
5 See David Brown and Ann Loades (eds.), *The Sense of the Sacramental*, London: SPCK, 1995, pp. 3–6.
6 Thomas Traherne, *Centuries of Meditation*, London: Mowbray 1975, 1, 31.
7 English editions, Jürgen Moltmann, *The Coming of God: Christian Eschatology*, London: SCM Press, 1996, and Karl Rahner, *Foundations of the Christian Faith: An Introduction to the Idea of Christianity*, London: Darton, Longman & Todd, 1978.
8 Richard Sennett, *The Conscience of the Eye: The Design and Social Life of Cities*, London: Faber & Faber, pp. 6–10.
9 Carol Lake, *Rosehill: Portraits from a Midlands City*, London: Bloomsbury 1989.
10 See for example, Zygmunt Baumann, "Utopia with no *topos*," *History of the Human Sciences*, 16(1) (2003), pp. 11–24.
11 On Christian engagements with postmodernity, see, for example, Philip Sheldrake, "Postmodernity," in Philip Sheldrake (ed.), *The New SCM Dictionary of Christian Spirituality*, London: SCM Press, 2005 (in North America, *The New Westminster Dictionary of Christian Spirituality*, Louisville, KY Westminster John Knox Press); F. B. Burnham (ed.), *Postmodern Theology: Christian Faith in a Pluralist World*, San Francisco: HarperCollins, 1989; Michel de Certeau, *The Mystic Fable*, Chicago: University of Chicago Press, 1992; Paul Lakeland, *Postmodernity: Christian Identity in a Fragmented Aged*, Minneapolis, MN: Fortress Press, 1997.
12 See T.J. Gorringe, *A Theology of the Built Environment*, Cambridge: Cambridge University Press, 2002, p. 192.
13 See Rowan Williams, *On Christian Theology*, Oxford and Malden, MA: Blackwell Publishers, 2000, p. 65.

Select Reading

Ackroyd, P., *The Life of Thomas More*, London: Random House, 1999.

Amin, A., "The good city," in *Urban Studies*, 43(5–6), 2006, pp. 1009–1023.

Amin, A., "Collective culture and urban public space," in *City*, 12(1), April 2008, pp. 5–24.

Amin, A. and Thrift, N., *Cities: Reimaging the Urban*, Cambridge: Polity Press, 2002.

Appadurai, A., *Modernity at Large: Cultural Dimensions of Globalization*, Minneapolis: University of Minnesota Press, 1998.

Arendt, H., *The Human Condition*, Chicago: University of Chicago Press, 1958.

Armstrong, R. and Brady, I. (eds.), *Francis and Clare: The Complete Works*, New York: Paulist Press, 1982.

Ashley, J. M., *Interruptions: Mysticism, Politics and Theology in the Work of Johann Baptist Metz*, Notre Dame: University of Notre Dame Press, 1998.

Atkinson, D., *The Common Sense of Community*, Demos Paper 11, London: Demos, 1994.

Augé, M., *Non-Places: Introduction to An Anthropology of Supermodernity*, London and New York: Verso, 1997.

Augustine, *St Augustine: City of God*, edited H. Bettenson, London: Penguin Classics, 1984.

Bachelard, G., *The Poetics of Space*, Boston: Beacon Press, 1994.

Barman, C., *The Man who Built London Transport: a Biography of Frank Pick*, London: David & Charles, 1979.

Baumann, Z., "Utopia with no topos," in *History of the Human Sciences*, 16(1), 2003, pp. 11–24.

Bede, *Ecclesiastical History of the English People*, London and New York: Penguin, Revised Edition 1990.

Berleant, A., *The Aesthetics of Environment*, Philadelphia: Temple University Press, 1992.

Bertrand, D., *La Politique de S. Ignace de Loyola: l'analyse sociale*, Paris: Editions du Cerf, 1985.

Betz, J. R., *After Enlightenment: The Post-Secular Vision of J.G. Hamann*, Oxford: Wiley-Blackwell, 2009.

Bitel, L., *Isle of Saints: Monastic Settlements and Christian Community in Early Ireland*, Ithaca, NY: Cornell University Press, 1990.

Boff, L., *Trinity and Society*, New York: Orbis Books, 1982.

Bonaventure, *Bonaventure: The Soul's Journey into God; The Tree of Life; The Life of St Francis*, ed. E. Cousins, New York: Paulist Press, 1978.

Brown, D. and Loades, A. (eds.), *The Sense of the Sacramental*, London: SPCK, 1995.

Brown, P., *Society and the Holy in Late Antiquity*, Berkeley: University of California Press, 1989.

Brown, P., *The Making of Late Antiquity*, Cambridge, MA: Harvard University Press, 1993.

Brueggemann, W., *The Land: Place as Gift, Promise and Challenge in Biblical Faith*, Philadelphia: Fortress Press, 1977.

Buchanan, I., *Michel de Certeau: Cultural Theorist*, London: Sage Publications, 2000.

Bultmann, R., *Jesus Christ and Mythology*, New York: Scribner, 1958.

Burton Russell, J., *A History of Heaven: The Singing Silence*, Princeton, NJ: Princeton University Press, 1997.

Burton Stone, N. and Hart, P. (eds.), *Thomas Merton: Love and Living*, New York: Harcourt Brace Jovanovich, 1979.

Buttimer, A., "Home, reach and the sense of place," in A. Buttimer and D. Seaman (eds.), *The Human Sense of Space and Place*, London: Croom Helm, 1980.

Bynum, C. W., *Jesus as Mother: Studies in the Spirituality of the High Middle Ages*, Berkeley: University of California Press, 1984.

Calvin, J., *Institutes of the Christian Religion*, Grand Rapids, MI: Eerdmans, 1995.

Calvino, I., *Invisible Cities*, London: Random House, 2001.

Camille, M., *Gothic Art: Visions and Revelations of the Medieval World*, London: Weidenfeld & Nicolson, 1996.

Canter, D., *The Psychology of Place*, London: The Architectural Press, 1977.

Carey, J. (ed.), *The Faber Book of Utopias*, London: Faber & Faber, 2000.

Carrette, J. R., *Foucault and Religion: Spiritual Corporality and Political Spirituality*, London and New York: Routledge, 2000.

Casanova, J., *Public Religion in the Modern World*, Chicago: University of Chicago Press, 1994.

Casey, E. S., "How to get from space to place in a fairly short stretch of time: Phenomenological prolegomena," in S. Feld and K. H. Basso (eds.), *Senses of Place*, Santa Fe: School of American Research Press, 1996.

Cassian, J., *John Cassian: Conferences*, ed. C. Luidheid, New York: Paulist Press, 1985.

Castells, M., *The Power of Identity, The Information Age: Economy, Society and Culture*, Volume 2, Oxford: Blackwell, 1997.

Castells, M., *End of Millennium*, Oxford: Blackwell, 1998.

Chitty, D., *The Desert A City: An Introduction to the Study of Egyptian and Palestinian Monasticism*, Crestwood, NY: St Vladimir's Seminary Press, 1995 [1966].

Cohen, D., *Household Gods: The British and their Possessions*, New Haven, CT: Yale University Press, 2006.

Commission on Urban Life and Faith, *Faithful Cities: A Call for Celebration, Vision and Justice*, London: Church House Publishing, 2006.

Cortone, N. and Lavermicocca, N., *Santi di Strada: Le Edicole Religiose della Città Vecchia di Bari*, 5 volumes, Bari: Edizione BA Graphis, 2001–3.

Cowan, P., *Rose Windows*, London: Thames & Hudson, 1979.

Davies, J.G., *The Secular Use of Church Buildings*, London: SCM Press, 1968.

Davis, W. A., *Inwardness and Existence*, Madison: University of Wisconsin Press, 1989.

de Certeau, M., "Practices of space," in M. Blonsky (ed.), *On Signs*, Oxford: Blackwell, 1985.

de Certeau, M., *The Practice of Everyday Life*, Berkeley: University of California Press, 1988.

de Certeau, M., Giard, L. and Mayol, P., *The Practice of Everyday Life*, volume 2, Living and Cooking, Minneapolis: University of Minnesota Press, 1998.

de Certeau, M., *The Mystic Fable: The Sixteenth and Seventeenth Centuries*, Chicago: University of Chicago Press, 1992.

de Certeau, M., *Heterologies: Discourse on the Other*, Minneapolis: University of Minnesota Press, 1995.

de Certeau, M., "How is Christianity thinkable today?" in G. Ward (ed.), *The Postmodern God: A Theological Reader*, Oxford; Blackwell, 1997, pp. 142–55.

de Certeau, M., *The Capture of Speech and Other Political Writings*, Minneapolis: University of Minnesota Press, 1997.

de Certeau, M., *Culture in the Plural*, Minneapolis: University of Minnesota Press, 2001.

de Gruchy, J., *Reconciliation: Restoring Justice*, London: SCM Press, 2002.

Dodaro, R., "Augustine's secular city" in R. Dodaro and G. Lawless (eds.), *Augustine and His Critics*, London and New York: Routledge, 2000, pp. 231–59.

Duby, G., *The Age of Cathedrals: Art and Society 980–1420*, Chicago: University of Chicago Press, 1981.

Dyson, R. W. (ed.), *Aquinas: Political Writings*, Cambridge: Cambridge University Press, 2002.

Eco, U., *Art and Beauty in the Middle Ages*, New Haven, CT: Yale University Press, 1986.

Eliade, M., *The Sacred and the Profane: The Nature of Religion*, New York: Harcourt Brace Jovanovich, 1987.

Ellul, J., *The Meaning of the City*, Grand Rapids, MI: Eerdmans, 1970.

Fitzgerald, T., *The Ideology of Religious Studies*, Oxford: Oxford University Press, 2000.

Foucault, M., *Discipline and Punish: The Birth of the Prison*, London: Penguin Books, 1991.

Francis of Assisi, *Francis and Clare: Complete Works*, ed. R. Armstrong and I. Brady, New York: Paulist Press, 1982.

Frugoni, C., *A Distant City: Images of Urban Experience in the Medieval World*, Princeton, NJ: Princeton University Press, 1991.

Furbey, R., "Urban regeneration: reflections on a metaphor," in *Critical Social Policy*, 19(4), 1999, pp. 419–45.

Furbey, R. and Macey, M., "Religion and urban regeneration: a place for faith," in *Policy and Politics*, 33(1), 2005, pp. 95–116.

Ganss, G. (ed.), *The Constitutions of the Society of Jesus*, St Louis, MO: The Institute of Jesuit Sources, 1970.

Gibson, K. and Watson, S. (eds.), *Postmodern Cities and Spaces*, Oxford: Blackwell, 1995.

Gill, R., *Moral Communities: The Prideaux Lectures*, Exeter: Exeter University Press, 1992.

Gorringe, T., *A Theology of the Built Environment: Justice, Empowerment, Redemption*, Cambridge: Cambridge University Press, 2002.

Graham, E. and Lowe, S., *What Makes a Good City? Public Theology and the Urban Church*, London: Darton Longman and Todd, 2009.

Grange, J., *The City as Urban Cosmology*, Albany: State University of New York Press, 1999.

Gunton, C., *The Promise of Trinitarian Theology*, Edinburgh: T and T Clark, 1997.

Gunton, C., *The One, The Three and The Many*, Cambridge: Cambridge University Press, 1995.

Gurevich, A., *Medieval Popular Culture: Problems of Belief and Perception*, Cambridge: Cambridge University Press, 1990.

Haight, R., *Christian Community in History*, volume 2, New York: Continuum, 2005.

Harrison, C., *Augustine: Christian Truth and Fractured Humanity*, Oxford: Oxford University Press, 2000.

Harrison, M., *Bournville, Model Village to Garden Suburb*, Chichester: Phillimore, 1999.

Harvey, D., "The right to the city" in *New Left Review*, 53, 2008, pp. 23–40.

Hauerwas, S., *After Christendom? How the Church is to Behave if Freedom, Justice and a Christian Nation are Bad Ideas*, Nashville: Abingdon Press, 1991.

Hawkins, P. S. (ed.), *Civitas: Religious Interpretations of The City*, Atlanta: Scholars' Press, 1986.

Heidegger, M., *Poetry, Language, Thought*, New York: Harper & Row, 1975.

Herbert, M., *Iona, Kells and Derry: The History and Hagiography of the Monastic Familia of Columba*, Oxford: Oxford University Press, 1988.

Himes, K. R., *Modern Catholic Social Teaching: Commentaries and Interpretations*, Washington, DC: Georgetown University Press, 2005.

Hollenbach, D., *The Common Good and Christian Ethics*, Cambridge: Cambridge University Press, 2002.

Hornsby-Smith, M., *An Introduction to Catholic Social Thought*, Cambridge: Cambridge University Press, 2006.

Hudson, W. S. (ed.), *Walter Rauschenbusch: Selected Writings*, New York: Paulist Press, 1984.

Hughes, G. J., *Aristotle on Ethics*, London and New York: Routledge, 2001.

Hughes, K., *Early Christian Ireland: Introduction to the Sources*, London: Hodder & Stoughton, 1972.

Hughes, K., *Church and Society in Ireland AD 400–1200*, Aldershot: Variorum, 1987.

Hughes, K. and Hamlin, A., *Celtic Monasticism: The Modern Traveller to the Irish Church*, New York: Seabury Press, 1981.

Ignatius of Loyola, *Saint Ignatius of Loyola: Personal Writings*, ed. J. Munitiz and P. Endean, London: Penguin Classics, 2004.

Jacobs, J., *The Death and Life of Great American Cities*, London: Random House, 1993 [1961].

Jencks, C., "The iconic building is here to stay" in *City*, 10(1), April 2006, pp. 3–20.

Johnson, E., *She Who Is: The Mystery of God in Feminist Theological Discourse*, New York: Crossroad, 1996.

Kardong, T. C. (ed.), *Benedict's Rule: A Translation and Commentary*, Collegeville, MN: The Liturgical Press, 1996.

Katz, P., *The New Urbanism: Toward an Architecture of Community*, New York: McGraw-Hill, 1994.

Kerr, F., *Theology after Wittgenstein*, London: SPCK Press, 1997.

Kotkin, J., *The City: A Global History*, New York: Random House, 2006.

Kramer, V. (ed.), *Turning Towards the World: The Pivotal Years 1960–1963*, The Journals of Thomas Merton volume 4, San Francisco: Harper, 1996.

LaCugna, C. M., *God for Us: The Trinity and Christian Life*, San Francisco: HarperCollins, 1993.

Lake, C., *Rosehill: Portraits from a Midlands City*, London: Bloomsbury, 1989.

Landry, C., *The Creative City: A Toolkit for Urban Innovators*, London: Routledge, 2008.

Lane, B., *The Solace of Fierce Landscapes*, New York: Oxford University Press, 1998.

Lawless, G., *Augustine of Hippo and His Monastic Rule*, Oxford: Clarendon Press, 1987.

Lawrence, C.H., *The Friars: The Impact of the Early Mendicant Movement on Western Society*, London: Longman, 1994.

Lawrence, D., *Bright Underground Spaces: The Railway Stations of Charles Holden*, London: Capital Transport, 2008.

Leadbeater, C., *Civic Spirit: The Big Idea for a New Political Era*, London: Demos, 1997.

Lefebvre, H., *The Production of Space*, Oxford: Blackwell, 1991.

Le Goff, J., *Medieval Civilisation*, Oxford: Blackwell, 1988.

Le Goff, J., *The Medieval Imagination*, Chicago: University of Chicago Press, 1988.

Le Goff, J. (ed.), *The Medieval World*, London: Collins and Brown, 1990.

Lofland, L., *The Public Realm: Exploring the City's Quintessential Social Territory*, New York: Aldine de Gruyter, 1998.

Louth, A., *The Wilderness of God*, London: Darton Longman & Todd, 1991.

Lucas, T. M., *Landmarking: City, Church and Jesuit Urban Strategy*, Chicago: Loyola University Press, 1997.

Lyndon, D. and Moore, C.W., *Chambers for a Memory Palace*, Cambridge, MA: MIT Press, 1994.

Macqueen, A., *The King of Sunlight: How William Lever cleaned up the World*, London: Bantam, 2004.

McDannell, C. and Lang, B., *Heaven: A History*, New Haven, CT: Yale University Press, 1988.

McElrath, D. (ed.), *Franciscan Christology*, New York: Franciscan Institute, 1980.

McGinn, B., Meyendorff, J. and Leclercq, J. (eds.), *Christian Spirituality I: Origins to the Twelfth Century*, New York: Crossroad Publishing, 1985.

McIntosh, M., *Discernment and Truth: The Spirituality and Theology of Knowledge*, New York: Crossroad, 2004.

Malpas, J. E., *Place and Experience: A Philosophical Typography*, Cambridge: Cambridge University Press, 1999.

Markus, R. A., *The End of Ancient Christianity*, Cambridge: Cambridge University Press, 1998.

Markus, R. A., *Christianity and The Secular*, Notre Dame, IN: University of Notre Dame Press, 2006.

Martin, T., *Our Restless Heart: The Augustinian Tradition*, London: Darton Longman & Todd/ Maryknoll, NY: Orbis Books, 2003.

Martin, T., "Augustine and the politics of monasticism" in J. Doody, K.L. Hughes and K. Paffenroth (eds.), *Augustine and Politics*, Lanham, MD: Lexington Books, 2005, pp. 165–86.

Mayernick, D., *Timeless Cities: An Architect's Reflections on Renaissance Italy*, Boulder, CO: Westview Press, 2003.

Mendieta, E., "Invisible cities: a phenomenology of globalization from below," in *City*, 5(1), 2001, pp. 1–25.

Merkle, J. A., *From the Heart of the Church: The Catholic Social Tradition*, Collegeville, MN: Liturgical Press, 2004.

Merton, T., *Conjectures of a Guilty Bystander*, New York: Doubleday, 1966.

Merton T., *Ishi Means Man*, Greensboro, NC: Unicorn Press, 1976.

Merton, T., *The Collected Poems of Thomas Merton*, New York: New Directions Publishing, 1980.

Milbank, J., *Theology and Social Theory: Beyond Secular Reason*, Oxford: Blackwell, 1990.

Moltmann, J., *History and the Triune God: Contributions to Trinitarian Theology*, London: SCM Press/New York: Crossroad, 1992.

Moltmann, J., *The Coming of God: Christian Eschatology*, London: SCM Press, 1996.

Moore, R. I., *The Formation of a Persecuting Society*, Oxford: Blackwell, 1994.

More, Thomas, *Utopia*, edited by E. Surtz and J.H. Hexter, in "The Complete Works of St Thomas More," New Haven, CT: Yale University Press, 1965.

Morris, J., *F.D. Maurice and the Crisis of Christian Authority*, Oxford: Oxford University Press, 2005.

Morris, R., *Churches in the Landscape*, London: Dent, 1989.

Mugerauer, R., *Interpretations on Behalf of Place: Environmental Displacements and Alternative Responses*, Albany: State University of New York Press, 1994.

Mumford, L., *The Culture of Cities*, London and New York: Harcourt Brace, 1970 [1938].

Northcott, M., "A place of our own?" in P. Sedgwick (ed.), *God in the City: Essays and Reflections from the Archbishop of Canterbury's Urban Theology Group*, London: Mowbray, 1995.

O'Daly, G., *Augustine's City of God: A Reader's Guide*, Oxford: Oxford University Press, 2004.

O'Rourke Boyle, M., *Loyola's Acts: The Rhetoric of the Self*, Berkeley: University of California Press, 1997.

Panofsky, E., *Abbot Suger on the Abbey Church of St Denis and its Art Treasures*, Princeton, NJ: Princeton University Press, 1979.

Pawson, J., *Minimum*, London and New York: Phaidon Press, 2006.

Peake, L., "Smashing icons," in *Will Alsop's SuperCity*, Manchester: Urbis, 2005, pp. 39–49.

Pearson, P. (ed.), *Thomas Merton, Seeking Paradise: The Spirit of the Shakers*, Maryknoll, NY: Orbis Books, 2003.

Pohl, C. D., *Making Room: Recovering Hospitality as a Christian Tradition*, Grand Rapids: Eerdmans, 1999.

Raedts, P., "The medieval city as a holy place" in C. Caspers and M. Schneiders (eds.), *Omnes Circumadstantes: Contributions Towards a History of the Role of the People in the Liturgy*, Kampen: Uitgeversmaatschappij J. H. Kok, 1990.

Raguin, V. C., Brush, K. and Draper, P. (eds.), *Artistic Integration in Gothic Buildings*, Toronto: University of Toronto Press, 1995.

Rahner, K., *The Trinity*, London: Burns & Oates, 1970.

Rahner, K., *Foundations of the Christian Faith: An Introduction to the Idea of Christianity*, London: Darton Longman & Todd, 1978.

Raitt, J. (ed.), *Christian Spirituality II: High Middle Ages and Reformation*, New York: Crossroad Publishing, 1987.

Richards, S., *Le Corbusier and the Concept of the Self*, New Haven, CT: Yale University Press, 2003.

Ricoeur, P., *Time and Narrative*, Volume 1, Chicago: University of Chicago Press, 1984.

Rogers, R., *Cities for a Small Planet*, London: Faber & Faber, 1997.

Rose, G., "Diremption of Spirit," in P. Berry and A. Wernick (eds.), *Shadow of Spirit: Postmodernism and Religion*, London: Routledge, 1992.

Sacks, J., *The Home We Build Together: Recreating Society*, London and New York: Continuum, 2007.

Saliers, D., "Liturgy and Ethics: Some New Beginnings," in R. Hamel and K. Himes (eds.), *Introduction to Christian Ethics: A Reader*, New York: Paulist Press, 1989.

Sandercock, L., *Cosmopolis II: Mongrel Cities in the 21st Century*, London and New York: Continuum, 2003.

Sandercock, L., "Spirituality and the urban professions: the paradox at the heart of planning," in *Planning Theory and Practice*, 7(11), 2006.

Schama, S., *Landscape and Memory*, London: HarperCollins, 1995.

Schmemann, A., *The World as Sacrament*, London: Darton Longman & Todd, 1965.

Schreiter, R. J., *The Ministry of Reconciliation: Spirituality and Strategies*, Maryknoll, NY: Orbis Books, 1998.

Schreiter, R. J., *Reconciliation: Mission and Ministry in a Changing Social Order*, Cambridge, MA: Boston Theological Institute Series, 2000.

Sennett, R., *The Uses of Disorder*, New York: Norton, 1990.

Sennett, R., *The Conscience of the Eye: The Design and Social Life of Cities*, London: Faber & Faber, 1993.

Sennett, R., *Flesh and Stone: The Body and the City in Western Civilization*, London: Faber, 1994.

Sennett, R., *The Fall of Public Man*, London: Penguin Books, 2002.

Sennett, R., *Together: The Rituals, Pleasures and Politics of Cooperation*, London and New York: Allen Lane, 2012.

Sheldrake, P., *Living Between Worlds: Place and Journey in Celtic Spirituality*, London: Darton Longman & Todd/Cambridge, MA: Cowley Press, 1995.

Sheldrake, P., *Spirituality and Theology: Christian Living and the Doctrine of God*, London: Darton, Longman & Todd/Maryknoll, NY: Orbis Books, 1998.

Sheldrake, P., *Spaces for the Sacred: Place, Memory and Identity*, London: SCM Press/Baltimore: Johns Hopkins University Press, 2001.

Sheldrake, P., "Reading cathedrals as spiritual texts," in *Studies in Spirituality*, 11 (2001), pp. 187–204.

Sheldrake, P., "On Becoming Catholic People" in P. Murray (ed.), *Catholic Learning: Explorations in Receptive Ecumenism*, Oxford: Oxford University Press, 2008.

Sievernich, M., "The evangelization of the great city: Ignatius Loyola's urban vision," in *CIS Review of Ignatian Spirituality*, Volume XXVI, 3, number 80 (1995), pp. 26–45.

Simons, W., *Cities of Ladies: Beguine Communities in the Medieval Low Countries, 1200–1565*, Philadelphia, University of Philadelphia Press, 2003.

Spohn, W., *Go and Do Likewise: Jesus and Ethics*, London and New York: Continuum, 1999.

Stanworth, H., "Protestantism, anxiety and orientations in the environment: Sweden as a test case for the ideas of Richard Sennett," in *Worldviews: Environment, Culture, Religion*, 10(3), 2006, pp. 295–325.

Tanner, K. (ed.), *Spirit in the Cities: Searching for Soul in the Urban Landscape*, Minneapolis: Fortress Press, 2004.

Vivian, T. (ed.), *Journeying Into God: Seven Early Monastic Lives*, Minneapolis: Fortress Press, 1996.

Walker, A. (ed.), *Spirituality in the City*, London: SPCK, 2005.

Walker, A. and Kennedy, A. (eds.), *Discovering the Spirit in the City*, London and New York: Continuum, 2010.

Ward, B. (ed.), *The Wisdom of the Desert Fathers*, Fairacres Publications 48, Oxford: SLG Press, 1986.

Ward, G., *Cities of God*, London: Routledge, 2000.

Ward, G. (ed.), *The Certeau Reader*, Oxford: Blackwell, 2000.

Ward, G., "Michel de Certeau's Spiritual Spaces," in I. Buchanan, ed., *Michel de Certeau – In the Plural*, special edition of *The South Atlantic Quarterly*, 100(2), Spring 2001, pp. 501–17.

Webster Bartlett, D., *The Better City: A Sociological Study of a Modern City*, Los Angeles: Neuner Company Press, 1907.

Weil, S., *The Need for Roots*, London and New York: Routledge, 1997.

Williams, R., *On Christian Theology*, Oxford: Blackwell, 2000.

Williams, R., *A Silent Action: Engagement with Thomas Merton*, Louisville: Fons Vitae, 2011.

Wilson, C., *The Gothic Cathedral*, London: Thames & Hudson, 1990.

Wilson, G. H., "Songs for the city: interpreting Biblical psalms in an urban context," in S. Breck Reid (ed.), *Psalms and Practice: Worship, Virtue and Authority*, Collegeville, MN: The Liturgical Press, 2001.

Worcester, T. (ed.), *The Cambridge Companion to the Jesuits*, Cambridge: Cambridge University Press, 2008.

Zizioulas, J., *Being as Communion*, New York: St Vladimir's Seminary Press, 1985.

Index

The Spiritual City: Theology, Spirituality, and the Urban, First Edition. Philip Sheldrake.
© 2014 Philip Sheldrake. Published 2014 by John Wiley & Sons, Ltd.